What readers say ...

"For years I've been in and out of the 'tool shares in this book. I read it first for myself, my friends and famil... it again for ministry, meetings and marriage counseling. The biggest vulnerability I witness in church communities is the danger of having no effective framework for good listening. Here it is. Impeccable!"

—Ben Dake, Pastor Nestucca Valley Presbyterian Church Pacific City, OR

"Why Don't We Listen Better? is a sensible guide to transforming verbal confrontation habits into good, healthy communication. Best of all, it comes with a Talker-Listener Card that provides a handy tool for practice."

—Ben Vose, retired teacher. Astoria, OR

"What an eye-opener! When I started the book I thought I was a good listener. Now I know better. I am a card-carrying listener/talker now. Insightful, thought provoking and thoroughly enjoyable to read."

—Jim Misko, author of *As All My Fathers Were* and other fiction & non-fiction books. Anchorage, AK

"Dr. Jim Petersen presents us with an exceptional set of tools for improving communication and enhancing relationships. His uniquely challenging style clarifies...the best of the teaching-learning processes ...I predict this book will find a wide readership by all who teach counseling and psychotherapy. Also, every church, school, medical group, and work groups in business and industry will gain much with Jim's coaching."

—John L. Butler, Clinical Professor of Psychiatry Emeritus Oregon Health & Science University. Portland, OR

"The Talker-Listener Card is a helpful adjunct to therapy...clients are specifically reminded of how to carry their experience from therapy into other important relationships."

—Donald W. Swan, Psychologist. Beaverton, OR

"At last! The ingenious little card gets its due. I have used them for years. I keep one by each phone to remind me to be present in conversations with friends, family and clients. They enhance relationships with children (especially teenagers), with partners, and with parents. Why Don't We Listen Better? will open your eyes (and ears) to a new world of effective communication techniques."

—Pam Gross, author of *Want to Find a New Better Fantastic Job?* Founder of CareerMakers. Portland, OR

"Dr. Petersen has developed a dynamic and easy to use system for improving and managing communication. It should be required reading for every educator and anyone else interested in improving their relationships."

—Patrick Stone, author of *Blueprint for Developing Conversational Competence*, Clinical Assistant Professor of Education Washington State University. Vancouver, WA

"The Talker-Listener Card is a simple idea that is enormously useful! I have used it and the book to great effect in many areas of ministry... pre-marital counseling, deacon training, Stephen Ministry, and youth ministry."

—Laurie Vischer, Associate Pastor, Westminster Presbyterian Church. Portland, OR

"This book addresses a serious problem in churches: people tend to talk at each other and rarely listen attentively. Without the skills this book teaches, congregation members tend not to know one another well enough to build true caring relationships; and congregation members are not as friendly to visitors because they do not offer real attentiveness to newcomers."

—Sandra Larson, Co-Pastor McKenzie Valley Presbyterian Church Waterville, OR

"I teach Interpersonal Communication and my students are required to read your book *Why Don't We Listen Better?* and write a report. I have to say that this book has changed their lives and you have given them some incredible tools to use. Many state that their marriages are improving and they are better prepared to serve their clients. I keep the TLC in my counseling office and use it often! I feel blessed to have your book to help my clients and students."

—Deborah Pinkston, Psychologist Northwest Counseling, Inc. Bentonville, AR

From on-line comments and emails

"Love, love, love this book!"

"I have never read anyone's work who had such a grip on how people get along through talking and listening. Petersen will teach you a few moves that will help you get along better with others. It is worth its weight in gold."

"This book is a journey into self-discovery focusing on communication techniques that promote healthy relationships." *John*

"I can't understand why it doesn't say 'Millions Sold' on the cover. The contents, like many counseling materials I review, sound "corny" at first glance, but the truths contained therein are priceless!" *Joel*

"I was assigned this book as part of a grad school course. At first glimpse, I thought it was too simple a text-book. Ha! I was wrong! The concepts and practices of the book are amazing tools which will change the way you communicate daily, or in dyads or groups to pursue better human understanding. This book is on my mental list of most life-impacting reads ever. Love it!" *Annette*

"Thank you so much! Your book *Why Don't We Listen Better?* revolutionized my life and the lives of those around me!"

"Well written and easy to read...A great book for couples struggling with communication issues...my significant other and I really benefited from this book." *Kathy*

"If I could be Queen For A Day, I'd ask that everyone learn the techniques presented in this book, and be a 'card-carrying' listener." *Maren*

"Your techniques work and have been a great tool for me in both counseling and coaching."

"Using the Talker-Listener process saved my marriage several years ago and continues to help my husband and me communicate hot button topics with each other. We tend to start arguing and then bring out the card, not what is suggested, but once the card is there in the middle it kind of becomes a referee in our exchanges. We play by the rules, no one gets hurt and problems are solved." *Deb*

"Yes, my mother was right, I DID need to read this book. Actually, EVERYONE should read this book. And now that I've read it, I need to go buy my own copy to keep on hand."

"This is a fabulous book. I teach some classes on communication for my church and this is one book I put in the hands of every student. Its humor and dandy little illustrations make it a hit." *Melissa*

"Brings new understanding to how people communicate. Explains barriers to understanding and how to overcome them. It is simply a must for any counselor." *Ramona*

"I downloaded your book with the intent of using it as a resource when teaching communication skills to my college management classes. I'm enjoying the content and could have used your suggestions related to old people and boring stories earlier today during lunch with my mother."

"I am so thankful to my university for having me read the Petersen text. Every household should process it. I just told my husband that this book is amazing and that it's like this man is in my head."

"I have found myself trying to mentally use the TLC and it has shocked me how poor I was at it, and how little I was actually listening to others."

"I've been married sixty years and now I realize I have a lot of catching up to do." *A retired guy*

"I enjoyed Dr. Petersen's use of humor in this book. He took an often light-hearted approach to many serious issues that impact people's abilities to communicate and listen effectively. He also offers a lot of useful advice...I found a lot more useful tips...than I have in many similar books." *Brandi*

"Before studying the book, I thought my husband was the problem in our marriage. Turns out I'm a lousy listener. This may have saved my marriage."

"Jim Petersen does a wonderful job of explaining how we go "flat-brained" when we're under stress or under attack, and I love that he also gives concrete steps and techniques to use to recover from that and open communication lines back up by really and truly LISTENING to what other people are trying to tell us."

"I have read through it at least two times. It came to me as part of graduate course material. The message of the book was fantastic. It deepened an understanding of "to understand, then be understood.""

"It really can speak to a person and help them view his/her life in a whole new light. It also helps to put words to feelings that otherwise have not been expressed before."

"My communication will never be the same! Thank you, Dr. Petersen. This book has already helped me see communication in a whole new light." *William*

"I have learned so much from your writings! I have read the book but will continue to read it over and over!"

"Good read for those looking to be better listeners." *Andre*

"Dr. Petersen's book finally gets to the bottom of much of our communication struggles. Without placing blame on anyone, his insights may be the one tool we have all been looking for, to be heard and to finally understand one another." *Barbara*

"Great book! Everyone should read it for their own benefit and it just might benefit those they care about as well." *Bonnie*

"Great book! Highly recommend, it has tremendously improved my listening ability and people around me are much more open and there is a lot less conflict."

Why Don't We Listen Better?

Communicating & Connecting in Relationships

Second Edition

Jim Petersen

Doctor of Ministry

Licensed Professional Counselor

Petersen Publications

Why Don't We Listen Better?
Communicating & Connecting in Relationships
Revised & Expanded

Books available at discounts for bulk purchases for gifts, educational needs, or fundraising. A free PDF of *Listening through a Mealtime Game* and *Listening through Difficult Discussions* can be ordered by contacting the author.

ISBN 978-0-9791559-5-6 (Trade Paperback)
ISBN 978-0-9791559-6-3 (eBooks)
Copyright © 2015 by James C. Petersen
Talker-Listener Card Copyright © 1980, 2007, 2015 by James C. Petersen

Second Edition – Seventh Printing

This publication is designed to describe the author's view of communication and relationships. Examples cited are composites based on the author's experience, not on any particular counseling situation with a person or couple. Some personal examples are real but modified for the sake of anonymity. If any seem familiar, it may be because what is most personal is also most universal. This book does not replace or substitute for professional advice or services. Any information received from this book is not intended to be used in diagnosis, treatment, or as a cure. The book is sold with the understanding that neither the author nor the publisher is engaged through this book in rendering professional advice or services.

The Library of Congress has cataloged this edition as follows:

Petersen, Jim.

Why don't we listen better? : communicating & connecting in relationships / Jim Petersen. -- Second edition. -- Portland, OR : Petersen Publications, [2015]

pages ; cm.

ISBN: 978-0-9791559-5-6 (paperback) ; 978-0-9791559-6-3 (eBook)

1. Listening. 2. Interpersonal communication. 3. Communication in families. 4. Communication in marriage. 5. Interpersonal relations. 6. Social skills. 7. Life skills. 8. Self-help techniques. 9. Self-actualization (Psychology) 10. Psychotherapy--Aids and devices. 11. Counseling--Aids and devices. I. Title.

BF637.C45 P445 2015
153.6/8--dc23   1505

Ψ Petersen Publications
Portland, OR 97210 USA
Jim@PetersenPublications.com

My love to Sally,
without whom
this edition, too,
would never have
been written.

Dedication

I dedicate this book:

To every one of you who yearns for deeper connections with people, who wishes to get along better with them, and wants to do what you can to enrich their lives.

To those of you who listened to me with a challenging acceptance. It touched me, grew me, and held me together.

To all of you who let me in on your lives — your struggles, your failures, and your successes. I am privileged and grateful.

To you the readers of *Why's* first edition and the many who joined me in learning to listen better.

And for all of you:

May you not only listen to those around you, but hear them in a way that encourages creativity, collaboration, and mutual growth. May your footprints increasingly lead others on to paths of love and justice.

Jim

Why a Second Edition of "Why"?

My readers often tell me that the Talker-Listener approach to communicating between people causes true transformation in their lives. *"Listening into love,"* some call it or *"A journey into a higher quality of life."* They mention self-discovery and healthy relationships.

This second edition moves more explicitly into techniques and situations that can create, nurture, and support such deep changes. No book alone can change lives and I don't pretend that this one will. But those who not only read, but practice and incorporate creative listening into their lives may find themselves impacted beyond expectation.

This is my hope for you readers of this second edition. But if that's too much, I hope the flat-brain theory, the tango, the card, and the practical listening techniques will lighten your path through life and broaden the smile on your face. That would be enough for me.

Specifically, instead of one chapter of listening techniques late in the book, I spread them throughout to get you practicing sooner. The more complex ones come later.

I beefed up *Managing the Flat-Brain Syndrome,* that is, how to enable growth in ourselves and others.

I added more *Communication Traps,* those common mistakes we unknowingly make that cause us trouble with those close to us. One we often make with youngsters (and adults) is *Asking for one-word answers.* And I take on that relationship-shattering urge we have to fix our partners' problems in *Fixing it — "I want a consultant, not a husband (wife)."* This one can be a game-changer in a relationship.

I expanded the decision-making processes for individuals, couples, groups, and in counseling in *Listening Techniques for Moving On.* We also look at *Motivation Levels* and *Balance Scales* for weighing decisions.

Instead of an index I've given you an expansive table of contents so you'll be able to find the sections you want later when you need them.

Jim Petersen

Contents

PART ONE:
Options in Communicating

1

Communication Became Important to Me

ONE NIGHT YEARS AGO, I pulled a rain slicker over a thick wool sweater to protect me from a skin-soaking coastal storm. I pushed the back door open, leaned into the wind, and sloshed to my car to respond to a call for help. A couple in my parish was near coming to blows.

My windshield wipers struggled against the Oregon downpour as I drove toward their home. This couple had been fighting like that "dark and stormy night" for years. Way before smart phones, this battle began over whether he should have stopped and called her when he realized he would get home late from a business trip. He didn't call and she jumped all over him — again.

Sitting on their couch I watched the rainwater drip off me onto their carpet. I felt helpless. My seminary training in Greek, Hebrew, theology, Bible, and church history hadn't prepared me for this job. As a young pastor I was painfully aware I didn't have the right tools to help when my parishioners couldn't get along with each other. I didn't know how to help them build loving relationships.

I didn't have a clue what to do for this couple, so I just listened. After they told their sides of the story, each of them looked at me as though I could solve the problem with a few magical words. I stared down at the carpet and noticed the dripping had stopped. Then I did what seemed to make sense. I translated back to them what I heard, both the words and intentions beneath them.

To him I said, *"Your wife is saying, when you didn't call, it made her feel unimportant to you. The later it got, the more worried she became. Finally, she panicked, imagining you hurt, lying injured in a muddy road-side ditch. Sounds to me as if she cares about you."*

And to her, *"He understands how afraid you get. He was trying to get home to you as quickly as he could so he didn't take the time to find a phone booth and call. On the other hand, when you get on his case for not calling he feels trapped, like you don't trust him and are trying to control him. Sounds to me as if he cares about you."*

Somehow, it worked.

In my struggle to apply love that evening, I discovered that while I could hear undertones of what they were saying, they couldn't hear each other well at all. They failed to hear the hurt and caring in their spouse's anger. They seemed blocked by insecurity, anger, habit, and even more, their need to win the argument.

However, they could hear what the other tried to say when they heard it translated through me, perhaps because they had no need to defend against me.

In time both storms settled. As the couple recognized that they both hurt, they grew in their concern for each other. They rediscovered how much they cared for one another. Their need to win subsided.

This experience gave me a clue how powerful good communication can be. It is the oil that lubricates the engine of relationships. Without it the engine seizes and grinds to a halt.

Nearly five decades later, couple counseling still thrills me when an angry pair begins to hear the hurt and caring under their partners' words. Sometimes, they end up in tears when they move beneath the complaints and jabs to rediscover, to their surprise, that their partners not only care for them — but still love them.

Good communication matters even when close-in intimacy is not your goal. Listening well can improve how effectively you work with your business associates, co-workers, and community volunteers. It helps keep friendships vital and even makes a difference in casual relationships where you merely want ease. It grounds effective counseling, teaching, selling, conflict resolution, parenting, and learning.

I learned some of this early

I grew up the middle one of three boys. Two girl cousins lived across the street. The five of us bounced back and forth between homes. Each of us chose where to eat depending on who was fixing liver and onions, who baked cakes, and who was in trouble with whom. Aunts and uncles, other cousins, friends and strays collected around our homes.

We never ate a holiday dinner with fewer than twenty people. We jockeyed for attention, teased and sparred, argued, and protected ourselves with "friendly sarcasm." Most of us talked better than we listened, though we appreciated each other and would defend the family against any outside criticism.

As a somewhat shy highschooler in the middle of that mayhem, I often found myself listening as others went on and on, wrapped up in their own thinking. I learned that listening pays dividends. Occasionally, someone would visit who seldom got along with anyone. They took to me and I liked that. At first, I hoped it meant I was particularly charming and likeable. I soon figured out they liked me because I listened to them. (Don't we all like an audience?)

I observed that while others avoided grumpy people, all I had to do to reduce their grump-factor was to ask questions and let them tell me their stories. As I listened, one of the payoffs for me was that these folks became more interesting. I also found that after I paid enough attention to their personal and political tirades, they became more receptive to me. (My lesson: Listen first; talk second.) I could toss in my views and even argue some, as long as I didn't go on long enough to steal their stages.

Communication balancing

I learned the value of communication balancing:
- Listen awhile.
- Talk until the other person almost stops hearing.
- Listen until the person calms enough to hear again.

I sensed that most people were more interested in telling their stories than hearing mine. And to be honest, I was more interested in telling mine than hearing theirs. While I relished times when others tried to understand my stories, I came to value even more, friendships where understanding worked both ways.

Listening deeper

I wanted to be liked. I never did enjoy conflict or when people were angry with me. But at a deeper level I liked it even less when tense situations were ignored. Those times hung heavy in the air and soured the atmosphere for me. I couldn't relax and enjoy interactions when the real issues were hidden underneath what was being said and done. That felt way too manipulative and bunched my insides.

I made it my mission to deal with those unpleasant situations by surfacing under-the-table problems so they could be dealt with. I experimented with versions of my "grumpy people technique," that is, ask questions, listen awhile, surface hidden issues, and wait for my time to talk.

I soon discovered that chronically angry people harbor hurt feelings under their anger. So, when I encountered these unpleasant folks, I put my stubbornness to work. I determined to listen until I dug deep enough to understand what made them feel, think, and act the way they did.

To my surprise, something strange happened. I began to care for the grumps, and often, even to like them. C. S. Lewis pinpointed what I experienced. Lewis said in effect:

> *Don't wait until you love people to act on their behalf.*
> *Act on their behalf, and you will come to love them.*

When I took time to understand others, it not only benefited them, it benefited me. I grew to accept a wider range of people and to enjoy most of the unlikely and unlikable among them.

I became motivated by the pure joy of connecting at a deeper level with people and wanted others to be able to do the same. I still do. That's why I wrote the book.

During my final edit of the first edition, I woke early from a dream where I was puzzling with people who were busy judging the motives and behaviors of others. This book had become so much a part of me, that even in my dreams, I was working to help the judgers see and feel what was inside the folks they were judging. I longed for them to listen and understand, because I knew that if they did, they would stop putting others down. (How's that for a dream?)

Real listening gets us inside each other. There seems to be something in such human connection that touches and changes us (for the better). I don't know, maybe it's that when we get far enough inside someone else, we see and connect more with ourselves. So how can we do anything then but be supportive of others?

What's ahead?

Ever since my first dinner table reflections, I have observed people, studied, experimented with different ways of communicating, practiced a lot, counseled, taught, led business and college workshops, and nurtured the growth of these insights. In this book I intend to share my current thinking, hoping you will find it as helpful in your lives as I have in mine.

Most people think they listen well, but don't

One of the most frequent comments I've heard since first publishing eight years ago was this: *"When I started the book I thought I was a good listener. Now I know better."* Not listening well causes a lot of unnecessary confusion and pain. Experience also tells me that people who are willing to work at listening better can improve their relationships across the board.

While better communication skills do improve relationships, they are not the entire picture. I am putting in your hands a practical "how to" guide to help improve your listening and talking skills, but I intend to take you deeper than that.

The need-to-win and put ourselves above others in relationships causes even more problems than shoddy communication. If we learn to recognize this tendency, we have a chance to set it aside and move into more meaningful connections with family, friends, and co-workers.

This revised and expanded edition includes three major sections, each one broken into chapters with many bite-size pieces for you to chew on. At the end of each chapter I've added a listening technique for you to start practicing. They will get more complex as you go and later in the book I'll group them for easier use. However, they are not directly related to the chapters they follow. I want you to have enough for a wide variety of situations.

(If you have an urgent need for help in a relationship, turn immediately to the first few **How to Listen Better: Techniques.***)*

PART ONE moves on from here with a communication chapter on connecting and disconnecting in relationships and then introduces my (kiddingly serious) *"Flat-Brain Theory of Emotions."* It explains how our emotions, thinking and relating abilities work and how what goes on inside us comes out in the ways we communicate and act.

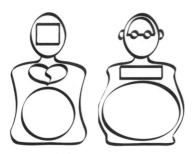

Then the Flat-Brain Syndrome shows why it's so difficult for us to listen, think, act, or even relate to others when our emotions go on overload. It will make it easier to accept ourselves (and others), when we're out of whack — very important. It will also illustrate how, when we're upset and out of phase, good listening helps return us to whatever is normal for us.

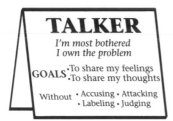

TALKER

I'm most bothered
I own the problem

GOALS
• To share my feelings
• To share my thoughts

Without
• Accusing • Attacking
• Labeling • Judging

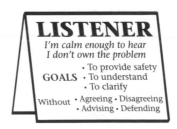

LISTENER

I'm calm enough to hear
I don't own the problem

GOALS
• To provide safety
• To understand
• To clarify

Without
• Agreeing • Disagreeing
• Advising • Defending

PART TWO discusses the use of the Talker-Listener Card, a radical departure from "everyone talking at once with no one really listening." The Talker-Listener Card facilitates a "taking-turns" method in communication. It reminds us to listen first, and talk second.

PART THREE begins with my ten favorite communication traps, includes more essential Listening Techniques, wraps up with extended examples using the Talker-Listener process, and a closing section on growing to become "people in whose presence good things happen."

To get the most out of this book

The book is designed to be read in short sections. While it builds throughout, you can easily revisit pieces by using the detailed *Table of Contents,* which I prefer to an index. Even after all this time, I find that going over the material again and again causes me to rethink how I relate to others. I also find that reading the listening responses aloud helps embed them in my mind. Hearing myself say them makes them more likely to pop up when I need them.

Couples report that it's best to read the book together, because when you ask your partner to read a book "to improve our communication," it usually creates defensiveness. Your partner hears, "Our trouble is your fault and I'm going to use this book to fix you." And so arguments escalate over who needs help, who has read how much, what the book said about whom, and who "really cares" about this relationship. One partner reading and passing on the ideas, often sets up skirmishes and defensiveness.

I don't want you arguing over the book.

Instead, offer, "I'm going to read this book that says we can quit arguing by listening better. Sounds impossible to me, but I'd like to try taking turns reading it aloud. I think we could have fun with it. And who knows? We might get along better and I'd like that. How about Thursday evening or Saturday morning?"

words matter

Couples who spend time reading the book together hear each other say the listening responses. They sense what works and what doesn't. And yes, to answer the question you may have in your mind (that I've been asked tons of times), even if your spouse/partner refuses, read it yourself anyway and practice the methods.

Why? When you change, your relationships will change. You'll be less defensive and your partner will feel heard, get calmer, and think straighter. But more on that later.

You'll notice repetition as you work your way through the book — that's intentional. Sometimes, I'll take a concept to a deeper level. At other times, use it as a gentle reminder of just how hard it is to change thinking and behavior. I'll often put an idea in more than one way in order to get through to readers who learn differently.

I wish you well as you embark on an effort to overcome the combative communication habits our culture drums into us. I hope this book will assist your journey of self-discovery, increase your understanding of people, and make your relationships more what you want them to be.

I also hope you have fun with it. May you hear and be heard in ways that deepen your connections and increase your commitment to constructive living.

The next chapter will take us deeper into communication and connecting in relationships, but for the moment, dive into the first listening technique.

─── ∞ ───

How to Listen Better: Technique # 1

Many of the skills I'll include have been around long enough to become part of a generic pool and you'll recognize them. Some I modified. Others I created. They all work at times, if not overused.

In the listening examples I use an odd punctuation mark *(...?)* to indicate that good listening includes a gentle accepting style. You catch and hand back what the talker is saying without strong statements or pushy questions. The ellipses *(...)* suggest incompleteness, while the question marks *(?)* encourage a slight rise in tone at the end of the listening response. Together they signal an open-ended inquiry to reduce the talker's fear of judgment and reprisal.

We'll start with *acknowledge.* It helps people accept themselves and feel real support from the listener — a foundation of good listening.

👂 Acknowledge

> ■ *Use words, tone, and body language to **acknowledge** it's okay for the talker to feel or think the way he/she does. It usually takes just a few words and an inviting, bite-your-tongue, patient attitude.*

"Ah, so you're irritated...?" Or, *"Mmmm, unhappy about that...?"* This form of acknowledging is a non-argumentative, non-judgmental acceptance of what the talker feels or is trying to say. (Neither agreeing nor disagreeing.)

When a child skins a knee and is crying, parents feel called upon to debate whether the pain level is worth "the carrying on." It rarely helps. If you say, *"Oh, it can't be that bad!"* you'll get an argument and louder bellows. The youngster will have to prove his knee does hurt "that" much. Instead, try this: When the child sniffles, *"It hurts."* You **acknowledge** softly, *"Mmmm, ouch...?"* Or, nod and say, *"Mmmm, it hurts...?"* And he/she will likely nod and say, *"Yeah!"* heading right back outside to play.

Sometimes we youngsters and adults just need to have our feelings acknowledged. Then we can move on, knowing our emotions are okay and that we're not alone with them.

Your spouse says, *"I'm frustrated. I don't want to go to work tomorrow."* It does not help to say, *"But we have bills to pay and you should be thankful for having a job in this economy, and don't forget I have to work at a rotten job too."*

To simply **acknowledge** may be all that's necessary. Try saying: *"Tough work day to face huh...? Bet you'd rather go to the beach...?"* Then bite your tongue and listen some more. This acknowledges the pain and allows its level to subside. It also makes room for the talker to go on, feel understood, and not be alone in frustration.

Or your partner comes home babbling about a new purchase. You don't have to ask, *"But how much did it cost?"* Try, *"Wow, you really sound pleased and excited...?"* And then listen some more to share in the excitement.

You might go back and repeat the acknowledging responses out loud. Get used to them rolling off your tongue with that little rise at the end. Then find an opportunity to **PRACTICE** with someone close, the grocery clerk, a co-worker, on the phone with a telemarketer. (I shouted "practice" because I want to emphasize it takes pots of practice to change personal patterns. Making changes takes work.)

Again, practice until you get comfortable using **acknowledge** and until your responses begin to sound like you.

2

Communication — Connecting & Disconnecting

THE WORD COMMUNICATION derives from the root "to commune." It has at least two levels — sharing information and connecting with others. For the spiritually-minded, overtones of "to commune" suggest that at a higher level people connect in a health producing way with other people, nature, and God as well. For the otherwise-minded, these same overtones may suggest the deep growth producing connections with people that can result from what psychologists call the "unconditional acceptance" in therapeutic relationships.

Two levels of communication

Level one communicating gives and receives information and discusses points of view. At this level, when we ask where the copy machine is, who decides on vacation schedules, or how much fifteen percent of the dinner bill comes to, all we care about is getting the facts. Here, factual exchanges work.

However, even when the primary goal of exchanging information is met, if the exchange is too brief (for us) or a tone of voice seems brusque, we may leave the conversation feeling unsatisfied. We might wonder:

- *"Can we work together?"*
- *"Do we even want to work together?"*
- *"Do we trust each other?"*
- *"Are we friends?"*

Since most of us yearn for personal connection, level one information exchanges by themselves can complicate matters. When we sense that others don't care what we think or feel, discussing points of view easily turns into arguments. To the disconnected person a simple question of curiosity like: *"Why are you doing it that way?"* can sound like: *"Look stupid, you're doing it wrong."*

Level two communicating goes deeper than words. It moves us toward more satisfying relationships where we develop trust, intimacy, and personal sharing. Level two connects us at a level of feeling and spirit where strangers become friends.

At level two, information sharing becomes easier, clearer, and the process more forgiving. We give each other more slack, the benefit of the doubt, and expect honorable intentions.

For example: Look at this shortened interaction between a frustrated computer owner and a tech support person. The computer owner phones and says, *"I just spent an hour trying to get my Wi-Fi connection to work. You've got to fix it."*

Techie responds, *"Your wireless isn't working? That must be really frustrating."*

Owner: *"You bet I'm frustrated. No e-mail and I can't do my business research on the web."*

Techie: *"Sounds bad for your business. So, tell me what your system is doing, what you've tried, and let's see if we can get you back online."*

When the caller senses that the tech is on his side, he feels like he's not alone with his problem. He feels supported even if the computer's problem can't be fixed without serious expense. This situation might have turned sour if the tech had not listened with care and moved the conversation from information sharing to a personal connection.

Feeling heard and understood has a lot to do with whether or not personal connection happens. We humans want to know that people care about us, value us, and take us seriously. (And, of course, we want our computers fixed too.)

13

When we don't hear each other

Talking and listening to each other ought to help us get along. Right? Often wrong. We picked up our ways of communicating automatically from others. We learned by observation, osmosis, and imitation. Unfortunately, many of us learned ineffective methods.

The people we copied learned the same way we did. So it's a waste of time trying to blame our predecessors, ourselves, or each other. I suppose someone long ago traded trying to understand for trying to win, and we've been paying the price ever since.

Many of you experienced communication as I did at my home dinner table with everyone talking at once and no one really hearing each other. How many times have we left such conversations with a vague sense of un-fulfillment, feeling that we hadn't connect with anyone?

How about the social times when we're visiting before a soccer game, being friendly at an office party, or making coffee time conversation? People standing around, waiting for an opening to start or finish their stories. I've watched myself get frustrated through five grandparents' stories about their grandkids, hoping for a chance to share the (important) news about my (special) granddaughter. So I jump into a crack in the conversation to talk, but if I take a breath or hesitate, I lose my place to someone else's straight-A student, tennis elbow, or trip to France.

We've all heard people grouse after parties, meetings, and coffee breaks: *"I'm not going back. Small talk is such a waste of time."* Were they complaining out of hurt feelings, because no one showed enough interest to listen to them?

Such conversations can be pulled apart and written side by side in unrelated columns. Timing is about all they have in common. They do little more than bounce off each other. Check this disconnection example:

Jack: *"I've had a tough week with my boss."*

　　Jill: *"Thank God it's Friday."*

Jack: *"This guy's a killer — too many unrealistic expectations."*

　　Jill: *"I can't wait to get home and start painting my house."*

Jack: *"It's a relief to get out of the office and away from him."*

Jill: *"Hope I get it painted before the rain sets in."*

Jack: *"I don't know if I can go back to work next week."*

Jill: *"If the painting doesn't get done, the repair costs will double later."*

Jack: *"Oh, ah, Jill, have a good weekend."*

Jill: *"See you Monday, Jack."*

Jack and Jill's dialogue could be read together as a conversation or split apart as two individual stories, each independent of the other. They both talked, and neither listened to (nor cared?) what the other was trying to say.

Notice that we're observing a trivial everyday conversation, nothing unusual, but if the concerns were serious, the "missed" communication would have been a much bigger problem. Would you risk sharing anything important with either Jack or Jill, if all your exchanges worked like that?

When you want a listener and get a pool-grabber

We all have times when something is troubling us, when we want a listener and need to talk it out. But, sometimes the person we choose not only doesn't listen, but takes the conversation off in a completely different direction — theirs, not ours.

Imagine preparing to dive into your brand new above-ground swimming pool. On to the diving board you go. You spring from the board, soar into the air, and begin a beautiful swan dive. You look into the sky, straighten downward in perfect entry position, only to discover the pool is gone. You either suspend in mid-air or splat on concrete. Your neighbor grabbed your pool, dragged it into his/her backyard and is now swimming in it.

That's the way it feels when we try to share something that matters to us, only to find that someone else used *our* story as a springboard to dive into *their* story.

Spring-boarding happens in conversations ranging from telling a funny story about our children to discussing serious crises in our lives. It's bad enough when we try to talk about our struggle with the school bureaucracy and another parent switches the discussion to their exceptional child. But when we need to talk about a failing marriage and someone springboards into their best purchase on eBay, our frustration can grow exponentially.

When others change the subject from our concerns to theirs, we learn not to risk going off our diving boards with them around. We may even begin building walls around us for protection against them.

In reality, we stop sharing *what* matters to us with those *who* matter to us. In fact, those who don't listen eventually become those who *used to* matter to us.

Being heard

In contrast to not being heard, when someone acknowledges what we said and wants to know more, we find that being listened to warms the heart and makes our day. *"Oh, really? Tell me about your granddaughter...?"* Or, *"About this problem with your boss...?"* Or, *"How much are you worried about painting your house before the rain sets in...?"*

It's no big surprise when we don't connect with strangers, but it can be distressing when it happens with people closer to us. When we expect intimate relationships and end up feeling alone. It just doesn't feel right.

Ever wonder why so many people pay professional counselors to listen to them, when they have friends like us? In part, perhaps because most of us think we listen well, but don't. We still use the same listening techniques we grew up with and have not replaced them with better ones. Three-quarters of good counseling is just good listening. Master these techniques and fewer of those around you will need to pay for expensive listeners.

Poor communication blocks access to the deeper relationships we want and our friendships remain distant and impersonal. Such frustration and isolation may be reason enough to sort out better intimacy-producing skills. Speaking of such, check the next listening technique and then get ready for a treat with my *Flat-Brain Theory of Emotions.*

—— ∞ ——

How to Listen Better: Technique # 2

Have you listened to someone who's upset and nothing seems to help? When this happens to me, I get nervous. I want to start giving advice or avoiding the issue. (Not helpful.) That's when I remind myself to use this second technique, ***repeat accurately,*** (over and over).

🕪 Repeat accurately

■ *Repeat the last paragraph, the last sentence, or the last word (or two). Use the very same words, phrasing, and intonation the talker used.*

The key here is accurate repetition (no spin), but that's tougher than it sounds. When we first try to ***repeat accurately,*** we routinely alter the content of what other people say. We shade their meaning to make them sound worse and us better. We can also do that with tone of voice or body language. (Though, sometimes we spin it the other way to make us look worse and the other better.)

A wife complains, *"You care more about your job than for me. You always put your boss' requests ahead of mine."* Her husband slants his listening response to make him and his position look better: *"So I hear you saying that I work hard to raise money for our family and that I do what my boss wants because he puts the bread on our table."* (How's that for sneaky arguing when he should have been listening?)

People are usually so unaware of giving biased feedback that when someone points it out, they can hardly believe they're doing it. I like to practice this technique in listening workshops, because it's so easy to recognize when someone else skews a talker's meaning, but so difficult to catch when we do it ourselves.

Talkers are really troubled by this skewing habit, or more accurately, "skewering" habit. But when we ***repeat accurately*** without distorting ▸ their views, talkers feel safe with us and arguments diminish. Doing this requires objective observation and practice.

The husband above could ***repeat accurately*** by saying, *"It seems to you that I care more for my job than I do for you and that I always put my boss' requests ahead of yours...?"* Hear how much cleaner that is? It's more respectful of the talker's point of view and it doesn't sneak in the listener's bias.

A friend says, *"She took everything in the divorce. I was so angry with the way she treated me, I could have murdered her!"* To **repeat accurately** we might say, *"She took everything in the divorce. You were so angry with the way she treated you, you could have murdered her...?"* Or, *"...so angry with the way she treated you, you could have murdered her...?"* Or, *"...could have murdered her...?"* Or, just *"...murdered her...?"*

He might go on, *"Well not murder of course, but I was angry. I don't want to be treated that way anymore."* And we repeat his modification, *"You don't want to be treated that way anymore...?"* Or just, *"any more...?"* He'll calm down a little, and go on clearing his head — which is what we want listening to accomplish.

It would not have helped if we'd said: *"Oh, you really aren't upset enough to hurt anyone."* He might have tried to convince us otherwise (not helpful).

Slipping our nervous argument into the feedback would have discounted the intensity of his thoughts, his hurt, and his anger. It would not have reduced his anger, nor helped him move toward a more reasonable solution.

If we catch ourselves trying to play down the harshness of an angry comment, it may mean that we're uncomfortable with anger ourselves. As listeners our denial of anger can leave other people stuck in theirs.

So when all else fails, *repeat accurately.* Clamp your hand over your mouth and *repeat accurately* again, and again, until glimpses of clarity shine through. Surprisingly, the logjam usually breaks. The talker calms down, thinks straighter, starts coming up with possible solutions. (And we get thanks for helping.)

Repeat accurately is one of my favorite listening skills. It's easy and it works. It has bailed me out of many difficult situations. This empowering technique is amazingly simple and effective — nearly magic.

3

The Flat-Brain Theory of Emotions

MY CAREER WITH A specialty in communication philosophy and practice taught me much about how people really operate. I found that while we struggle to understand ourselves, we are routinely confused about the difference between a feeling and a thought, and how our feelings and thinking relate to each other. Both emotions and thoughts are part of how we operate, but trying to describe behavior as either emotional or rational doesn't seem to help. Most psychological language adds little clarity and lacks the practical simplicity necessary to help us understand how we operate or how to get along better.

I also observed that feelings and thoughts are really different from each other and yet affect each other significantly.

Here's how it works. If we feel guilty, we think we are guilty and tend to act in a guilty fashion. Feeling guilty is an emotion. Whether we think we are actually guilty is a thought. I've found it helpful to distinguish between the two when deciding what to do with them.

If I figure out that I feel guilty because of some early programming I've given up, then I can let the guilt feelings go. If I'm actually guilty of hurting someone, then I can apologize or make amends.

As I began to get a handle on this process, I grappled with ways to make it clear to my personal growth classes. A graphic model formed in my mind to show how feelings and thinking are different from each

19

other and yet interact. Over a long time the models developed and were sharpened by class reactions.

Result: The Flat-Brain Theory of Emotions, which starts here in Chapter 3. It begins by picturing how we operate when our brains are functioning well (not flat) and goes on in the next chapter to portray what I call the Flat-Brain Syndrome, that is, how we operate when an overload of emotion "flattens our brains." Beyond that, the following chapters will cover handling the effects of flat brains on individuals and their (our) relationships.

In my experience, understanding how this mixture of thinking and feeling affects us and our relationships goes a long way toward reducing clashes and disconnections. Such understanding helps us accept ourselves and others. It gives clues about how to communicate our concerns and how to listen so others can calm down, think, and act more clearly.

Join me now for a "serious, tongue-in-cheek" look at how our minds and emotions interact and how we can learn to relax and accept ourselves and others more easily.

Stomach functions

That big circle in the stomach area is where I locate feelings, because that's where I notice butterflies before public speaking and feel pangs of hunger that tempt me away from writing toward the refrigerator. You may locate your feelings elsewhere, but for convenience, I'm going to stash them in the stomach.

Stomach functions consist of our emotions or feelings — those inner nudges that let us know when we're uncomfortable, happy, excited, interested, attracted, irritable, angry, resentful, frustrated, curious. Feelings are our internal responses to the world around us, to what we're thinking, and to our bodies. (For simplicity I use feelings and emotions interchangeably.)

The round container suggests that emotions by nature are the personal part of us. They connect us with each other, because we all experience them. You and I may enjoy different things, but the "enjoying" part is the same. Because I enjoy steelhead fishing even in a freezing downpour, I feel a connection to the golfer who has fun sloshing along under a huge umbrella.

Heart functions

We relate with our heart functions. I put a yin-yang squiggle inside the heart to suggest that "it takes two to tango," that you and I both have something to offer, and that we can learn from each other.

Healthy heart functions give and receive concerns, suggestions, and support and are ready to consider many options and possibilities. Healthy hearts recognize that we don't possess "the whole truth," but are confident both in owning our views and remaining open to the views of others, a rare maturity in our contentious world.

The yin-yang divided heart reminds us how essential are the twin qualities of owning our views and staying open to others in building friendships and human communities.

Head functions

The head functions incorporate thinking, planning, remembering, reviewing, deciding, rationalizing — what we consider the logical part of us. The brain processes what we see, hear, feel, remember, and imagine. It picks up messages from the emotional system inside our skin and the world of people and events outside. It decides what to do with the input. The brain can create and problem-solve.

I've drawn square corners and hard lines to suggest that head functions are the computer-like, non-personal part of us. Relating to people based on logic/thinking alone rarely builds close relationships.

Understanding and directing your emotions

While many people are frightened of emotions or consider various ones either good or bad, I believe they are involuntary and perhaps even innate or God-given — simply there for us to use. If I think of any emotions as bad, then I'm under the gun to get rid of them. At times I've struggled with desire, jealousy, and anger, often unsuccessfully. (Perhaps you know someone who has too?)

I prefer to think of feelings as pure energy. We can choose how to direct their energy. As with the gasoline in a tank, we can choose to use the power to drive a hurt child to a hospital or to run over someone.

The emotions I used to consider "bad," I now work at directing. For example, when angry with someone, we can work to improve the relationship, punch the person out, talk with a counselor, cook up a storm, mop a floor, or mow a lawn — our choice.

While many of us might prefer to choose which emotions to have, it doesn't work that way. When we try to push our emotions in a particular direction, it usually has the opposite effect. Deciding not to be attracted to someone when we are, to like spinach when we don't, or to feel a particular way because we think we should, rarely has much positive impact on our feelings. Emotions don't react well to pressure. Trying to force an emotion out of our systems is like trying not to think of a giraffe.

In general though, we can choose to ignore them (to our detriment), to withhold them from others (so people neither know us nor feel close to us), to let them take over and run us (often disastrous), or to direct them wisely.

What helps with emotions?
- Recognize them.
- Accept them (until we relax).
- Decide what to do with their energy.

I'm convinced we can use any of our emotions to build or destroy. If we recognize and accept them, we can choose to act on them in compassionate, responsible, constructive, and creative ways, making a more hospitable world.

Does thinking affect our feelings?

While we can't directly change an emotion, what we think may affect how we feel — our heads can affect our stomachs. When we fill our minds with good thoughts about people, life, universes — sometimes our feelings get on board and catch up.

When I visualize a peaceful warm sunset in Kauai and put myself in the picture, I tend to become more relaxed and happy. I also notice a growing twinge of yearning to be there, which just might instigate a plan and a call for airline tickets or maybe a less expensive drive to the beach or a walk in a park.

Thinking healthy creative thoughts can have a positive impact on our emotional systems and consequently on our actions. If I keep someone's best interests in mind, I grow to care more for them and as a result, may act in a more helpful way.

When we perceive going to the dentist as painful, we can get frightened. If we learn about newer numbing treatments and rethink our perceptions, we may come to see the process as painless, which can allow our fears to settle some. As we think through ideas and situations, our perceptions can change and so will our feeling responses to them.

Someone may say, *"You made me angry!"* Or we might think a movie made us sad, but people and situations do not make us feel a certain way. People react differently to the same stimuli. Rather, how we think about a situation causes our reactions. The idea that changing the way we think alters the way we feel is the base for cognitive-behavioral therapy. An ancient philosopher suggested, *"Whatever is true, whatever is just, whatever is pure, whatever is lovely, whatever is commendable...think about these things..."*

Sometimes our first impressions of people result in our disliking them. When we get to know them better or have a meaningful experience with them, our reactions may change. We could get to like them, and perhaps even fall in love with them. (Of course, it can work the other way too.)

Rationalizing stirs our disconnections

Our culture tends to over-value the rational part of us and devalue and ignore the emotional. Since emotions are the driving energy for most of our decisions and behavior, we are set for trouble.

Many of the people who value logic/thinking very highly are chagrined that their spouses, partners, or co-workers are not equally excited about that quality. Women (and some men) often feel distanced from "Logic Man (Woman)" and prefer dealing with a feeling person with whom they can more easily connect in a personal way. A whole person includes both feeling and thinking, emotion and logic. It takes both to build human connection.

To our detriment, we overlook our emotions by rationalizing them. Some say that rationalization is America's favorite indoor sport. We buy a new car. We say, *"Keeping the old car on the road was breaking the bank. It spent more time in the shop than in my garage. Besides, new cars get better mileage."* Sounds rational, but truth be told, we'll never save enough on gasoline and repair bills to pay for the new one.

What's going on here? We don't want to admit we *tired* of messing with the old one and simply *wanted* a new car. Many of us like to think that our decisions are based more on our heads than on our stomachs. But, when it comes to buying things we want, we seem infinitely capable of manufacturing lists of reasons to justify most any desire-driven purchase.

We also rationalize to cover uncomfortable emotions with a coating of logic. We get to a meeting late and are embarrassed, but we don't admit that. We say instead, *"Sorry for being late, traffic was terrible."* We rationalize (cover) our discomfort by presenting extenuating circumstances (thoughts about traffic).

Then three others at the same meeting immediately come off the floor to ease their guilty feelings about times they've been late: *"Oh right, the traffic is getting worse all the time." "I have to leave earlier than ever to get anywhere." "Remember when you could get across town in just a few minutes — now it takes..."* Sounds like "tag team rationalizing" designed to skirt acknowledging our emotions.

We rationalize faster than we do about anything else. Covering in this low-level way puts distance between us. It masks our feelings. It keeps us removed from the personal part of us and as a result, it keeps us distant from each other.

How's it all supposed to work?

One simple theory of behavior suggests that we humans move from a state of bother to a state of calm. For example: We get curious (bothered). We jump on the internet and Google the topic we're interested in (behavior). We get the info and we relax (calm). Or, we become concerned about hungry children (bothered). We research helping agencies, send a check or go to a rural community to teach agriculture (behavior). We settle down (calm). Our emotions fuel deciding and acting. They make bodily changes in us (heart rate, breathing, etc.) to allow us energy to do what we want to do.

Emotional energies motivate and move us. When heads notice that stomachs are getting active (anxiety, love, excitement, hurt), then we decide whether to tell anyone and/or act further on any of those feelings.

Heart functions allow us to be open with others and to collaborate with them, thus multiplying our individual abilities to build a better world and enjoy life.

Human beings have enough caring for people, concern for the environment, curiosity to learn, desire for justice, worry over the way things are, and broad interests to right the wrongs in the world. We could take on everything that needs creating, organizing, building, or beautifying. However, you may have noticed that a lot of us are not getting along well enough individually or together to pull this off.

What's that about? The Flat-Brained Syndrome will suggest that the heads, hearts, and stomachs of the world are getting overloaded or short-circuited somehow and not working well together. We'll look at what we can do about that on a personal level.

Where do stomach, heart, and head talk fit?

Communication is the lubrication designed to keep our functions of stomach, heart, and head working separately and together. The way we move into personal connection and cooperation with people is primarily through communicating. Sharing what's in our internal processes of stomach, heart, and head can open us up and move us toward connecting better with others.

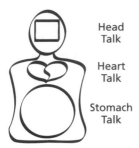

Head
Talk

Heart
Talk

Stomach
Talk

Stomach, heart, and head talk each call for a particular kind of recognizable language:

- **Stomach talk** puts our *feelings* into words. It describes what's in our emotion containers. Feelings are by nature non-debatable — they just exist. If we say, *"I'm too warm (cold), irritable, excited, angry, as anxious as a new student in school, frustrated, pleased,"* or, *"I hate anchovies,"* what can anyone say, but, *"Oh."* Stomach Talk shares what's inside us, connects us with others who have similar feelings, and tends to keep us out of arguments.

- **Heart talk** puts our *ownership* and *openness* into words. It makes clear that we're describing our own concerns and views (not everyone's or the correct ones) and that we're leaving room for other thoughts (which are likely different and may be illuminating to us). When we say, *"This is how it looks to me..."* we leave an opening for how it looks to others.

- **Head talk** puts our *thoughts* into words. It describes what we're thinking, our perceptions — roughly factual stuff. It by nature is most always debatable. We can argue "facts" ad infinitum: Someone says, *"The sky is blue."* Another responds, *"But, there's a grey cloud on the horizon that means rain."*

Language that communicates best, that is, connects us with others at a deeper level, includes elements of all three — our views (head), how we feel about them (stomach), and ownership of our concerns and openness to another's concerns (heart). We'll go into more detail on the three elements in *Chapter 12 TLC – What Does the Talker Do?*

As we come to understand how important it is to remain open to others and the difference between thinking and feeling, we can use that information to improve our interactions.

In the next chapter I invite you to look at and chuckle with me about how our emotions get the better of us and bump us into the Flat-Brain Syndrome. But first, here's to fine tuning our attempts to *acknowledge* and *repeat accurately.*

—— ∞ ——

How to Listen Better: Techniques # 1 & 2 (revisited)

Hopefully, you've practiced *acknowledge* and *repeat accurately* and had great success. However, it might or might not have gone that well?

So, here's the **New Listening Techniques' Warning Label:**
Often when folks start practicing, they parrot the lines:
"And how does that make you feel?" **or,** *"So, I hear you saying...?"* **Great listening responses, but they use them over, and over, and over, and over until "listened to" wants to throw the askers down the nearest elevator shaft.**

Why the negative reactions, when we are "just trying to be better listeners?" Three reasons:

1. Too much repetition grates. Imagine the sound a violin would make, if the bow had only one or two gut fibers? The fullness would be lost, replaced by sounds akin to fingernails scraping a chalkboard (shivers my backbone). It takes more than a couple fibres in our bows to provide decent feedback (30+ listening techniques coming).

2. New skills often sound phony. The new ones we try will neither feel right to us nor sound like us to others — until we get better at them. Be willing to sound odd. What seems natural now is simply what you got used to years ago. With practice, new responses will begin to sound like you.

3. People get rattled by change. So, change in us will stir anxiety in our friends, family, and co-workers — until they get used to it. Even if some of them have been asking you to be a better listener, listening more will jar them. Their anxiety will often surface as resistance or accusation. Don't be surprised if your attempts at listening net negative responses at first. Be patient and don't give up. Your attempts may take some time to produce results.

If your first tries bring negative reactions, best not defend yourself: *"Well, you always said you wanted me to listen, and now that I'm trying, you've changed your tune. You just wanted your own way."*

If you do slip into defending, others will remain convinced that they were right, and that, *"You will never change."*

What can you do when others react negatively? Listen more, *acknowledge* their resistance and *repeat accurately,* like: *"You seem irritated with me that I'm parroting something out of a book and don't sound like myself...?"* Bite your tongue and be ready to *acknowledge* and *repeat accurately* until they calm down enough to listen to you.

My experience tells me that we improve our relationships primarily through effective and respectful listening. But again, keep in mind that new behaviors do not come easy for us, or those around us. It takes self-awareness and practice.

And your assignment (mission) for the end of this chapter (if you should choose to accept it) is to use *acknowledge* and *repeat accurately* — more. They are foundational.

4

The Flat-Brain Syndrome

NOW, LET'S TAKE THE Flat-Brain Theory of Emotions a step further, into the Flat-Brain Syndrome. It shows what happens to us when our systems go out of whack. For example:

- Our stomachs expand with an overload of mixed emotions.
- They press the heart functions into bricks in our chests, sending our relating abilities south.
- The upward expansion flattens brains against the tops of our skulls, forcing our thinking, hearing, and seeing off kilter.
- When flat-brained we can't hear well, see accurately, think straight, or act sensibly.

We'll have a little fun with this model and pick up some clues about what to do about flat-brain fallout (yours and someone else's).

Stomachs overload

Most of us have hurt-feeling residue from earlier painful situations that weren't unloaded well enough. The hurts arose from feeling inadequate when big people could do everything better than we could, from red check marks on school papers, from adolescent anxieties over who likes whom better, from worry over arguing parents and world crises, and from whether we'll find a job, or ever get married.

29

These lumps of hurt feelings clutter our emotion containers and don't leave much room for current stomach activities — falling in love, anger, committing to life direction, fear, joy, or any emotions that move us along toward decision-making and action.

Then something happens to upset us even more — hurt from an unkind remark, worry about finances, news about a medical issue, fear of public speaking, shock over a near accident, serious infatuation.

 The disturbance gets added to our stomach containers, expanding them beyond their normal sizes, like tumors, gradually pressuring internal organs, perhaps even squeezing them between ribs. It pushes everything out of place. We feel awkward, uncomfortable, and slightly off-balance. Women who've experienced pregnancy have no trouble getting this picture.

Whenever emotion containers expand, normal activities or conversations take a turn for the worse. If a husband hugs a wife (friendly+) who is full of worry about a sick child, he may get rebuffed (as cuddled ribs pinch organs) with the comment, *"How can you think of sex at a time like this?"* Emotions under pressure can turn explosive, like steam in a pressure cooker. Jammed-up feelings often cause us to blurt them. We lose our ability to do stomach talk, that is, describe our feelings.

Feelings under pressure tend to produce edgy, erratic behavior, where we take them out on others, rather than sharing them. In a corporate setting, this can create chaos. It can even turn deadly, as in "going postal."

In the packed gut, feelings mush together and lose clarity. We may know that we're "really upset," but not be at all clear what kind of upsets we have or, much less, what caused them. It's no wonder we get touchy and feel like exploding when we're on system overload.

In addition, warm friendly feelings get displaced by strong negative ones, that is, they get pressed flat against the inside of the container walls. Emotions need room to flex for us to "feel" their movement. That's why resentments need to be unloaded before we can "like" our spouses again after a conflict.

At times I've counseled a long-term-conflict couple for months before the hurt, angry one had an inkling of a warm feeling toward the other. It took time to unload the fat belly, to relieve the resentments before "liking" could peel off the container walls and move enough to be felt again.

Hearts turn bricklike

When stomachs bulge they squeeze the heart functions up into the chest cavity. The yin-yang squiggle blurs and disintegrates. We cease to be open to other people or to varied options. We can't give or receive suggestions. And our ability to cooperate vanishes. Shades of grey disappear into black and white. So it's: *"Knuckle under or fight?"* — *"Deed them the company or get rid of them?"*

When bothered, our hearts spread and turn brick-like, which pretty well describes my ability to make small talk with folks before speaking to a large crowd. When an upset is more serious than pre-speech jitters, we lose self-confidence, our friends seem more like enemies, and we can feel quite alone.

Any ability we had to use heart talk, to share and be open with each other morphs into put-downs, absolute statements, and resistance. Collaborative inclinations go up in smoke.

And brains go flat

Expanding bellies push up through our bodies, until the pressure hits our brains, flattening them against the tops of our skulls. Brains are designed to work well when shaped like short fat footballs (or the squares in my pictures), but not when squashed. Flat brains create serious defects in our head functions.

Flat-brained folks tend to think that others are the problem. *"I wouldn't be upset if you would just be different than you are."* Quite logical, if you have a flat brain and your thinking is askew. Any wonder that people who are fat-bellied, hard-hearted, and flat-brained don't focus well on us and when we are that way, we can't focus on them either?

When I have to introduce people to each other or to a crowd, I get uneasy. The uneasiness hits my brain, which goes flat, twisting my memory chips. *"I want to introduce my good friend, ah, ah... we fish together, been through thick and thin, ah, ah..."* How embarrassing! My name-memory-bank gone. Later, when I relax, I can almost feel my brain un-flattening and the name dropping onto the back of my tongue.

For many students timed-tests stir enough anxiety to flatten brains and crash memory banks. Everything they learned the night before is ir-retrievable, until they are drinking coffee and relaxed after they bombed the tests.

Our thinking goes funny, that is, it resembles the emotions in our stomachs. If we're excited, we think, *"There are no mountains we can't climb."* If depressed, *"Life is not worth living."* If suspicious, *"Someone tried to scuttle us."* And if angry, *"Other people caused all our problems."*

When flat-brained we say crazy things that seem reasonable to us at the time. But later, when our brains aren't flat, they seem as out of line to us as they did to others.

For example: After we say something in anger, we try to repair the damage by saying, *"I didn't mean what I said when I was angry."* But, it doesn't help, because they (and we) know we did mean it at the time. Everyone believed it because our words, tone of voice, tight-jawed body language, and finger waving produced a congruent message.

When you understand the flat-brain syndrome, you can carefully and respectfully listen to the person you hurt, and then say: *"I meant those awful things when I said them. My emotional system had overloaded and my brain went flat (I was nuts, off-balance, crazy). I'm afraid I say dumb stuff when I'm flat-brained. But now that I've calmed down and my brain is working again, I don't mean what I said anymore. I apologize for saying what I did and for hurting your feelings. Now what I mean is..."*

Falling in love, too, can make brains really flat. In the early throes of infatuation we promise to climb the highest mountains and swim the deepest oceans for our beloved, yet later when our brains un-flatten, we have trouble taking out the garbage (or listening patiently).

I don't think it makes sense to hold what people say or do against them, when their brains were flat. If we realize everyone gets flat-brained — says hurtful things and damages people — we will better be able to accept people and discover forgiveness as a two-way street. Someone said, *"The more you understand people, the less there is to forgive."*

The "three-day-return law" allows for changing our minds after major purchases. It recognizes, accepts, and acts on the reality of the flat-brain syndrome. Perhaps we could apply a version of the return law to things people say and do when flat-brained. After three days we could go back and check to see whether we or they still really mean what was said or done.

Hearing is skewed

Imagine what flattening a malleable brain against a skull might do to eardrums. As a child on a family vacation in Yosemite, I enjoyed watching the tourist-fed squirrels. One bolder and fatter than the rest, would stay and eat a little longer, then waddle toward safety under the cabins. To get there he had to go between a couple of two by fours, making his crawl space a tight one and five-eighths inches. As he flattened from football to waffle, his fat little body pressed out in all directions.

A similar sort of squirrel squeeze happens to our brains. They flatten and spread equally in all directions, putting pressure on eardrums from the inside, turning them into tone-deaf misinformation gatherers.

Wonder why we have trouble listening to each other? People with flat brains and crushed eardrums simply don't hear well.

What we hear is affected by how we are feeling. For example: A wife's question asked out of curiosity: *"Do we have enough money to go to the beach this weekend?"* when heard by an insecure flat-brained husband, could sound like: *"You never will make as much as the guy I should have married."*

Or, if I'm excited about the possibility of you going fishing in Alaska with me and you say, *"I'll think about it,"* the hope-full pressure on my ear drums causes me to hear: *"Sure, when do we leave?"* And I mistakenly make airline reservations and start packing.

To test the flat-brain effect on ears, try explaining something logically to a person who is upset. Very little you intend to say gets through. A youngster coming home from school in tears, cries, *"The teacher yelled at me in front of my class."* We try to explain that teachers have bad days too. The child hears: *"She wouldn't have yelled at you if you didn't deserve it. We're on her side."* Flat-brained young people don't hear any more accurately than adults who are fat-bellied, hard-hearted, and flat-brained.

Seeing is distorted

You guessed it. The same goes for the eyes. The fault line across the bottom of a flat brain is at eye level, so the brain presses on the eyeballs from the inside.

When I'm uptight about being late, having a helpful gas station guy show me a map does minimal good. Little penetrates through my eyes and not only do his vocal directions fuzz over, but I can't remember more than two turns. The flat-brained syndrome strikes again. (Thank goodness for technology and a GPS to rescue me.)

I've noticed that flat-brained folks often have eyes that bulge a bit — a little pressure from the inside. Take notice the next time you hear someone say, *"You're always late!"* Or, *"I just caught my first salmon in years!"* Or, *"I didn't do that!"* Or, *"I've decided to divorce my overbearing spouse!"* I'll bet you'll see bulging eyes.

In pre-marital counseling, a common experience for me is asking a couple with differing backgrounds, interests, educational levels, hobbies, and attitudes about children how they will handle their differences. They answer in effect, *"We're in love. That's all that matters!"* When I notice the slight bulge in their eyes, I have a pretty good idea about the state of their eardrums. I say to myself, *"Mmmm. Serious cases of flat-brainitis. They can't see, hear, or think straight."*

Incidentally, I'm still researching to see if this term might just have come from the Latin *flotabrainaura*, but in any case, I know there is no point in showing them statistics about their poor chances of working out a successful marriage or talking to them about conflict resolution and joint decision-making. Why? Because nothing much is working above their mouths.

What I do is ask them to talk about when they met, their resistance to parents and friends who said it wouldn't work, their fear that if they lose this one they'll never find another one, or whatever is in their emotion containers. When enough emotional steam escapes through their mouths, their brains un-flatten, and their eyes return to normal size. Then I can talk and help them think about what it takes to put a complicated relationship together.

It takes unloading stomachs to allow head functions to work, but that's getting ahead of myself. Let's look at the mouth.

And the mouth works overtime

So a flat brain damages thinking, skews hearing, and distorts vision, what about the mouth? Check my favorite drawing: With the brain flattened against the top of the skull, there's more than enough room for the mouth to work freely (and it usually does).

Note however, that the mouth is connected to a defective brain. In this condition, while it can be useful in unloading pressure from the stomach, it's not very good at conveying reliable information.

So again, when people are flat-brained, please don't hold what they say against them. And don't hold hurtful things you say or do against yourself either. Remember, we all get flat-brained (but most of us recover).

One of the beauties of the Flat-Brain Syndrome is that it is so non-judgmental. It describes a state we all experience. I'll bet you recognized yourself in parts of it. I hope you smiled when you did. It's meant to give you a tool for lightening tense situations. And it works.

The people around me use this common language. And I can just see people relax when someone says, *"My brain is flat."* Then others think: *"Oh, that's the problem. I know about that. I'll cut you some slack or listen awhile."* This accepting process keeps us from misreading each other's flat-brain behavior and gives us room to work out our upsets.

Families and work groups alike find that a common understanding of the flat-brain process helps them diffuse uncomfortable situations and allows them to work together better.

True and not true

I had just finished describing the Flat-Brained Syndrome to a class of about fifty people, when a young nurse in the back of the room raised her hand and asked, *"Is this a new physiological theory developed since I finished my training five years ago?"* After the chuckling in the room settled, I answered that it's one of those theories that is both true, and not true at the same time.

While the Flat-Brain Syndrome isn't hard science, it does describe how we operate. Our ability to act with emotional and logical clarity diminishes. In the middle of the last century a psychiatrist said about a sudden increase of emotional energy (falling in love) or anxiety, that, *"It has more than a little in common with a blow on the head."*

When the Flat-Brain Syndrome strikes, it engages the body in what I call The Flat-Brain Slump. We'll hit that in the next chapter and look at ways to unhook from both the Syndrome and the Slump.

How to Listen Better: Technique # 3

We'll take a break now to review my *para-feeling* listening technique.

✆ Use para-feeling

■ *Put the talker's feelings (emotions) into your words.*

Paraphrasing is a commonly taught listening device, but it doesn't distinguish between emotions and thoughts. For practical clarity, I prefer to split paraphrasing into *para-feeling* and *para-thinking.* The two terms remind us that when someone is talking, both are there, whether expressed or not.

"Para" means alongside or next to. We put the emotions we hear from talkers into our words. In contrast to *repeat accurately,* it gives them a different look.

Naming feelings makes them less scary and gives talkers more ability to use their energy. When they hear their feelings come back without judgment, it lets them know that what they are feeling is understood and okay.

Expressing feelings is like releasing steam from a pressure cooker. When cooking, if too much steam builds up inside the pot, it either causes an explosion with potatoes hitting the ceiling, or an implosion, where the potatoes go to mush. Emotionally, putting feelings into words keeps them from exploding all over anyone close by or damaging our insides.

People who express their feelings rarely get ulcers. (Though, if they take them out on others, they may become "ulcer carriers," that is, giving them to everyone within earshot.)

Even when a talker doesn't put feelings into words, the tone or body language may give you a clue. Use *para-feeling* to put your best guess into your words. For example, if a spouse looks harried or says, *"I'm glad you came home early,"* try *para-feeling*: *"It seems like you're really happy to see me...?"* Or, *"I'll bet you're relieved to see anyone over three feet tall...?"*

Releasing feelings works equally well whether we name our own, or others do it for us. Having listeners put our feelings into their words even helps when we don't recognize them or have trouble describing them. When someone identifies our feelings (*para-feeling*) and we nod in assent, our emotional levels recede and our brains begin to work better.

Poetic or dramatic language often works when using *para-feeling*. Someone says, *"This is one too many times for me to have trouble with this car,"* you might reply poetically: *"You sound so fried you could go up in smoke and blow away...?"* Or, dramatically: *"You're so upset you could run that stupid car off a cliff...?"*

Whose feelings are they?

Be careful not to accuse talkers of having certain feelings. Rather, in an easy, open way ask if that is what they feel. Remember, the feelings are theirs. That makes the talkers experts on how they feel. Do not argue about feelings: *"You are too angry!"* If you do, you've quit listening and started trying to win. And never say they shouldn't feel the way they feel: *"You're angrier than this situation is worth!"* Or, give advice: *"You know, anger never helps. Get over it!"*

Some of us learned that certain emotions, like anger, hate, lust, or pride are taboo. So when we have such feelings, we can't accept those words to describe them. If you say, *"You sound really angry...?"* and someone responds, *"No, I'm not!"* your ***para-feeling*** didn't work. Then try again: *"Well, so not angry, but maybe bugged, or a little upset...?"*

When you are listening to people who resist specific labels for their emotions, poke around gently and experiment, until you find words they are comfortable using to describe their feelings.

When ***para-feeling*** helps us label and describe feelings, they become less scary and more manageable. So we can better direct them toward effective living. And speaking of manageable, let's look at Managing the Flat-Brain Syndrome.

5

Managing the Flat-Brain Syndrome

THE PRINCIPLE WE'LL work on here is that what's going on inside us (emotions-attitude-thinking) effects how our bodies behave. And vice-versa, what our bodies do on the outside (posture, tone of voice, etc.) affects our insides (emotions-attitude-thinking). That interaction causes us trouble when we don't understand it and gives us options for handling ourselves better when we do.

It's really clear when we're watching someone else that their bodies and facial expressions speak volumes. Their slumping body might tell you, *"I don't feel good about myself."* Or their drumming fingers, *"I'm irritated."* Jumping up and down smiling suggests, *"I feel great!"* Or, *"I'm so excited!"* Or depending on how hard they stomp, could imply, *"I'm furious!"*

You could use *para*-feeling to check this out: *"Looks like you feel bad about yourself...?"* Or, *"You seem irritated...?"* Or, *"Wow, you're on top of the world...?"* **But, remember you are** asking the talker if your observation fits, not telling him/her what their body is communicating, because that would be talking (focused on your point of view), when you should be listening (focused on theirs).

Balanced body posture

The Flat-Brain Syndrome effects the body's look and posture. To illustrate, I'd like you to try a balanced body position first.

Balanced

For the balanced pose, stand up, pull your stomach in, tip your pelvis and buttocks forward, bending your knees slightly. Straighten the small of your back, chest out, pull your neck back and balance your head over your spinal column. Let your arms hang freely at your sides. With your knees slightly bent put your weight on the balls of your feet with your heels lightly touching the floor.

Notice the comfortable in-balance feeling. You can breathe well and see ahead clearly. With this bent knee balance, you can move easily in any direction. And you are "no pushover." If bumped or jostled, you can adjust easily and catch yourself without falling.

Hold this posture for a minute or two and pay attention to how you feel. It tends to create a sense of confidence and strength. Compare this to the way beginning little leaguers play infield positions. They think it looks "cool" to bend over, putting hands on their legs above the knees, locking their knees back with their weight on their heels. But when they need to move to the right or left to go after a ball, they must first bend their knees and get up on their toes. Then they can move toward the ball. It takes two motions (time lost) and the ball whips past them. (You might try it.)

So we teach them to "go ape" — hands ready off the legs, knees bent forward, weight on the balls of their feet and toes, prepared to move either direction with one motion. Set to go. The balanced pose I'm suggesting is an everyday adult version of this at-ready stance.

Slump

Now try the Flat-Brain Slump

As you look at the illustration, imagine a basketball in your belly. To make room for it shift your pelvis and rear-end back, pooch out your tummy so the small of your back caves in. You may feel a little twinge of discomfort in your lower back (a hint of what can happen with constant emotional pressure).

When your stomach goes out and your butt and pelvis go back, your knees lock back, slowing the blood flow to the brain, which can cloud thinking and even cause one of the Queen's finest to faint. Your weight settles on your heels. In this position with your knees locked you can't move quickly. A little shove and you're off your feet — a pushover.

Drop and round your shoulders forward, giving the sensation of carrying the weight of the world on your shoulders. Pull them down a little more and your lungs will compress, so you can't breathe deeply.

Tip your head forward. Your eyes will see only what is near you on the ground. Pebbles (in life) will look like rocks (or boulders). You lose perspective. Maturity requires seeing the long view, how present crises compare with future goals.

Tipping your head and shoulders forward puts strain on your neck, in time producing neck pain and headaches. Jutting your chin out, stretching your vocal chords, makes your voice sound thin and raspy. In years past, when not sure of my sermon prep, I'd anxiously lean forward, "leading with my chin" — vulnerable and by the end of my delivery, hoarse.

In the slump arms tense and lift, pointing forward. When we're upset we have a strong tendency to point at others (judge them) and see them as the cause of our problems.

The Flat-Brain Slump damages coordination and diminishes self-confidence. We don't see, hear, or think clearly. We bump into things and tend toward being accident-prone. Insurance companies know that when people go through major upsets, such as grief or divorce, their driving habits degenerate.

Pecking orders

While the Slump reduces our ability to function well, it also effects how others treat us. Not good. My family moved off the farm into town when I was nine, taking some chickens with us. The chicken yard pecking order always fascinated me. The top-dog chicken pecked all the others, the second pecked the rest, and on down the list, until one chicken was pecked by all of them, and often did not survive.

The most-pecked chicken scurried (and slumped) around the yard, almost attracting trouble. A dog who messes in the corner and then skulks (slumps) away from the sound of your footsteps, doesn't invite petting, but rather almost asks for harsh words. There is something about the look that draws a negative response. (And the same for us too?)

As a young pastor it rattled me to visit hospitals during non-visiting hours. After harrowing put-down encounters with a few Nurse Ratchet types (who'd likely been pecked by both doctors and patients), I took time to think it through. I visualized a white-haired master of the pulpit I knew walking down a hospital hallway to call on a parishioner in off hours. The nurses and staff would part like the Red Sea. How come? We were both ordained and on "missions of mercy." What was the difference? Simple. He walked as if he belonged there. No slump. (So I learned to walk tall and the pecking stopped.)

But, it happened again one day on my way home from a camping vacation. I wheeled into a hospital to visit a new mother. I hadn't shaved, was sunburned, wearing shorts and sandals (pretty disreputable). I approached the Pink Lady at the visitor's desk and asked for my parishioner's room number. *"You'll have to come back during visitors' hours!!!"*

Oops, I realized I not only looked scruffy, but timid (vacation relaxed) as well. I straightened up, pulled my chin back, established eye contact, and said, *"I'm her pastor."*

"Oh, sorry!" she said. *"You can't tell by looking anymore. Room 453. Down the hall."*

Think about this the next time you take a purchase back to a store. The counter person who's been jumped on all day is looking for someone to take it out on. If you let your anxiety about being there cause you to slump, you'll be the one.

Can you minimize the Flat-Brain Slump?

Can you influence the way you feel about yourself and the way others treat you? Sure, you can. I don't care whether you begin from your outsides or your insides. Either will get you started. If you change what's going on inside you, your body's posture and the impression you give will change. If you change your body posture, it will affect how you feel on the inside and how others react to you. Best yet, over time, you can work on both.

Change from outside in

It's clear that when we are happy inside, we smile on the outside. But let's look first at changing our outsides to affect our insides. Sometime when you are down, try holding a pencil crosswise in between your teeth, forcing your facial muscles up, causing a sustained smile. What you do outside may produce an emotional lift inside.

We can reduce some of the effects of the Flat-Brain Slump like I did for the Pink Lady above. I straightened up and took on a balanced look, like I belonged there. We can practice the balanced position, shaking ourselves loose, taking deep breaths, and talking with fully supported voices. Moving in a balanced, non-push-over way will not only make us feel more confident, but will communicate strength to others.

There are some fine Ted Talks about body language on YouTube. They suggest that we can make ourselves appear less confident or powerless by sitting or standing scrunched in on ourselves in a closed posture, like we're playing solitaire on a smart phone. Practicing an open stance with outstretched "victory arms" can help break us out of the slump and convey the impression that we can manage our lives well.

Studies show that two minutes of holding an expanded body posture with outstretched winning arms before an interview changes not only how the interviewer sees us, but our body chemistry. It measurably increases testosterone and decreases cortisol, preparing us, male or female, for handling a challenge. Slumping in on ourselves reverses the chemistry and gives us a sense of powerlessness.

Striking the "Wonder Woman pose" may not pump up our emotional systems right away, but don't let that slow you down. The body language folks encourage us to *"fake it until we make it."*

We can act strong and capable even though we feel weak. Doing so will display confidence to others and eventually we'll come to believe it and be it ourselves.

I like putting it this way: *"Straighten up physically and grow into it emotionally."*

When we move with a balanced look, people won't have the same urge to kick us that they would if we trudged slumpily up to them. It even works over the phone. My Sally says, *"When you face a difficult conversation on the phone, stand up, feet apart, head up. You'll do better."* When I stand tall, wide, and ready on the tennis court, I find that it increases my confidence (and my opponent's wariness).

Change from inside out

 You can use the book's listening techniques to encourage fat bellies to subside, hearts to un-harden, and brains to get square again. When that happens, bodies straighten up and carry off everything they do better.

A look at the Flat-Brained Syndrome suggests four goals to help move others (and ourselves) back to relatively normal functioning. Listening well goes to work on insides by reducing emotional disturbance, clarifying thinking, increasing self-confidence, and building supportive friendships. These help us stand taller, function better, and improve our relating abilities.

The four basic goals in listening (counseling)

1. Reduce emotional disturbance

Look at the stomach: Like an electrical storm in a computer, too much mixed emotional energy in people produces erratic behavior. You can help reduce this emotion overload by helping people *acknowledge* and release their feelings.

If they expel some of their upset, there'll be less pressure on their brains. They'll be better able to decide what's best, whether to take a long walk, mow a lawn, tell someone what they're angry about, negotiate a new plan, go see a lawyer, sleep on it, or gather more information.

2. Clarify thinking

Likewise when stomach containers expand and brains go flat, people get confused. They see few alternatives and can't accurately assess themselves or their situations. Folks have trouble making good decisions unless they can think clearly.

Good listeners help them see the interaction between their feelings and thoughts, their actions and the actions of others, and themselves in their situations. This clarity will enable them to see new options and make more constructive decisions for their lives.

3. Increase self-confidence

When people get upset and confused, their self-confidence erodes. If you listen to them with respect and don't take over their problems, you'll make it clear that you believe they can manage their own lives. That builds their self-confidence and gives them more strength to carry out the options they choose.

4. Build supportive friendships

When people are muddled, they feel alone, which makes any problem seem more daunting. Listening builds friendships so people don't feel isolated. When they sense a friendship connection, they find new support, and the courage to go on.

When you are flat-brained yourself, you can go a long way toward moving back to normal functioning by concentrating on the first two goals and using the listening techniques on yourself. Then when you can, find yourself a good listener to hear you through your flat-brain periods. (We'll talk later about training a friend to be your "go to" listener.)

When you take time and learn to skillfully listen to others, you will help make this four-way magic happen for them. You'll be part of building confident people whose feelings and thoughts are clear, who have solid friendships, whose bodies reflect their self-confidence, and who can manage their lives well.

And now with an enriched understanding of what listening can do, let's return to skill building with another listening technique. After that we'll encounter a head-on collision between two people with flat brains.

— ∞ —

How to Listen Better: Technique # 4

The second part of paraphrasing shifts the focus from the talkers' feelings, in *para-feeling*, to their thoughts, by *para-thinking*, though the technique is similar.

𝕊 Use para-thinking

■ *Put the talker's thoughts, which include ideas, views, observations, facts, and perceptions, into your own words.*

When you put people's thoughts into your language, they can hear them better. When they hear their thinking come back, filtered through your words, they can tell very quickly what they do and do not mean.

For example a talker says, *"I don't know whether I want to be a salesman or not. I think I'll hold off on taking that selling class."* If that doesn't make sense, you might say: *"You should take the class to find out if you like selling."*

But, this argument would likely bring resistance, *"I don't have time to find out whether I like selling. You know about our finances. I need to make money now."* If instead you used ***para-thinking,*** you could respond: *"So it doesn't make sense to you to take the sales course until you figure out what you want to do with your life...?"*

Hearing their own words coming back to them, he/she might say, *"Right. (Pause) Though maybe taking the course would give me a clue about whether I could sell and whether I'd like it."* Putting the talker's ideas into your words helps them see gaps in their thinking so they can sharpen their thoughts themselves.

To clarify thinking is a process

Clarifying our thinking has several stages. Thoughts form in our heads. We think about them, revise them, and roll them around in our minds to sharpen and polish them. The more often we come back to them the clearer they become.

Saying our thoughts out loud is almost magical in helping us to refine them. Our brains react differently when we take our thoughts in through our ears, instead of just thinking them silently inside.

Para-thinking adds to the magic. When someone para-thinks back our fuzzy, silly, or unrealistic thoughts (or cracker-jack ones), it helps us to see that ourselves. When we hear someone else put our thoughts into their words, we discover yet a new level of clarity, objectivity, and validation that we can't get by ourselves. Such feedback helps "separate the wheat from the chaff."

When you use *para-thinking* with people you care about or on yourself, it will help clarify the thinking processes. Such clarity opens the door to new thoughts, options, and actions.

6

The Flat-Brain Tango

Now for a look at what happens when we encounter people with that cluster of symptoms I've called, "The Flat-Brain Syndrome." A flat-brained person approaches and the music begins for "The Flat-Brain Tango."

The plot thickens. Will we help him or her calm down, think straighter, and relate better or will we catch what they have?

"Flat-Brain" in the picture represents someone who is depressed, excited, angry, happy, fearful. Their system is on overload and the mouth tends to enter hyper-drive, making it difficult for those nearby to remember it is connected to a flat brain and fat belly. This person can infect every one at a party, in an office, or on your block with *flatbrainitis*.

But the more pressing issue comes one-on-one. The negatively-loaded flat-brainers are more of a problem than the positives. They are "on the peck" as my family used to say. The air hangs heavy around such folks, making it hard for those in the area to breathe, think, and not get defensive.

The person named "Thud" represents us, relaxed and happy with stomach, heart, and head working well. But when F-B's three functions go on overload, the emotional disturbance (1) jolts his/her head (2) and

the attached mouth opens sending a verbal accusation (attack) toward Thud.

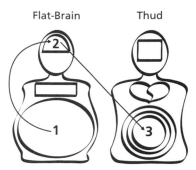

The opening salvo might sound like:
*"You don't pay me enough for the job I'm do-
ing."* Or, *"I'll tell you how we are, my husband just died."* Or, *"Why did you order that
green couch?"* Each one is loaded with un-
described emotion and hidden accusation.
When someone hits you with one of these, you'll recognize it by the sinking
feeling in the pit of your stomach (3), which I call "the thud experience."

To illustrate, we'll follow the business accusation example. The hit in the
gut activates Thud's flat-brain process (3
& 4). So what happens? Well of course,
a defense (attack) (5): *"We're paying you
all the company can afford."*

Does that help? Certainly not.
When we defend ourselves, we attack
the very people who already have fat bellies, hard hearts, and flat brains.
We add to their upsets, reducing even more their abilities to cope.

Keep in mind that though we call
it "defending ourselves," defense and
attack are identical. A mortar fired in
defense maims and kills as thoroughly as one fired in attack. The same is
true for relationships. You can see it
here. Defending ourselves by hitting
Flat-Brain in the stomach increases F-

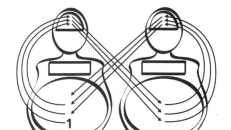

The Flat-Brain Tango

B's pain, which flattens his/her brain even more and activates another
round of defense (attack). And the dance goes on.

This flat-brained tango between people is like escalation between
countries. You add a few soldiers at the border. We bring in a tank or
two. You deploy some guided missiles. We ... and pretty soon it's all-out
war. How often have we watched that between people and countries?

So Flat-Brain responds: "The company has plenty to spend on your long lunches and travel."

And Thud defends: "But, I'm producing enough to warrant them."

F-B: "Right. It helps when you're part of the boss's family."

Thud: "Family or not, your production doesn't merit an increase."

F-B: "Your so-called production is all in your head."

Thud: "And *you don't work here anymore. You're fired.*"

A courtroom culture

Another name for the flat-brain tango might be "courtroom." We can't turn on television without finding lawyers, juries, and judges battling for victory. Winning seems to be everything. TV reared some of us with *Perry Mason, Matlock,* and *LA Law,* hit its stride with *The Practice, Judging Amy,* countless versions of *Law and Order,* struck our funny bones with Boston Legal, and upped the drama with *The Good Wife.*

Legal thrillers roll off bookstore and library shelves and download to fill our electronic screens. There are and will be more shows and books subtly training us in the art of personal warfare.

TV parades celebrity criminal cases in tiresome detail until the public says it can hardly bear it, yet advertisers know the ratings — people watch by the hour. Even "regular" people get in on the act, agreeing to have their minor skirmishes settled by robed actor-like lawyers. The flat-panel screen and legal thrillers groom us to practice a litigious style of communication.

Our cultural norm says that when attacked, we have "the right to defend ourselves." Does that improve relationships? Such courtroom escalation creeps in to how we relate. It turns a lot of communicating into win/lose games.

Many of us find it hard to talk without accusing, or listen without defending, and so goes the Flat-Brain Tango.

A common courtroom-kitchen exchange starts when she accuses: *"You're late for dinner again."*

He defends: *"What's the point? You never have dinner ready when I get home."*

And she: *"The point is, you are never here for me or the children."*

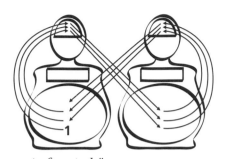

He: *"Somebody's got to make a living. You don't bring in any money."*

She: *"I thought you wanted me to be a stay-at-home mother."*

He parries: *"Right. You watch TV all day. Our house is a mess and the kids are out of control."*

We all know the courtroom games so well, if you scratch one of us, you'll find a prosecuting attorney or defense lawyer right under the surface.

Our defensiveness is so pervasive it even raises its ugly head when we talk about the weather. A person looking at the sky says, *"It's going to be a hot one today."*

Without missing a beat someone within earshot counters with, *"See those clouds. Looks like rain. Better not forget your umbrella."* Low-level defensiveness perhaps, but argumentative and alienating just the same.

Such edgy defensiveness exacts a high cost in relationships. Even at this low level, it's no fun. It undermines our being relaxed with each other. We don't think or act as well when we operate in a self-protective mode.

When we judge others or get judged ourselves, we are immediately into a courtroom dance, where accusing and defending, winning and losing become the music.

The result: We don't let ourselves get close to people who judge us and those whom we judge stay away from us as well.

Courtroom or collaboration?

In business when someone makes a mistake, others often make accusations like: *"You're wrong again." "Another stupid mistake." "Are you trying to ruin the company?"* In courtroom thinking we make a case, determine guilt, and exact punishment.

Compare this approach to a healthy partnership in which the shared intention is to collaborate for the good of the company. Comments might sound like: *"Let's describe the situation accurately so we can understand it and fix any fall-out from the mistake." "Let's figure out how it happened so we can avoid it next time." "If we understand everyone's strengths and weaknesses, we can work together better and make this business more successful."*

One approach is judgmental; the other is not. Courtroom puts down; collaboration builds up. The latter seeks ways to work together. It is a version of win-win. While courtroom conversations may look like win-lose, more realistically, they're lose-lose.

The flat-brain tango is as costly in business as it is in personal relationships. Keeping everyone pulling in the same direction matters in both, as it does in running non-profits, the church, government, and all forms of collaborative human endeavors.

I hope you will be able to recognize the flat-brain tango when you feel it coming (the thud reminder). It's the first step to gaining the know-how to get out of it and move into cooperative, more enjoyable relationships.

—— ∞ ——

How to Listen Better: Technique # 5

The next listening technique (*alternate feelings and thoughts*) will give you a clue about helpfully handling the Flat-Brain Tango. And we'll hit it again harder in the next chapter.

👂 Alternate feelings and thoughts

> ■ *Don't let talkers stay focused too long on either their feelings or their thoughts, that is, their stomachs or their heads. Carefully move them back and forth between the two.*

Feelings are personal reactions to situations and they motivate behavior. Thoughts are observations and interpretations about what's going on in those situations. They help us determine behavior.

When talkers dwell on how depressed they are (feelings), they get more depressed. When they lock into a litany of complaints about their spouses (thoughts), they get angrier by the minute. If they stay focused on either one, emotional intensity increases, clear thinking decreases, and the ability to learn from experience diminishes.

When you help talkers **alternate feelings and thoughts,** you help them see how each one effects the other.

When you hear a feeling, if you listen carefully, you'll find it accompanied by a thought. When you hear a thought expressed, you'll be able to find a feeling lurking beneath it. When you hear a feeling without a thought, or vice versa, you're getting only half of what's going on in the talker and your talker might be in the same boat. Part of good listening is to help people recognize their feelings and thoughts and to clarify the interactions between the two.

Gently guiding folks back and forth between their stomachs and heads produces growth. Because feelings and thoughts are connected, it takes surfacing both to gain clarity and make way for good decision-making. These will mix *para-feeling, para-thinking, acknowledge, repeat accurately, and explore the future.* (**Explore the future** is **Technique # 30.**) For example:

Talker: *"The jerk threw an ashtray at me. He's always doing stupid things like that."*

Listener: *"So he threw an ash tray at you...? Did that frighten you...?"* (moves from thinking to feeling)

Talker: *"It scared me first, then I got angry."*

Listener: *"So you were really scared and angry...? What did you do then...?"* (moves from feeling to thinking)

Talker: *"After I ducked, I yelled at him and broke his favorite golf club."*

Listener: *"Broke his favorite golf club...? How did that feel make you feel...?"* (moves from thinking to feeling)

Talker: *"A lot better."*

Listener: *"Mmmm...? Better...? Then what did you do...?"* (moves from feeling to thinking)

Talker: *"I took a walk around the block to calm down."*

Listener: *"Did the stroll relax you...?"* (from thinking to feeling)

Talker: *"No it didn't. I got irritated again when I remembered how much I paid for his golf clubs."*

Listener: *"So remembering about breaking his expensive club really bothered you...? What do you think about it now...?"* (from feeling to thinking)

Talker: *"Well, the club isn't important, but my marriage is."*

Listener: *"So trashing the club doesn't matter, but you are concerned about your marriage...?"* (from thinking to feeling)

Talker: *"Yes, I want to turn it around before it gets any worse."*

Listener: *"Sounds like you want to save your marriage...? What can you do about it...?"* (moves from para-feeling to explore the future or nexting.

Talker: *"Yes, I do. I guess I'm ready to call a marriage counselor."*

Listener: *"Do you have one in mind or would you like a referral...?"*

The listener helped the talker alternate feelings and thoughts, that is, "label, define, and describe" them. This helps talkers see how their feelings affect their thinking, behaviors, and situations; and how their thoughts, behaviors, and situations effects their feelings. As a result, the talker calmed down, thought more clearly, and moved toward a solution.

Incidentally, when you find yourself uptight and confused you can use this method on yourself. Gently move yourself back and forth between your emotions and your thoughts, between your personal reactions and your situation, until you relax and think more clearly.

My favorite psychiatrist repeatedly urged his counseling students to, "label, define, and describe." It just fits here.

For simplicity you can **alternate feelings and thoughts** by using **para-thinking** and **para-feeling.** It works like a charm and allows emotional energy to subside and thinking to clear, which can produce new insights and behaviors.

Now let's see how to get out of the flat-brain tango.

7

Opting Out of the Flat-Brain Tango

WHEN WE CATCH OURSELVES slipping into the Flat-Brained Tango, can we stop and de-escalate the situation? Yes we can, but it means giving up what seeming advantage we get out of arguing and trying to win.

Victors or friends?

The classic *Pink Panther* movie, starring Peter Sellers as the clumsy Inspector Clouseau, included a scene where the wily rogue plied the gorgeous young princess with charm and fine champagne. David Niven played the charmer and Claudia Cardinale the charmee. Towards the end of the evening, after considerable wooing and intoxicating, she raised a pointed question, *"Now that I've become vulnerable, I guess we'll find out whether you are going to be victor or friend."*

This pinpoints a fundamental issue: Is the goal in our relationships to be victors or friends? Will we let our insecurities drive us toward winning and control, or will we risk trying to hear and understand each other so that we can act together for mutual good?

I remember (embarrassed) one of my early marriage arguments over purchases. I won because I "argued better." I've since learned that arguing better isn't always beneficial. While the sewing machine I advocated might have been technically the best available, the purchase didn't consider the needs and desires of the principal user, my wife. (She never used it as much as she had wanted and it remained a reminder of a power decision fiasco.) Our relationship suffered, because I won and she lost.

And in relationships someone winning most often makes everyone a loser.

The need to win

I'm not talking here about those times when winning may be essential to living lives of integrity, to protecting our families, or to maintaining a healthy society, because certainly, there are times when fighting is essential. But deciding which of these are critical issues is made more difficult by our unhealthy need to win (and be right). The need to win can get in the way of our doing what's best for people.

The difference between an unhealthy need to win and a healthy drive to win, shows up most obviously in sports. Winning at any cost (need to win) includes using drugs, cheating, and even intentionally injuring other players. A healthy competitive drive to win includes hard training, concentration, investing full energy, and even owning up to a bad line call that favors the opponent. We applaud such straightforward competitiveness and call it sportsmanship.

While most of us share a desire to win, for me, it turns into an unhealthy need to win when it is additionally fueled by anxiety — where we "must" win to assuage our insecurities and prove ourselves, even at the cost of fair play. I recently photographed a novelty store picture of two people face-to-face, yelling at each other, each shouting a version of, *"I'm not arguing. I'm just explaining why I'm right."* Neither had a clue how their flat-brained need to win prevented them from seeing that they were in fact arguing and trying to win over the other.

This kind of winning is about gaining power over people. This negative need to win in relationships shows up when we put winning arguments ahead of treating others with respect, when we interrupt folks with a barrage of facts, when we give up discussing issues in favor of attacking character and motives, and when we defend ourselves by belittling others.

Are these short-lived victories — putting ourselves up by putting others down — ones that we can give up in favor of messy and risky experimental cooperation?

This unkind and unhealthy part of us seems deeply ingrained

But, it is possible to counter this urge, to avoid painfully escalating en-counters like the stormy night episode. As I worked with people I began to see this underlying issue: That chances to deepen our connections come as we gradually let go of our need to win. But to acknowledge this negative part of us and stop it from spoiling our relationships, requires serious self-examination and constant vigilance.

When we recognize our tendencies to relate to each other in this courtroom-like manner, we have identified the enemy. Giving up our defensiveness lets us hear the hurt and caring hidden beneath someone else's anger. Then we can begin to turn destructive win-lose games into come-alive cooperation.

In short, we can go for being *friends*, rather than *victors*.

Handling a "thud"

But how do we do it? For starters, when we sense a thud feeling, we reframe it. Instead of going into auto-defense mode and making the situation worse, we see it as our bodies telling us that a new response is needed to help a hurting (attacking) person.

If you want to shut off the music and de-escalate the flat-brain tango, no-tice the thud and don't defend yourself. While I'm afraid that escalation in our culture is "normal" behavior, we have the option of what a management expert called "deviant" behavior — a deviation from the norm (a mathematical phrase). 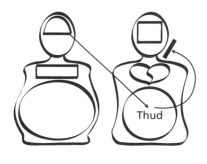 That is, not doing what everyone else does, but unlearning those parry-ing patterns of communication and trying new ones.

I invite you to join me in a radical attempt at "deviant" behavior. I'm suggesting that we shift our goals from winning to understanding and move from courtroom to partnership in our relationships.

This is a fundamental attitude adjustment. It also could be called putting love into action.

Again, feeling the thud is your first clue that the other person has a problem and therefore needs your help. A friend said this is one of the most useful book ideas for her: *"Now when I feel a thud, I think, oh, this person's got a problem and needs help."*

However, when we experience a thud, our immediate tendency is to think that we have a problem and need to defend ourselves. If the thud shakes us up enough to flatten our brains, then we do have a problem, but our problem is different from the one that Flat-Brain hit us with.

So now there are two problems, Flat-Brain's and ours. If we focus on ours, we end up escalating the situation and providing no help to the other person with their problem.

When I notice the sinking sensation in my gut and feel like defending myself, before my brain goes completely flat, I try to remind myself that what I expect of myself is not "standard" cultural defensiveness, but rather "deviant" behavior.

I've been struggling with this for years. Some days I pull it off. On others, when my brain goes flat, I botch it completely. But then I try to figure out how to rebuild something out of the rubble.

Do I deserve a shot?

Feeling the thud raises a basic question for me: Do I deserve it? Do I in particular have it coming? I've thought that over pretty carefully and here's my thinking: We all do some good and some bad. We don't do all the things we should and we do things we shouldn't. As near as I can tell, none of us does everything right. So we all share some guilt. As a result, none of us deserves to be judge over the rest of us and all being in the same boat, none of us has being judged coming any more than anyone else.

I figure I'm a basically nice person, that is, a BNP, and as far as I'm concerned, that goes for you too. So, we don't deserve getting worked over and as a result, have no need to defend ourselves. We're free then not to get wrapped up in our own guilt. And especially, we ought not be wallowing in our guilt when there are fat-bellied, hard-hearted, and flat-brained people who need our help.

If we keep that in mind when our insides go thud, we can refocus on dealing with the dance, Flat-Brain, and his/her problem.

Changing communication habits

How do we begin to change old habits? First we recognize and admit that we are often more interested in our point of view and getting our way than in building rapport and finding out what anyone else thinks and feels.

Wait a minute before you say: *"Not me. I'm really interested in what others have to say."* Think back. Have you ever noticed that when others are talking, your mind tends to jump ahead to what you think?

We often frame arguments while waiting for others to quit talking. Some call this "ritual listening." It looks like listening, but it's not. It's waiting for the other person to pause or take a breath so we can get our point across (and win). The result: We pay attention to what we want to say. We don't focus on what other people are trying to say. (For more on *ritual listening,* jump ahead to: **Chapter 17 – Avoiding Ten Communication Traps.**)

Being good listeners requires shifting focus from our interests to the interests of others. It means concentrating on their thinking rather than your own.

Try it in your next conversation with a friend, relative, or business associate. Set aside your own concerns. Ask yourself what they are thinking, what their concerns are, and why they are acting the way they are. See how long you can stay focused on their perceptions rather than on what you want to say or on what is going on with you. You may be surprised at how hard it is for you to hear them out.

The double-reverse-twist

When someone with a flat-brain starts the tango with me, I use the **double-reverse-twist** to stay out of it. Follow the numbers and the arrows on the line to see how it works for me:

I start with a quick look at my stomach (1): *"Ugh, I've been hit (thud feeling)."* I follow that acknowledgement with an actual "gulp" (2). It stops the jolt before it flattens my brain by giving me the physical

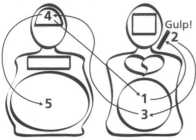

sensation of swallowing the urge to defend myself.

I check back with my stomach (3). What does being hit mean, if I'm a basically nice person (BNP) and don't have it coming? Aah, F-B can't see or remember that I'm a friend, that we're in this together. Must be a flat brain (4) or he/she'd know better than to attack me. He/she has a problem.

Keep following the line. Where does the flat brain (4) come from? I remember. The stomach must be on overload (5). For me, nearly having a flat brain from the attack, I gradually unfold this process into understanding and dealing with what's going on between F-B and me.

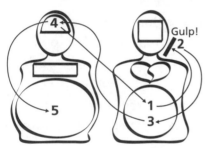

Let's use the same illustration and put words to the ***double-reverse-twist.***

Follow the line again:

Flat-Brain: *"You don't pay me enough for the job I'm doing!!!"*

Thud: To myself (1) I say, *"Ugh, I've been hit* (thud)*."* If my brain is in danger of flattening beyond usefulness, I relieve my stomach by saying, *"Oops, that blew my mind. Give me that again…? I don't want to misunderstand you…?"*

F-B: *"You don't pay me enough and I need a raise!!"*

Thud: I gulp (2) and stop it from taking out my head functions. I remind myself I'm a BNP and F-B doesn't realize that (3). I also think: This valuable employee must be really upset to attack like that. I catch my breath and then follow the Double-Reverse-Twist line to F-B's flat brain (4) and repeat accurately what I find there: *"So, you're not getting paid enough and need more money…?"*

F-B: *"Right on! This cheap company doesn't take care of its employees."*

T: I acknowledge the head (4) and shift toward the stomach (5) where the heat is coming from: *"Sounds like the way the company treats its employees makes you really angry…?"*

Acknowledging what's bothering F-B, begins the downshift from anger to resentment: *"Yeah. I've never liked the way it treats family and others who work here differently."*

T: This little shot at me (boss's family) shakes me enough that I need to recycle through steps (1) to (3) before I can again focus on (4). To myself (1) I say, *"Ugh. Hit again."* I do another gulp (2). To myself (3): *"Hitting a BNP means F-B is still really upset and flat-brained."* Then I can handle getting back to (4) again: *"So the company's nepotism hasn't helped (para-thinking)...?"* Then I'd go for (5): *"Sounds like it has irritated you for some time. (para-feeling)"*

F-B: *"Well it has. I like working here, but I'm struggling financially and need to figure something out."*

(This conversation would take longer, but I shortened it to illustrate the process.)

Reflecting head, stomach, and heart talk

Once I get the ***double-reverse-twist*** rolling, then I gently move Flat-Brain back and forth between head talk (4) and stomach talk (5) *(alternate feelings and thoughts)*. That helps F-B reduce emotional buildup and clarify thinking.

Growth (therapy) happens when a person moves back and forth between head functions (4) and stomach functions (5), the two worlds of thinking and feeling. Remember, practicing *para-feeling, para-thinking,* and *alternate feelings and thoughts*? Really useful here.

While moving back and forth between head and stomach is basic, an occasional detour through the heart functions is helpful to humanize the absolutes popping out of Flat-Brain.

When Flat-Brain said, *"You don't pay me enough for the job I'm doing."* Thud might have led F-B through the heart (4 to 6) by saying, *"So you think you're not getting paid enough for your work."*

Or, when F-B said, *"This cheap company doesn't take care of its employees."* Thud could say (4 to 6), *"It looks*

61

to you as though this company doesn't take care of its employees." Or, you could say (5-6), *"You're pretty upset with the company. It looks to you as though…"*

Diving through heart talk like this can help F-B see that his views are his and not everyone's, or the absolute truth.

This helps reactivate his heart functions. He'll become more aware that he's describing his own concerns and more open to the views of others.

(For more on including heart talk, check ahead for **Technique # 24 – Reframe the Rigidity.**)

Let's dance to a new song

> *When your stomach goes thud*
> *And your brain goes flat,*
> *When your eyeballs begin to bulge*
> *And your ears start to close,*
> *When you want to defend yourself*
> *And attack someone else,*
> *Don't.*
> *Swallow hard,*
> *gulp it down,*
> *And do the double-reverse-twist.*

Someday, I think I'll set that to music.

How to Listen Better: Technique # 6

When communication attempts get muddled and sticky, I resort often to *decode* as one of the most effective and simplest listening techniques to master. It's a winner in defusing the Flat-Brain Tango.

Decode

- *Decode messages by checking your translation with the talker. Say, "What I heard you say was (fill it in). Ask: "Is what I heard what you meant…?"*

Our culture teaches us to "encode" messages, that is, to say something a little off from what we mean and to listen for what we expect, rather than what the talker intends. So, we neither say what we mean nor hear what is said. This double filtering makes communication difficult unless we learn to listen below the surface.

The *"Meant, Said, Expected, Heard Syndrome"* shows what happens to the messages we send and receive.

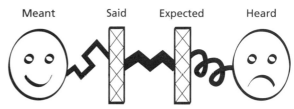

For example: An exchange between a husband and a wife: The husband **meant** to say to his wife, *"Honey, I was thinking about how much I love you and appreciate you for what you do for me and the children. I want to do something nice for you. I want to give you a break and take you out to dinner and that movie you've wanted to see."* But, what he actually **said** (after being filtered through his defensive grid) was, *"If you can get a babysitter, I'll take you to that movie you've been bugging me about."*

The wife figures that even though he's been distant all week, he'll want sex this Friday evening. She listens for what she **expected.** What she **heard** (after being filtered through her defensive grid) was: *"I suppose I'll have to take you to dinner and the movie you've been nagging about to warm you up for later."* She responds to what she **heard,** *"No way. You're not buying me off. You've been an absent husband and father all week."*

Befuddled, he says, *"Why are you so angry? I just told you how much I love you."*

And she replies, *"You did not. You just pressured me for sex."*

It might have helped if he'd not encoded the message and clearly stated what he **meant**: *"Honey, I've been really busy and tied in a knot over work lately, and you've been understanding with me and carried more than your share with the children. I appreciate it and want to do something to let you know I'm grateful. If you would like a night out, I'll get a babysitter and take you to dinner and a movie. And you can relax."*

It is possible for us to say things directly if we take the time to be clear about what we really want to say. (If in a hurry, check **The EHJs of balanced communication** in Chapter 12.)

It might have helped if she'd listened, that is, used **decode**, and asked if what she **heard** is what he **meant** to say: *"What I **heard** was, 'If you give me what I've been nagging about, will I come through with sex tonight…?' Is that what you **meant**…?"*

Then he could have clarified: *"Sorry, that may be close to what I **said**, but it's not what I **meant**. I intended to say that I'd noticed how you covered for me this week and carried extra weight with the offspring. I want to do something to show my appreciation. I thought you'd like me to take you to*

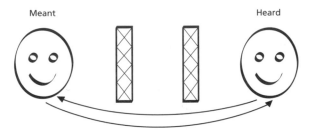

Meant   Heard

dinner, because I know you like to eat food you didn't have to cook and get a break from being a mother. And I remembered there was a movie you wanted to see."

She responds with *para-feeling and para-thinking,* *"So you're trying to tell me you appreciate me and think I'd enjoy a night out…?"* And he says, *"Un-huh."* And she says, *"Well, I'm glad to hear that and sure, I'd love to. Let's go."*

When what someone says makes you feel defensive (thud), try **decode** and find out what message the person is really trying to convey. Say and ask: *"What I heard was (fill it in) … Is that what you meant…?"*

Working together, it's possible to get beneath what was **said** and **expected**, to what was actually **meant** and **heard**. What makes the difference is taking the time to **decode** what one person **meant** and to find out what the other person **heard**. When we move together to identify those, we develop that elusive understanding that keeps you out of useless arguments and heals relationships.

No one knows what anyone actually said?

How often have you heard conversations like this?

Sam: *"You didn't say that."*

64

Emily: *"I did too."*

Sam: *"Look, I remember what I heard. My ears and memory work just fine."*

Emily: *"I'm the one who said it. I should know what I said."*

Don't waste time or emotional energy on this kind of argument ever again. Let's be real here. No one knows what either person really **said**. One of us remembers what we **meant** to say, not in fact what we **said**, and the other remembers what we **expected** to hear, not what was actually **said**. What we remember is skewed by our intentions or our expectations. So, no one of us can ever find out what was really **said**.

In addition, what was actually **said** doesn't matter anyway. People don't act on what anyone **said**, but rather on what they meant or what they heard.

From here on, the operative words are **heard** and **meant**. And again, to **decode** an encoded message, say and ask: *"What I heard was (fill it in)...? Is that what you meant...?"*

Notes

PART TWO:
The Talker-Listener Process

8

Going Beyond the Tango

So HOW DO WE replace the Flat-Brain Tango (everyone talking and no one listening) with a communicating style that un-flattens brains, makes information sharing clearer, builds empathy, trust, and cooperation, and puts the "commune" back in the word communication?

For me, the answer is the talker-listener process — taking turns talking and listening. My understanding of the process developed over years of trial and error. As it became clear to me that the roles of talking and listening were substantially different, I noticed that what we focus on, what we think about, and how we say it depends on which role we are taking. To pinpoint these roles to my classes I first wrote "Talker" and "Listener" on opposite sides of A-frame cards so we could practice switching roles and taking turns.

TALKER
I'm most bothered
I own the problem
GOALS •To share my feelings •To share my thoughts
Without • Accusing • Attacking • Labeling • Judging

LISTENER
I'm calm enough to hear
I don't own the problem
GOALS • To provide safety • To understand • To clarify
Without • Agreeing • Disagreeing • Advising • Defending

Gradually, I discovered "do's" and "don'ts" for each role. I passed out manila card stock and people folded and wrote the goals and rules on them. They found the cards useful in their homes and offices. I began to use them in marriage counseling, giving couples a take-home tool to help them communicate better, when I wasn't there with them.

Several years later, I decided to move from rough scribbled cards to professionally printed ones. I struggled to make the phrases on the card sharp and parallel. I took the mock-up to a workshop. It went over well, except for one phrase that nearly brought the participants off their chairs.

As a guide for the Listener I had written: *"It's not my problem."* They heard it as a put down: *"It's your problem, and you can stuff it."* After I finished the workshop I hurried to the nearest phone and called the graphic designer, who said, *"Too late. I already turned it over to the printer."* And I said, *"I'll have to eat the cost. Change the loser line to read, 'I don't own the problem.'"* The corrected card has worked well ever since.

Another note about "problem." It's not a negative, but merely an indicator of an issue or topic or concern you'd like to talk over or solve. (Can you tell I have a degree in mathematics?)

I've taught the Talker-Listener Card (TLC) method in workshops, parent/child relationships, couples' counseling, churches, school and university settings, city governments, small businesses, and large corporations. I have it printed on the back of my business card, so it's always available. Occasionally, people show me the worn and wrinkled cards they keep in their purses or wallets. Some keep them by their home phones or on their desks at work. Others give theirs away to people they feel need them more than they do. When they run into me, they ask for new ones.

This handy little tool, the Talker-Listener Card, has helped many people significantly improve their communication, their relationships, and the cooperation of their work groups.

Incidentally, if you are reading a print version and have lost the inserted TLC, there are cutouts in the back of the book. If you are reading an *electronic version* and/or want free printed copies or PDF downloads of the TLC, check the back of the book or our website for ordering options.

Taking Turns Seems Simple

Taking turns is essential to the Talker-Listener process. It may seem simple, but it is not. We learned the social-getting-along skill of taking turns in preschool. However, before we left grade school, many of us abandoned it for the more competitive skills useful in getting ahead of others.

I want us to apply our child-learned skill of taking turns directly to communication. If we can focus on one person's view at a time and establish human connection, we'll all feel heard, sense that we are valued, relax, feel safe, and function better.

The A-frame card works by folding it in the middle so that TALKER is on one side and LISTENER on the other. Placed between two people or used in a group, the Talker-Listener Card helps track whose turn it is to talk and whose turn to listen. It's like a game people choose to play together. It sets guidelines to aid participants with their roles and makes it easier to focus on one person at a time. The game-like quality can take the edge off the personal communication struggle and replace it with some friendly objectivity.

TALKER
I'm most bothered
I own the problem
GOALS · To share my feelings
· To share my thoughts
Without · Accusing · Attacking
· Labeling · Judging

LISTENER
I'm calm enough to hear
I don't own the problem
· To provide safety
GOALS · To understand
· To clarify
Without · Agreeing · Disagreeing
· Advising · Defending

Taking turns with the TLC works like this: One person talks; the other listens. When the talker finishes, so does the listener and the card is reversed. Then the person who talked first listens, and the one who listened first, talks. This works like an online keyboard Chat with a customer service tech: While you type a question or comment in your Send box, the screen indicates the tech is Listening. Then when you hit the Send button, the screen indicates the tech is Responding and you wait for the return message to be typed and sent to your screen. Hitting the Send button changes the direction of the communication, like turning the card. So you are either Responding or Listening, but only one at a time.

When you first use keyboard Chat it seems unnatural and mechanical, where only one person can type at a time. Similarly, when we first try taking turns with the TLC, it feels odd, but that's simply because we aren't used to communicating that way.

Imagine we are fishing together in Oregon. Standing hip deep in a wild cold river, I fight and land a fifteen-pound steelhead. Those big trout swim to the ocean and back to spawning streams, repeating the cycle several times. As a result of fighting ocean currents and predators, they become crafty and strong — one of the hardest fighting game fish to catch.

It's been awhile since I caught my last one. I'm so excited I have to talk to re-live the experience, even if you were there to see it. So I start babbling (stomach talk) to unload my emotion container. But an odd thing happens. When I pause for a breath, you grab the conversation and change the subject to a fishing memory of yours. Perhaps my steelhead reminded you of a larger one you caught last year, one you heard about, or "the one that got away."

Even though I'm too excited to listen (flat-brained), you launch into your story anyway. I stuff my story and off we go into one of those episodes leaving both of us feeling incomplete and unheard. Each of us sees our story as the most compelling as we toss pieces of our stories over the other's shoulders, each waiting for breaks to finish ours, as did Jack and Jill leaving work on Friday.

Don't beat yourself up when you think of how many times you've done this. Every time someone else catches a fish, I notice the same nearly uncontrollable memory surge (emotion) well up in me, jolt my brain, and I want to tell one of my stories. On good days I can remember to avoid talking when others need listening ears. On other days I still blow it.

One fish story at a time

We don't have to give in to the urge to take over someone else's air-time. If we communicated well about the fishing incident, that is, I finished my turn to talk (tell my story) before you started yours, it might sound something like this:

Me: *"Wow! Was that a fighter! Did you see her jump?"*

You: *"I came around the bend in time to see the last jump, how long did it take you to land it...?"*

Me: *"About fifteen minutes. Thought I was going to lose her when she got near that submerged branch."*

You: *"It'd be tough to lose a fish like that...? You more relieved or excited...?"*

Me: *"Excited. I haven't caught one in quite awhile. She's really bright, just in from the ocean."*

You: *"Bright as a new dime...? You going to keep it or release it...?"*

Me: *"This one's a hatchery fish, see the clipped fin? It's a keeper."*

You: *"You must be pleased...? What'd you hook it on...?"*

Me: *"Salmon eggs with chartreuse and fluorescent orange yarn — water's pretty murky."*

You: *"You use the yarn to make it tougher for them to spit the hook out or for the color...?"*

Me: *"Both, and I use salmon eggs for smell in the colored water."*

You: *"That makes sense...?"*

Me: *"Yeah, I'm happy my strategy worked."*

And finally, your turn begins: *"You know, that reminds me of one I caught last year..."*

Having pretty well finished a turn at my story, my ears and heart are open enough to take in your fish story. This process is like releasing steam from a pressure cooker. Being heard revives my capacity to listen to you, so I can ask, *"Where'd you catch yours...?"*

When we handle one fish story at a time, we can experience a level of satisfaction and connection that may not happen otherwise.

Good listeners improve our stories

Once at a preaching conference, I heard a nationally recognized African-American preacher discussing the "amens" and other vocal responses of his congregation during his sermons. Many of us were not used to such an interactive style.

He said, *"It isn't just up to preachers [talkers] to get the message across. We need help. Preaching takes a lot of work from the congregation too [the listeners]. After services sometimes my people say, 'We did good this morning!' Now that's real preaching when they feel like we did it together."*

The listener's job is more than waiting for people to finish their fish stories. A capable listener, like a midwife, helps people give birth to the feelings and thoughts inside them. It often takes time for talkers to become clear about what they are trying to say. Listening supports the process and helps them tell their stories. Such midwifing takes skill and patience, but it's worth it.

For talkers, sharing an experience with someone who is interested completes it. If no one listens or cares, the wonder of the incident somehow diminishes.

We can help other people round out their experiences by listening instead of interrupting. In return, we become closer to the talkers, as we share in the excitement of the birthing process.

Teeth marks in the tongue

When other people are talking, I find that my thoughts and feelings have a life of their own. They seem to want to butt into other people's talking time. They seem so pressing at the time, I want to say, *"That reminds me..."* and dive right into the middle of their paragraphs.

Recognizing our tendency to interrupt, change the subject, give opinions, make suggestions, or argue, gives us a chance to keep ourselves from leaning into someone else's sentences. When someone tells you about a death, a job change, or their two-year-old's accomplishments and you're struck by something more interesting, bite your tongue and listen.

Instead of talking, respond as a listener, *"Sounds like your friend's death caught you by surprise."* Or, *"How will this job change affect you?"* Or, *"Oooh, what a proud father...?"* Then bite your tongue again to keep from talking. If you absolutely can't stand waiting any longer, say: *"That reminds me of something, but we'll get to it later...? Please go on...? What happened then..?"*

Teeth marks in the tongue — signs of a good listener.

End arguing as we know it

Arguments occur when two views clash and a flat-brained tango begins. If I try to sell you my point of view, while you are trying to get me to buy yours, we're in trouble. I'll be waiting for you to pause so I can straighten you out. You'll be listening for a hole in my view so you can drive a truck through it. And soon we'll be trying to take each other apart.

If we take turns, that is, focus on one point of view at a time, we literally can't argue. Just as one hand can't clap alone, so one point of view can't produce an argument. It's like dropping one end of a tug-of-war rope.

Again, this may sound too simple to be true, but you and I can't argue if we both focus either on understanding your point of view or mine — one at a time.

If you want to stop arguing, you can. We can switch from leaning on others argumentatively to moving with them in cooperation, if we practice using the talker-listener process.

How to Listen Better: Technique # 7

When you are well into a turn listening, you may have a *guess* about what your talker is trying to say. You can use it to help him/her figure out where they're coming from without breaking into their turn.

Guess

- *After listening awhile, guess what's going on with the talker. Spell it out briefly. Ask the talker to try it on to see if fits.*

Guessing is a reality check for both you and the talker. Making a guess says to the talker that you are listening, interested, and thinking (engaged).

Try saying: *"I have a hunch about what may be going on with you. Let me lay it out for you and see what you think... Does that fit...?"* Or, *"From what you're saying, I'd guess that you might be ready for a job change...? How does that strike you...?"*

Note that (...?) makes it clear the talkers are the authorities on what's going on with them and are still talking (not you). To keep us from pushing our ideas on to the talkers, keep in mind that what we're doing is guessing. Not laying our "truth" on them. Our listening job is to help them find *their* truth. Then we won't get invested in our guesses and turn them into talking points (even though it's more fun to talk and hand our "truths" down from above).

An accurate *guess* matters little. While a good *guess* may open the door for talkers to see their situations through different eyes, guesses that are only partly right or even all wrong work too. They invite talkers to correct us or fill in what we miss.

Talkers may say in response to your guess, *"Mmmm, the first part missed a mile, but that last part really hits me. I'll think that one through."* Or, *"No, that's not it at all, but I'm beginning to see what the problem is. Thanks."*

Or, *"You may be right. I hadn't considered changing jobs, but that might solve a lot of the problems I'm facing. I'll think on it."*

Guess is a helpful listening technique because it encourages talkers to review and clarify their thoughts and often to take a step beyond the options they were considering. Now let's move a little deeper into the Talker-Listener Card.

9

The Talker-Listener Card

A FRIEND OF MINE CALLS the Talker-Listener Card "a foldable third person," that is, someone you bring in to moderate a difficult discussion. Introducing a third person into a conversation adds objectivity and puts us on our good behavior — the same thing that happened when I arrived to help the arguing couple that rainy night years ago.

At times we all can use a foldable third person to keep us honest and on target. If you and I agree to use the Talker-Listener Card, it links us in a common effort. We play by the rules of a game and take turns, instead of letting a discussion slip into misunderstanding and arguing like a couple of street fighters.

Using the TLC forces us to observe the roles we play. Placing the card between us takes some of the heat out of discussing difficult issues. It provides a little objective distance, because we are playing a game with rules and holding a serious discussion at the same time. This two-pronged action makes it harder to get caught up in an argument.

When we're playing a game with a little folded card between us, how can we take ourselves too seriously or our conversation too personally? The card reminds us that we can work and play together even when our opinions differ widely. As a reminder in more settings someone suggested I put Talker on one side of a necklace pendant (or coffee cup) and Listener on the other. How would that strike you?

Using the TLC opens the door to more effective conversations when someone needs to "talk things over." This worked many times for me in my last pastorate. Members of my congregation, who knew the method, would invite me to breakfast or lunch. After we ordered, they'd pull the TLC out of their pocket or purse, and set it on the table between us. I knew immediately that they had a concern to share or some kind of complaint. I'd think, "Oh boy, I'm going to get it now. Why do I teach this stuff?"

In a minute or two when my thud subsided, I remembered the ground rules were there for both of us. I couldn't use subtle attacking techniques to save my skin, because the TLC was there to keep me honest. Using the TLC made it safe for them to discuss something that was churning in their emotion containers. It insured that they would be fairly heard. After I'd calmed down, I was pleased that they had learned to confront me in a constructive way and that we were able to discuss contentious issues.

I knew that after I had absorbed a few emotional jolts in the process of understanding them, I would get my time to talk. They knew the rules applied to them too, so they would take their turn trying to understand me.

By using the Talker-Listener Card we had chosen cooperation over trying to win, partnership over courtroom. We had tacitly agreed up front not to argue, but to work toward understanding each other. Taking turns was the symbol for all that and what's more, it worked. It made it so much easier to collaborate for the good of the church, even when we held divergent views and concerns.

The TLC as intervention

While sitting in their living room late one afternoon, a couple who knew the TLC system forgot their training and slipped into a typical marital squabble. Their arguments grew fuzzier, their voices louder. As their quarrel escalated into the Flat-Brain Tango, they lost track of their initial concerns and their caring for each other.

In the kitchen their teenage son rummaged through the refrigerator. He could hear the rising voices. He hesitated, then walked through the living room, grabbed the Talker-Listener Card from its place on the mantel, set it on the couch between his parents, and circled back into the kitchen to finish making his sandwich. He never said a word.

The parents were exposed as if a mirror had been turned on them. They shuddered and smiled at each other in embarrassment and said, "Guess our brains went flat. Okay, let's take turns. Who talks first? Who can listen first?" Focusing on one point of view at a time, they soon resolved their dispute.

Old habits had surfaced and bumped this couple back into a familiar pattern before they realized it. With their son's simple act, the foldable third person intervened, allowing them to see what they were doing. Self-recognition makes better choices possible.

We all forget

Sometimes I forget what I teach. One evening driving home after attending a play, my wife asked whether I enjoyed it and what I thought about it. It always makes me feel good when she's interested in what I think and feel. So eagerly, I shared my reactions to the drama. Then I settled into what I thought was a companionable silence.

A ways down the freeway she said, *"This is when you turn the card and ask me how I liked the play. Remember taking turns?"* Fortunately for me, she was smiling and knows the Talker-Listener Card, sometimes better than I do.

I'd become so caught up in my own talking that I forgot to take a turn listening. I'm still learning too.

As we move along we'll focus more on listening than on talking, since most of us have more difficulty with listening. But I will also discuss how to take your turn talking in ways that have the best chance of being heard.

Getting ready to use the TLC

Begin by observing other peoples' conversations when you are not involved. Identify the roles, who's talking and who's listening, who's sending and who's receiving. You can tell by whose issues are being discussed.

The issue, concern, or story belongs to the talker.

Once you can recognize when other people switch their roles, move to your own conversations and observe the role changes between you and another person. See whether you are sending while the other person receives, whether the other is sending while you receive, or are you both sending with no one receiving?

The goal here is to develop skill as an observer while you are either talking or listening. It just takes practice.

Observing pays dividends

The act of observation puts distance between you and the heat of a conversation, creating some objectivity. This will help to keep your brain from going flat, so you can think, talk, and listen more effectively.

If you listen while the other person talks, you not only get a clearer picture of what the other is saying, but you gain time in the back of your mind to figure out what you think — before it's your turn to talk. This differs from ritual listening by its intent. Here, you are not trying to win, but to respond to what's really there in your talker.

When you observe that someone can't stop talking, an option is to choose to stop talking yourself and listen instead. Then when you observe the other person has finished talking and seems ready to listen, you can shift to talking and have a better chance of being heard.

We have little chance of changing our behavior unless we can calmly observe it. Improving communication skill depends on being able to accurately identify what we are doing, so we can choose other options, if they are needed.

Let's observe a phone conversation between forty-year-old, harried Mary, and her widowed mother, who lives across town:

Mary (talker role): "Oh Mom, my feet hurt. I spent all day shopping for a new sofa."

Mary's mother (also talker role): "Well, I don't get to shop at the big stores anymore. Since your father died, I'm stuck in this apartment."

Mary (talker): "But, you could get a driver's license. All your friends drive. They could take you shopping. I'd like to get a sofa before our anniversary party. It would make the living room more inviting. The old one looks pretty tacky."

MM (talker): "I guess I feel run down too. Sometimes your brother takes me shopping, but I hate *to trouble him. I know how busy he is. And you never seem to have time to take me anymore.*"

A pretty standard low-level flat-brain tango: Each person so focused on their own concerns, that neither pays attention to what the other is saying. They spring-board off each other's comments, right back into their own agendas, each delivering low-level thuds to the other.

The result? Both feel unheard and hurt because their concerns don't seem to matter to the other. Had the TLC been in sync with the conversation, it would have moved back and forth quick enough to make a good fan.

Let's try the conversation again using the Talker-Listener method. Observe the listening response to each talker statement and note the thud reduction:

Mary (talker): "*Oh Mother, my feet hurt. I spent all day shopping for a new sofa.*"

MM (listener): "*You must be really tired...? What kind of sofa are you looking for...?*"

Mary (talker): "*Something in green that would fit our living room. I want it before our anniversary party. The old one looks pretty tacky.*"

MM (listener): "*I'll bet you'd be glad to get it before your party...? The party seems really important to you...?*" (shifts role to talker) "*I can't get downtown to shop in the big stores anymore since your father died.*"

Mary (listener): "*Sounds like you feel pretty limited and lost without Dad...? That must be really hard for you...?*"

MM (talker): "*It really is. I didn't realize how much I depended on him. (Pause) Your brother takes me shopping sometimes, but I hate to ask him because he's so busy.*"

Mary (listener): "*I can't imagine what it would be like losing a husband after all those years...? It must make you feel good that (brother) Bill takes you once in awhile...? Sounds like you'd appreciate it if you and I spent more time together...?*"

MM (talker): *"Oh, yes I would, but I do know how busy you are."*

When each acknowledged what the other felt and thought, the pressure on their flat brains subsided. They also learned more from each other than they did in their first conversation.

This conversation would provide them a sense of connection instead of distance, as in the earlier conversation.

Telephone practice

The phone is great for honing observer skills. Keep a Talker-Listener Card next to your telephone. Practice by turning the card so the TALKER side faces the one who's talking. It won't be obtrusive because the other person can't see what you're doing.

You may be surprised at how rapidly the roles shift, how easily you both get caught up in expressing your views, and how little time either of you spends focused on what the other person is saying.

During face-to-face conversations, use the telephone observation model by mentally keeping the Talker-Listener Card between you and the other person.

If you can keep it in your mind's eye, you can monitor conversation flow, and know when to listen and when you can talk with the best chance of being heard.

Try the TLC with a "safe" friend

When you've observed enough to track the role switches, then try using the TLC with a friend who is patient, kind, and understanding — someone with whom you feel safe. It's best if neither of you has a flat brain on the subject you pick. Start slowly.

This can benefit you both. Because you each get a turn to talk about something that matters and have someone else really focus on what the two of you are thinking and feeling.

When you get together, explain the taking turns process. Ask if he or she will try it with you and be sure you have enough time to experiment. You may want to draw a quick flat-brain picture on a napkin by way of background.

If you get agreement, set the TLC between you and decide who talks first. Both of you be observers to note the role changes. Whichever of you first notices a role shift, turns the card, keeping the Talker side facing the new talker.

If you start to talk out of turn, say, *"Wait, it was your turn to talk, wasn't it...? You weren't finished yet...? Let's go back to what you were saying...?"* Or, ask, *"Who's talking and who's listening...? I think we lost track...?"* Then turn the card back so the original talker can finish.

This game-playing "give and take" makes it easier to hear another person's concerns. It can help keep you out of the courtroom and deepen your friendships.

For further practice with friends, family, or business associates try taking turns by using topics such as:

- What does (vacation or any other topic) mean to you?
- What traditions did/do matter most and least to you?
- What do you like and dislike about your (work, recreation, etc.)?
- What places in the world would you like to see and spend time
- in? What is it about them that grabs you?
- What places have been most meaningful to you? In what way?
- What people have most touched your life? In what way?
- What books, movies, ideas, or events have moved you?
- What would you like to be remembered for?

You could use questions like these to enliven your lunch breaks or family dinners. Conversations with meaningful personal sharing can significantly deepen our knowledge and our relationships.

A coffee house experiment

At times I find myself upset and/or confused about something in my life. It works for me to talk it over with someone who listens and helps me sort it out. So I call a friend to meet me over tea or coffee.

After I pay for our liquids of choice I set the TLC on the table between us and say, *"I need a listener to help me clarify an issue. See what the TLC says: When I'm the talker, it's my problem. You try to understand and clarify, that is, ask me questions and repeat back what you hear me saying. And please note the 'Withouts' at the bottom of the card: No agreeing, disagreeing, giving advice, or defending. I want to solve the problem myself. To do that it would help me to talk out loud and hear you feed back what I'm saying. Then when I'm finished, you'll get a chance to say what you think about my situation. We'll turn the card around and I'll listen to you. Are you willing to do this for me?"*

While they routinely say, *"Yes, of course,"* before I'm through my first paragraph they jump in with advice or an argument: *"But you could do..."* Or, *"Why don't you..."* Or, *"That'll never work..."* Or, *"Don't you think they had a reason for doing that?"*

So I turn the card around and say, *"I know this is hard, but you just switched from listening to talking. Remember, no agreeing, disagreeing, advising, or defending. Please, just ask questions; say back to me what you hear me saying; bite your tongue, and say, 'Un-huh' a lot. Okay to try it again?"*

I usually have to turn the card another time or two, but most people learn quickly. So, I talk, they feed it back, they ask a few questions, and I sort out my issues. When I'm clearer headed, I say, *"Okay, I think I've got it worked out. Thanks for listening. You've been really helpful. Now it's your turn. Is there anything you want to say about my situation or for that matter, about your situation?"*

Then I listen to them the way they listened to me. I might also add, *"I appreciate your listening to me. If you could use a sounding board anytime, I'd be happy to return the favor and be a listener for you."*

One time when I was in a decision-making bind and needed to figure something out quickly, I phoned someone who had recently taken my listening skills class, a real novice at the process. We met for lunch. He struggled to do what he'd learned: *"Oh, ah, okay. What's it about, Jim...?"* As we continued I could hear the words he'd learned in class. Being inexperienced, it sounded pretty stilted and canned.

Even though I could see what he was doing and knew where he learned it — it still worked!

What an experience. He practiced his talker-listener skills. I began to calm down and got a handle on my issue. I was surprised, pleased, and a little embarrassed that his mechanical yet earnest efforts worked for me.

Can you use the TLC with yourself?

Sometimes when I have something troubling me or a decision to make, no listener is available. I practice the method on me. Why not? We carry on internal conversations all the time, so why not use good listening skills on ourselves?

During an internal conversation I try to give up criticizing myself in a way that blocks creative thinking. I treat me as an accepting friend would. I ask myself questions and respond. I re-say my thoughts with different words. I move back and forth between my head and stomach, my thoughts and feelings, using the listening techniques in the book.

Gradually, I become clearer, more relaxed, and better able to make decisions. But, it doesn't always work. If I'm still too muddled, I call a friend and set a time later to trade some good listening. You might be surprised at how many of your friends would happily take you up on such an offer.

Some people can't listen

I was on a fishing trip with a friend who normally doesn't listen well, but I really needed to talk something out. He was familiar with the TLC, so I thought I'd give it a shot. When we stopped for breakfast I said, *"I really need to talk."* I described what I wanted: *"Ask questions, repeat what I'm saying, and don't argue or give me advice."*

He agreed, but immediately interrupted and started plowing me under with advice. After a couple of tries, I gave up and reverted to fishing talk. I'm sure he never noticed.

Some people don't seem to have the disposition to be listeners. Their own thoughts and feelings make so much internal noise, they can't hear anyone else. I see them with constant low-level walking flat brains, that disable everything above their mouths.

When I make the mistake of trying to share with one of them, I've learned after a bit to change the subject or ask them a question about their lives, and off they go to the races, enmeshed in their own worlds, seemingly impervious to anyone else's concerns. In spite of their paltry listening skills, I maintain some of these relationships with friends, co-workers, and relatives because we share interests, values, or work.

Cultivate some listening friends

A life accompanied by a few good listeners makes for less loneliness, clearer thoughts and feelings, and creative, collaborative living. The question, *"Who did you discuss important, personal issues with this year?"* was asked in a study in 1985 and again in 2004. Roughly three decades ago, the average answer was *"Three friends."* Two decades later, *"No one."* That is a scary loss!

If you don't have enough friends with whom you can "talk things over," you may want to connect with a few who are willing to learn with you how to be good listeners. If you do, then quickly tell them the flat-brain story, give them a Talker-Listener Card, and teach them how to use it, so you can exchange listening with each other.

How to Listen Better: Technique # 8

Asking questions is basic to good listening, but must be done carefully.

⑨ Play detective

> ■ *Ask questions to gather information. Sort, compile, and organize it so you and the talker can see it better. Fill in missing pieces and look for connections and relationships.*

Kinsey Milhone, the private investigator and hero of Sue Grafton's mystery series (*A is for Alibi,* etc.), describes a similar crime-solving method. As Kinsey gathers information, she writes each kernel on a three-by-five card. She stick-pins them to a large bulletin board so she can organize them in groups, see their relationships, notice the information gaps, and get a clue about the next questions to ask.

Every situation has a past, present, and future. Each area can be mined for important people, events, and influences. As you listen to fill in the information-picture ask what led up to this situation, what is going on now, and what the future ramifications might be. As the picture unfolds, the talker (and you) will better understand their struggle and see more options.

As a listener you are treating talkers as though they can think, observe, question, examine, and problem solve their own situations without falling apart. This process gives talkers the sense that they can impact their own situations. It lets them know you have confidence they can act in more creative ways in the future.

Use questioning carefully

A word of caution: Questioning can be misused. More often by men, though sometimes by women, questioning becomes a license to take over a conversation from the talker.

Rather than taking time to savor and soak in what the talker is uncovering, we can morph questions into judgments, jump ahead, or push for solutions: *"What did you do that caused the problem?"* Or, *"So you're upset? When are you going to get over it?"* Or, *"When are you going to call him and take care of it?"* Or, *"Why'd you do that?"* It is important to let talkers be where they are until they are ready to move on.

In bullying hands questions can turn into staccato attacks and battering rams.

For questioning to be helpful, it takes gentleness and patience. Good listeners really try to understand what is developing in talkers, rather than trying to force opinions on them.

Listen for clues: *"You said a couple of seemingly opposite things... What do you make of them...?"* Allow time for information to emerge. Listen for possible implications. Let silence provide space for the talker to reflect.

We often miss clues in what talkers are saying by jumping ahead to something we're focused on: *"So why did you spend so much money?"* *"Why"* questions not so subtly mask accusations, rather than seek more information.

Soften your questions with heart talk: *"So, I'm wondering if you have any idea about what's bothering you...?"* Or, *"I'm curious about...?"* Or, *"It seems to me that this matters to you...? Tell me how this is affecting you...?"*

When you play detective and personalize your questions to keep them from taking on a prosecutorial tone, you'll better be able to follow the leads that your talker provides.

This careful questioning mode turns up and fills in helpful information for you and the talker, all of which is helpful for making decisions.

In addition, you'll learn as you walk through the talker's life and your talker will be supported in his or her quest for clarity and direction.

10

TLC — Who Talks First?

WHEN YOU ARE READY to experiment further with the Talker-Listener Card, it's best to sit down with someone who's agreed to do it with you. For illustration in the next few chapters, I'll move back and forth between setting up a talker-listener practice session and some real situations you might experience or observe.

When you ask someone, tell them first that you want to talk something over with them, trying a safe method with no arguing, just an attempt to understand each other. Say: *"I want to try a Talker-Listener Card taking-turns-method with you. Are you willing to give it a try with me?"*

TALKER — I'm most bothered

Then look at the TLC together. The first step is to decide who talks first. If you both have something going on, figure out who's the *most bothered*, stirred up, or flat-brained. Let that person talk first, because he/she is least able to hear.

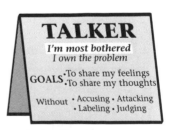

TALKER
I'm most bothered
I own the problem

GOALS · To share my feelings
· To share my thoughts

Without · Accusing · Attacking
· Labeling · Judging

"Bothered" here isn't necessarily a negative. It could mean concerned, excited, angry, happy, depressed, or worried. Talking first will un-flatten the brain, enabling the ears to take a turn listening later.

Sometimes deciding who's most stirred up is difficult because we don't recognize our feelings or haven't learned to communicate them.

Men tend to have more trouble with this and often will say, "I'm not really bothered. You talk first." Polite, yes, but notice how it's qualified with a "not really." While the "not really" means not bothered a lot, it still means bothered some, and that some may affect the eardrums enough to cause trouble hearing.

The best way I know to recognize and describe feeling levels is to rate them on a zero to ten scale — zero for no feeling and ten for enough energy to power a rocket. So "not really" isn't an eight on the scale, but probably somewhere between two and five.

What do we do about this?

Most people can attach a number to their emotional levels, so when you want to know how bothered a person is, first share your number, then ask: "So you're not 'really bothered.' How bothered are you? Give me a number between zero and ten...?"

And the other will say without hesitation, "Five (or whatever number fits)."

We all have an emotional level above which we can't listen effectively. One of you needs a number low enough to listen without getting distracted or argumentative.

Take a minute now to think about what your maximum feeling level number might be where you can still set aside your concerns and focus on someone else's. If you attempt a conversation when both of you are too distracted by your own agendas, then you're in for disappointment and probably a damaging disagreement.

LISTENER — I'm calm enough to hear

Once you've compared your feeling numbers, return to the card. The lower-number person says: *"You're a five and I'm a three, you talk first. I can listen a while."* Set the card so the Talker side faces the "five" person and the listener side faces the "three" person.

The least flat-brained person is acknowledging what's printed on the Listener side of the card — *"I'm calm enough to hear."* The listener sets his or her concerns aside for the moment, knowing that both will get turns to talk. The listener focuses first on the other's point of view and works to help sort out the talker's concerns.

Thud means listen

The need to use the Talker-Listener process is obvious when someone says, *"I'm upset. I want to talk with you."* Unfortunately, people usually don't give us such clear messages.

In the real world my gut tells me when another person needs to talk.

I meet a friend on the street who says, *"It's been a long time since you called me for lunch."* Or, *"You missed an important meeting last Tuesday."* Or, *"My wife died since I saw you last!"* Such comments register with that uneasy, vaguely accused, thud feeling. It usually evokes an urge to set the other person straight, to defend myself, or at minimum to talk rather than listen.

To apply love here requires giving new meaning to the pit-of-the-stomach thud. Instead of letting those feelings goad you into defending yourself, recast them as early warning signals that someone else is bothered and needs to talk.

Shift into a listening support mode, when you run into comments like those above. Say: *"Mmmm. A long time since we had lunch...? Have you wanted to get together...?"* Or, *"Was the meeting I missed an important one...? Did that cause difficulty for you...?"* Or, *"Your wife died...? You must be terribly shaken...? What happened...?"* Listening responses like these, open the way toward reducing alienation and increasing understanding.

Don't let a question mask what someone needs to say

Sometimes when people are bothered, they throw us off by asking questions. Grammatically, question marks call for answers, but often they hide what needs to be said. Questions like, *"Why haven't you called me?"* Or, *"Did you know I just got a new job?"* often disguise unshared concerns.

What lies under the questions is not clear. Are we in trouble with them? Do they want us to be more involved in their lives? Listen, clarify, and find out.

In this wife/husband encounter listen for the masked concern. She asks, *"Why did you ignore the children last night?"* This question could trigger the husband to defend himself (attacking her) when what she needs is an understanding listener (him).

If he gives a quick answer, *"Because they were a pain in the neck,"* he'll be talking not listening. As the tango begins she'll get even more upset because she didn't get heard. She'll likely get defensive (attacking him) because he judged (attacked) *her* children.

Often when someone asks a question, the first answer that pops into our minds may seem really important, but after listening awhile, it turns out to be irrelevant.

What the person says first, usually isn't what the person means or needs to say. Remember the listening technique, *decode?*

In the above case the wife didn't recognize she had something to tell her husband, so he didn't have a clue what she meant by her question. If the husband had responded as a listener, he might have asked, *"Are you irritated about how I handled the children last night...? Did you think I hurt their feelings...?"*

Then he'd find out what she needed to say, *"I'm worried about them. I think they were acting up because the dog died and they haven't had much chance to talk about it."*

Does the TLC help when only one person uses it?

Do both parties need to understand the talker-listener process for it to be useful? Certainly it's easier if both do, and especially if you use the Flat-Brain Syndrome to give you a common language to describe upsets. But it can be effective even when the other person doesn't know how to listen or understand what a flat brain is.

If we notice that someone is bothered, we can choose to listen first. When our turn comes to talk, we'll likely be more successful, because we'll understand their concerns and they will already feel heard. As a result they will be calmer and more able to listen to us.

How to Listen Better: Technique # 9

Many people think that single-minded is good, that they shouldn't have more than one feeling or motivation at a time. Either they should want this, or that, but not both. They assume they can't both love and hate people at once, love two people at the same time, or that if they do, there is something wrong with them. The **both hands** listening technique will help clear this confusion that gets in the way of their making clean decisions.

🜪 Both hands

- *Acknowledge the talker's mixed feelings by alternating hand gestures.*

To help talkers get comfortable with their mix of feelings, gesture back and forth from one hand to the other as you acknowledge all of their feelings.

In listening you might say to a guy: *"On the one hand you love her and on the other hand, you're afraid to propose to her...?"* Or, *"On the one hand, you could hug her and on the other, you want to yell at her...?"*

Here's an example of more than two feelings in the person you are listening to: *"On the one hand, you want to buy that expensive boat, and on the other, you want to save your money...? And then again, on this hand, you want to buy a new car, while on that hand, you want to reduce your mortgage...? Must be tough to be pulled so many ways at once...?"* By going back and forth between hands you can cover an infinite range of feelings, help your talker clarify their emotions, and relax about having more than one.

Physically, using **both hands** to *acknowledge* helps talkers see that it's okay to have more than one concern at a time. This listening technique legitimizes their several emotions so they can deal with them in making their decisions.

11

TLC — Who Owns the Problem?

ONCE YOU'VE ESTABLISHED who talks first, then you need to maintain clarity about who owns the problem you are going to talk about. So check the second lines under **TALKER:** *I own the problem* and under **LISTENER:** *I don't own the problem.* As noted earlier, by "problem" here, I don't mean to suggest something negative, but rather whatever concern or topic the talker wants to talk about.

TALKER — I own the problem

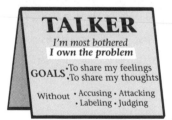

I own the problem means that I lead off and we talk about my issues, agenda, or story from my point of view. Both of us look through my eyes and experiences, not yours. When it is your turn to be the talker, we'll shift to your problem, that is, consider your concerns from your perspective.

Bouncing pronouns

Problem-ownership revolves around whose story we are discussing. Watch the pronouns. Let's say I tell you about my attempt to lose weight. You describe a foolproof method you know that could solve my weight problem. Note the ownership shift from *my* problem to *your* solution.

I own the problem also means the talker has responsibility for handling the issue. In this case, dealing with *my* weight is up to *me*.

If, as a listener, you remember this, you might ask about my frustration over my weight-loss attempts, what I've tried, what's worked, what hasn't, and what I'm considering. Then I'd be free to come to my own conclusions and put full energy into them.

For another look, let's change the problem to finances and from mine to yours. You as the talker say to me: *"What do you think I should do about my financial situation [problem]?"* I quit listening and start talking, *"Mutual funds are the only way that makes sense. Here's a list of the best..."* Notice how *I'm* deciding for *you* and *your* money.

I lost track of the fact that it is *your* life, not *mine*. While on the surface it appears that we're discussing mutual funds vs. other investments, actually underneath we're getting into a tug-a-war over who decides about *your* investments.

During challenging counseling sessions, I sometimes lose track of who owns the problem. I start leaning forward, working hard, coming up with solutions, trying to be helpful. I find myself explaining what they *should* do. I try to persuade and even push to get them moving (in my direction).

Once when I was working hard on his problem, the guy responded by sitting back and relaxing. He said, *"That'll never work. You don't know my wife. If you did, you'd know better than to suggest that."* That activated my observer role and I saw that I had leaned in while he leaned back, as if to say, *"Just try to solve my problem. You're so smart. Hah! You can't do any better with my life than I can."*

Fortunately, I recalled the LISTENER side of the card: **I don't own the problem**, leaned back, and handed the problem back to him. While I listened, he went to work and clarified his problem.

Such ownership issues fall under the "good fences make good neighbors" philosophy. While looking over your backyard fence, you can comment on your neighbor's peas and carrots, if you remember they are her peas and carrots. She gets to decide what to plant, how to make them grow better, and when to harvest them. You can help her think about them, but they are *hers*, not *yours*. (If you respect her ownership, she may even share some veggies with you.)

If you push her toward your ideas about her peas and carrots, you will have crossed the line (and the fence). Most of us instinctively feel this overstepping of boundaries. We don't like it when others tell us what to do about our lives. And what is worse, we often resist even when the advice makes sense.

The issue is deeper than pronouns

People never fully commit to *our* solutions for *their* lives. They only give one hundred percent effort to *their* solutions. When we grab responsibility for the problems of others, they usually stop working on them (and become irritated with us).

Why? Because they feel put down. By taking responsibility from them, we imply that they are not capable of managing their own lives. This can erode their self-esteem and hamper their progress.

When I first started pastoral counseling, I carried the problems of so many people, I almost went under myself. If they didn't get better, I got worse. Young and eager, I was confused about problem-ownership. Finally, I figured out that my life was the only one I had any chance of handling.

Perspective came when I discovered that most people have within them the resources to effectively manage their own lives. While they momentarily may be upset and confused, with support and clarification, they will find their strengths and handle their lives. This belief helps me keep ownership of problems where it belongs.

When someone tries to hand me their responsibility (or I try to grab it from them), I consciously give it back by saying something like: *"This is really a tough problem you have…? It looks as though you have been struggling a long time with your situation…? I don't have the answer…? Do you have any ideas…?"* Or, *"What are your options for handling the issues you've presented…?"* (pause) *"Do any of those look better to you than the others…?"* (pause) *"What would the costs and benefits be to you and others for the options you like best?"* (These listening techniques combine **Technique # 8 – Play detective** with **Technique # 11 – Admit ignorance**, and **Technique # 30 – Explore the future**.)

In counseling, when shifting the pronouns doesn't work, I lean back in my chair, bite my tongue, and say, *"Mmmm…?"* (**Technique # 10 – Hem and haw** follows this chapter.) If *my* urge to solve *their* problem gets too strong, I put my elbow on my chair arm and clamp a hand over my mouth to keep it shut, to stop me from coming up with *my* solutions to *their* problems.

That's when the magic happens. When I lean back, they lean forward and go to work on *their* situations.

Silence is a useful tool. It bothers most of us, so we tend to talk. When your friends, children, or employees want you to pick up responsibility for solving their problems, say: *"Mmmm..?. Tough problem...?"* and rather than letting the silence get you to talk, let it gently nudge them into talking about *their* solutions to *their* problems.

There are exceptions

Offering quick solutions can be useful sometimes — when someone asks: *"Where's the restroom?"* Of course the question of responsibility also shifts when your talker is seriously depressed, suicidal, or nearly violent. We may need to assume responsibility for the safety of that person and/ or others by taking the person to a hospital or calling the police, but these occasions are rare and temporary.

People generally respond better when we are responsible *to* them, not *for* them.

The four-alarm issue in problem ownership

Now that we've warmed to the ownership issue, let's get serious with the toughest side of it. Consider a situation where I'm angry with you. You didn't do what I expected and I forgot that my anger and expectations are my problem.

I'd prefer thinking that *my* anger is *your* problem. That would be convenient for me because *"If you would just shape up, mend your ways, and do what I expect you to do, then the problem would be solved. So see? It is your problem after all. Right?"*

Wrong. If I try to make my anger problem yours, then you'll probably become defensive or give in. In either case, I won't solve my problem, feel understood, or be any clearer about what's troubling me.

When my anger is directed at you, there's little chance you'll become concerned about me or what's bothering me. Your making lasting behavior changes toward me requires that you become concerned about me, not just knuckle under to me.

To illustrate, imagine a frustrated, angry husband saying, *"You're always late. You never plan ahead so you have enough time to get ready. If you would just plan a little, we wouldn't have to show up late to parties, miss the first scenes of movies, or walk into church after the first hymn."*

And she says, *"You only have yourself to get ready. I have the youngsters. And I'm not late that often anyway. Why can't you be a little more flexible or remember the children are yours too, and help?"*

This flat-brain tango could escalate for the rest of their married lives with them locking deeper into their arguments, neither feeling heard nor understood, and both believing their problems would be solved if the other changed.

It might be different if the wife listened: *"Sounds like it really bothers you to walk into situations late...? It must seem to you as though I'm always late and a little planning on my part would make your life more comfortable...?"* (para-feeling & para-thinking)

Or, it might be different if the husband listened: *"You sound irritated with me and overwhelmed handling the children on your own...? It must seem to you as though it's easy for me to be ready on time, because I don't help out much...? You figure the problem isn't that you are routinely late, but that I'm not very flexible and don't pick up my parenting responsibility...?"* (para-feeling & para-thinking)

If she listened effectively, she could help them both understand his concerns. Then he might realize that his upset over being late is his problem. He could even learn to handle it better by helping get the children ready or by the two of them taking separate cars. His awareness of options for handling his concerns might increase substantially. When people are stressed they see fewer options, if any, but when they are calm, the options suddenly become limitless.

If he listened effectively, he could help them both understand her concerns. Then she might realize that her upset over his lack of help and inflexibility was her problem. She could even learn to handle it better by talking with him about a more cooperative way of dealing with their children, by getting ready earlier, or by suggesting that they take separate cars. Her awareness of options for handling her concerns might increase substantially.

In addition, if she tried to understand what was bothering him, remembered she liked/loved him, and didn't resist his anger, she might become motivated to change her behavior to make him happier.

And, if he tried to understand what was bothering her, remembered he liked/loved her, and didn't resist her anger, he might become motivated to change his behavior to make her happier.

In communication crises like these, both techniques and attitudes need adjusting for real improvement (long term behavioral changes) to take place.

LISTENER — I don't own the problem

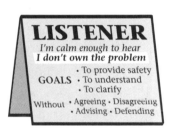

Keeping ownership in the lap of the talker is tricky. It's tough for many of us, because we want to be "nice" people who are helpful. And "helpful" often has meant giving advice and solving friends' problems. The card's *I don't own the problem* does not mean we don't care about people. It means we're committed to helping them focus on what they are doing about their situations.

Years of experience has proven to me that listening is a more effective and empowering way to help others than trying to solve their problems for them.

When we remain clear that we don't own the talkers' problems, we set aside our points of view, hot buttons, biases, and hobby horses. As we do we become more able to focus on their situations and get inside their perspectives. This provides talkers with the support they need to better take charge of their lives, make their own decisions, and commit themselves fully to them.

How to Listen Better: Technique # 10

Sometimes it gets really hard to listen because you want to solve someone else's problem. Can you **hem and haw** in a way that will help you keep from grabbing their problem and keep them focused on solving it themselves?

🎧 Hem and haw

- *When you feel the urge to answer, solve, give advice, defend, fill the talker in on who died of his/her dreaded disease, immediately bite your tongue, clamp your hand over your mouth, tap your pencil, clear your throat, clean your pipe, **hem and haw.***

As listeners we are there with talkers, not to take over problems, but to provide support so they can safely process their own thoughts and feelings and come up with their own solutions.

A management consultant I respect described "constructive hemming and hawing" as an effective listening device to keep talkers responsible for doing their own work. And it allows time for talkers to think out loud.

When you have an urge to jump in to your talker's time and take over their problem, constructively hem and haw. Stroke your jaw and say: *"Hmm...?"* Or, *"That's a tough problem...?"* Or, *"I'll be darned. I wonder what you could do about that...?"* Or, *"Mmmm. My goodness...?"*

While staying focused on the talker, keep your mouth shut. Stick a pencil in it and chew on it. Lean back in your chair, walk across the room, clear your throat, or turn back to your cooking. All these subtly remind both of you that this is the talker's problem to figure out, not yours. Do anything but take over the talking.

I love the phrase the fictional detective, Kinsey Milhone uses to describe how she keeps her interviewee talking. She makes "sympathetic noises." And remember, teeth marks in the tongue — signs of a good listener.

Hemming and hawing after school

Once in awhile youngsters will come home, sit at the kitchen table with a snack, and start talking about their school problems. If parents turn around, face them directly, and ask, *"Do you want to talk about it?"* Ninety-eight point three percent of them will retreat and say, *"Oh no, it's nothing. I can handle it."*

But instead, don't look at them. Keep on rattling pots and pans at the stove and say: *"Mmmm...? That's a tough one...?"* and then shut up. More often than not they will continue talking, feel heard, and relax. After awhile, when it's clearly your turn to talk, they may even be open to a suggestion or two.

Keep in mind that near-silence doesn't work as a listening technique if it's the only one you use. Talkers need to hear us feed back what they are saying.

Hemming and hawing gives you the listener something to do, rather than going with the urge to talk about your stuff or give advice. When you **hem and haw** and mix it with other listening responses, it will really help your talkers keep focused on discovering their options for their issues.

12

TLC — What Does the Talker Do?

SOMETIMES WHEN WE have trouble putting our concerns into words, we get frustrated and say, *"I know what I mean. I just can't say it."* I suspect the truth is, that we aren't sure what we mean, or we could say it. What we likely have is a mixture of feeling and thinking with its meaning still unclear to us.

Talking has two parts:

1. Determining what we think and feel.
2. Sharing that with someone.

This definition assumes that we aren't always clear about what we think and feel and need to talk out loud to clarify. This may be embarrassing for those of us who learned not to speak until we knew what we wanted to say or until we were sure we had the right answers.

However, when we realize we are unclear, we can choose to move toward clarity. Talking aloud with someone who feeds it back can be like projecting our digital images onto a big screen so the fine details and interrelationships become sharper.

Nothing makes a dumb (screwy) idea seem more sensible than keeping it trapped inside our heads. Getting our thoughts out into the light of day helps us see their pluses and minuses more clearly.

For me a dumb idea crumbles to dust when I hear it fed back in someone else's words. Conversely, an odd kernel of an idea can morph into sheer brilliance when someone reflects it back to me. Over the years, I solidified much of what I believe by listening to myself (but then, teachers and preachers get to do a lot of this). My views sharpened as others reacted and fed them back. Rough edges got knocked off, poor ideas fell aside, and my commitment to the better ones grew.

It's a relief to me when I share an idea and no one faints or goes on the attack. If we share our deepest desires and thoughts, and no one collapses, we become less afraid and more sure of ourselves. In addition, those who hear us find themselves trusting us more.

Good listeners are worth their weight in gold. They help us sharpen our insights and directions. But talkers have their work to do as well. In Chapter 3 we took a first look at stomach, heart, and head talk. (**Chapter 3 – Where do stomach, heart, and head talk fit?**) And here in Chapter 12 we'll look at them in depth as the talker's goals.

FIRST TALKER GOAL — To share my feelings

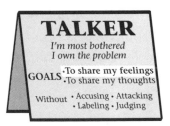

As talkers, how do we share our feelings and thoughts effectively? The best communicating attempts contain three parts — feeling, thinking, and an open kind of ownership. The first two components show up as goals listed on the Talker side of the card. The third is less obvious, yet important.

We'll look at how they impact communication, how they can work together, and how communication falls off when any of them is excluded.

To share my feelings means to describe our feelings (emotions) to a listener. These include, but are not limited to, excitement, depression, enthusiasm, concern, hope, anger, anxiety, attraction, irritation, fear.

Stomach talk

Stomach talk is not "spilling your guts." It is language that puts feelings into words. The E in the model stands for emotions.

While people who say they are going to spill their guts or "be perfectly frank," think they are expressing their feelings, they usually aren't. They are likely attacking: *"At the dinner party last night you were overbearing. You talked too long and too loud. You ruined it for everyone."* All the feelings in that attack are undercover and un-named.

Spilling our guts or being perfectly frank usually means taking our feelings out on people rather than sharing them with people.

To share my feelings or *stomach talk* describes what's inside me, rather than describing someone else. The difference is huge: *"I feel un-comfortable and insecure when I hear you say..."* instead of, *"You put me down."* The first describes the feeling that's in me and therefore, shares my feelings with you. The second is a thought that describes and ac-cuses you, and as a result, takes my irritated feelings out on you.

Feelings require very few words (usually one or two and less than five): *"I'm irritated..." "I don't like..." "I'm tired..." "I want..." "I'm in love, excited, angry, disturbed, depressed, turned on,"* etc.

Watch out for the dreaded "I feel that..."

Sometimes we confuse emotions with thoughts. We say, *"I feel that..."* We think we are expressing a feeling, but what follows is actually a thought: *"I feel that you drank too much and were all over Marcia at the party last night."*

Anything coming after *"I feel that..."* will be a thought (idea) that describes and/or judges behavior. It is a mild form of spilling your guts or taking your feelings out on someone. *"Feel thats..."* almost always lead to an argument or at minimum — avoidance.

Whether or not someone likes asparagus is a feeling and therefore, non-debatable. Whether asparagus is good or bad for us is a thought and can be debated: *"Asparagus has nutrients you need." "Asparagus needs hol-landaise sauce to taste decent, but has too much fat."*

At the party mentioned above, her thought/attack, *"I feel that ... you drank too much and were all over Marcia,"* could be debated into the next millennium. His thought/defense, *"My behavior was appropriate. Besides, how would you know? You were hanging out with Tom."*

If she had expressed her feelings, she might have said, *"I was feeling lonely at the party. I got anxious when you were talking with Marcia. Odd, that after so many years I still get insecure and jealous."* What a difference. The latter comments drop the thought (attack) and share her feelings. He might have been able to hear what she was saying without defending himself.

Sharing feelings is risky, but often worth it

As a self-protective device many of us learned not to share our feelings. By walling our feelings inside, we may protect ourselves against others, but often it is to the detriment of our relationships. Having said that, a person who enters this process as a talker does take certain risks that I don't want to minimize.

When we let our feelings and thoughts out into the open, people will react to them. If our listeners are inept, unhappy with us, distracted, or hostile, our attempt to clarify may not only fail, but could be used against us. As we share the personal part of us, we risk getting hurt, like the following:

- While trip planning a wife says, *"I'm really scared of flying."* The husband says, *"Oh, grow up."*
- Or a man shares, *"I think I might be falling in love with you."* And she says, *"Yeah, sure, you fall in love with anybody in a skirt."*
- Or a son shares, *"I'm scared about taking the tests the doctor recommended."* And his father says, *"You cry-baby. Be a man."*

Though it's risky, I often find that as I open up more with people, they open up more with me. Sharing is an act of trust that moves us toward intimacy. Allowing people to know how we feel lets them deeper into our lives, where they have a chance to care more about us and as a result, act more often on our behalf.

In short, no sharing, no caring.

While I encourage you to risk increasing the sharing level of your feelings in general and especially with those who matter to you, please take note: I am not suggesting that you share your feelings indiscriminately. Some folks operate so much in the courtroom that they'll put you down at any opportunity. So, keep your eyes open, select your confidants wisely, and choose the level at which you share your feelings with each different person.

SECOND TALKER GOAL — *To share my thoughts*

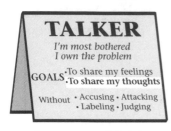

TALKER
*I'm most bothered
I own the problem*
GOALS
•To share my feelings
•To share my thoughts
Without • Accusing • Attacking
• Labeling • Judging

To share my thoughts means to describe developing ideas, points of view, concepts, philosophies, memories, questions, guesses, and accumulation of facts and fictions.

When we share thoughts, the sharing helps us and our listeners gain clarity about what we are thinking.

If we limit sharing to our feelings, then we don't give others a clue as to how we see life, what we think about it, or where we stand on issues. Saying, *"I'm happy to be here,"* doesn't tell you what I think about being here. I might be happy to be here (feeling), because I plan to rip you off and take your money (thought).

Head talk

Head talk is language that puts our thoughts into words. The J stands for judgments (thoughts).

The square's harsh edges hint that thoughts (judgments), expressed without feelings attached, tend to come across as accusing. Judgments without the inclusion of our feelings change in nature and become judgmental, because the personal part of us is left out.

For example if I say, *"So here we are at long last having dinner together."* This thought, without an expressed feeling, might sound as if I'm irritated with you because you should have invited me to dinner sooner. Anyone with normal insecurity could interpret it as an accusation and reply defensively, *"You could have called anytime. It's not my fault it took so long to get together."*

My feelings might have ranged from *"I'm really delighted to be with you; I've been looking forward to this for a long time."* To, *"I don't want to be here; I've been dreading it and can't wait to get out of here."*

Unless my tone of voice or body language clearly conveys my feelings, the other person is left to assume what's under my thoughts and that's usually trouble.

Without feelings expressed, thoughts leave the hearer hanging. When the feelings are unclear it leaves room for the hearer's insecurity to fill in the gap and convert what may be flat factual statements into complaints or accusations. It would have been much clearer had I said, *"I'm thrilled that at long last we're having dinner together. I've missed you."*

Compliments

Ever get in trouble when you were trying to be nice and give a compliment? He says, *"You look great in that dress."* This is a positive thought, appears to be a simple compliment, but on closer examination, it is one person judging another. Since we don't like to be judged, we tend to get defensive.

A typical response indicates that she felt judged: *"This old thing? I've had it forever, and you never noticed it."* She defended herself by attacking him.

Compliments without a feeling expressed are rarely received well. If he had included his feeling from the beginning, it might have gone over the way he intended, *"I really like the way you look in that dress. You look great."* His judgment is there, but it is softened and personalized by his feelings.

Or in another situation she says, *"You did it."* This thought, without her feelings expressed, sounds accusing. So he responds, *"I did not."* A standard defense. *"You did too." "Did not..."*

Think how this conversation might have gone, if she had said, *"I am so relieved that you did it. I didn't want to do it myself."* Note how including her feelings both softens and clarifies her thought.

You'd better include both feelings and thoughts in your statements, if you want to reduce the argument quotient, ambiguity, and the risk of misinterpretation.

Stop a second. Look back at that last statement, and consider it. Does it seem a little argumentative? Or, at least debatable? As a reader you might have been tempted to say, *"Yes, maybe, but why?"* Or, *"Doesn't really matter, why be so picky?"*

Here it is again, but with both feelings and thoughts included. See if it reduces the argumentative or judgmental quality: *"I'm excited to share what works for me. When I include both feelings and thoughts in my conversations, the argument quotient seems to be reduced so we have fewer misunderstandings and arguments. What a relief for me. I hope it works for you."*

Sharing thinking is risky too

In most situations, my preference is to share what I think, so that people react to what I really believe, rather than to their assumptions and guesses about my views.

When we say what we think, we take a stand. We risk being wrong or having people react negatively, and that's difficult. On the other hand, if we let others know when we're unsure of what we think, there's a chance they'll criticize us for inconclusiveness.

Keep in mind, it's easier for them to attack us than to deal with their own lack of certainty. If that happens, then listen more to understand the people who can't handle honesty. If that doesn't work, you may want to avoid them, or at least, avoid trying for an in-depth relationship.

While saying what we think often helps us and others figure out where we stand, I don't always describe my thinking or "tell everything I know." It is wise to consider that our thoughts might be hurtful, inappropriate, or poorly timed.

The principle that makes sense to me is to "speak the truth in love." This recognizes that we can use "the truth" to initiate constructive change and also, to bully or hurt people.

I believe we have a responsibility to decide what, when, and how we say what we think so that it has a chance to be helpful in building relationships and getting worthwhile things accomplished. When we do this, others may become uncomfortable with what we say, but then I figure we are not here to please people, but rather to act on their behalf.

THIRD TALKER GOAL — My

TALKER
I'm most bothered
I own the problem
GOALS • To share my feelings
• To share my thoughts
Without • Accusing • Attacking
• Labeling • Judging

Both goals for the talker include the word *my* to emphasize the importance of ownership and openness in communication. I call the qualities of ownership and openness "the human factor," that is, the part of us that accepts responsibility for what we're saying and yet leaves room for the other person in the conversation. Let's look at these two parts of the human factor.

Ownership

Ownership in communication means taking responsibility for the feelings and thoughts that are ours. When we speak, using "I" or "my," we make it clear that we are expressing our feelings and opinions and that we are including ourselves in conversations as people with something to offer. Many call this "using I statements."

For example, it helps to shift from *"The way the manager sees it..."* Or, *"Other people are saying..."* To: *"I'm uncomfortable with how it looks."* Or, *"My preference would be..."* Or, *"The way I see it is..."* These "I/my" statements make it clear that we are expressing our feelings and thoughts, not someone else's — and especially not "everyone" else's.

If I were to say to you as my boss, *"People are saying that you shouldn't have fired Fred,"* you wouldn't know what I think or how I feel. I'd be keeping you from dealing with me and pitting you against unknown people you can't deal with. You wouldn't know who's upset and disagreeing with you. You'd have no way to respond.

My talking about how others see you is at best impersonal and self-protective, and at worst, gossipy and manipulative.

Openness

Openness in communication makes it clear that we are open to other people, that they too are people who have something to offer. The human factor acknowledges that none of us knows "the truth." None of us sees, hears, or thinks perfectly. We each have limited perspective, affected by background baggage, experience, less-than-perfect eyesight, and faulty hearing.

However, even though we're all a bit flat-brained, we're still basically nice people (BNPs) and can learn something from each other.

Heart talk

Heart talk puts openness and ownership into words. The H in the symbol represents the human factor that opens the door to relating and collaboration.

Heart talk says, *"My point of view is..."* Or, *"It seems to me..."* Or, *"As I see it..."* Or, *"As I remember it..."* These phrases own my thoughts, yet leave room for yours.

Heart talk says, *"I think..."* instead of *"I know..."* Or, *"It looks to me as if you often do it that way."* Instead of, *"You always do it that way."* And heart talk says, *"It looks to me as though you may have goofed on that one."* Rather than, *"You goofed on that one."* Or, *"I don't remember you ever fixing the plumbing."* Not, *"You've never fixed the plumbing."*

While these may seem like subtle differences, the trouble becomes more obvious when we leave heart talk out of our communication. Absolute statements deny our ownership and leave no room for the other person's views. If someone says to me, *"You never help in the kitchen,"* there isn't much room for an exception. I might instinctively argue, *"Oh, but there was that one time I helped. It was in 1997, when..."*

I would feel less defensive if the person said, *"It seems to me that helping in the kitchen isn't your best thing."* (heart talk softening head talk) *"Most of the time I'm okay (or not okay) with that."* (stomach talk) *"But I would like it if you..."* (Stomach talk)

Television evangelists can leave heart talk out of their preaching. They proclaim, *"The Bible says..."* Or, *"The only way to believe is..."* Seems to me they drop the human factor, that is, I don't hear much heart talk.

When I listen to absolutist preaching, the hair on the back of my neck stands up. It sounds to me as if they're saying that their understanding is identical to God's, and if mine is different I must be wrong. As near as I can tell they make no room for the hearer to think differently (which I, for one, often do). They seem not in tune with French novelist and Nobel prize-winner, Andre Gide who said: *"Believe those who are seeking the truth. Doubt those who find it."*

As most people do, I feel better when I listen to speakers who use heart talk. Their inclusion of ownership and openness leaves room for me to feel strongly about my views and also more able to hear theirs.

When the human factor is evident, religious leaders say, in effect, *"This is very important to me, I believe the Bible says this... However, you may find different meaning in your faith or your philosophy, and I wish you well."*

Rather than, *"If you don't believe as I do, you are wrong and going to hell."* The latter seems to me to have shifted from sharing a judgment to being judgmental.

We all judge and draw conclusions about many things as we should. Being judgmental is different. It doesn't leave room for differing views. Strikes me that judgmentalism denies ownership, kills openness, puts us above others, and invites defensiveness.

In business, the process is the same, even if you have the authority to decide. If you want buy-in, you might say, *"I'm excited about this new concept. I believe my approach is best for the company. Let me tell you how I see it and then we'll look at how you see it,"* rather than, *"The only way our business will be successful is by adopting this strategy. Any other course will put us in bankruptcy."*

Heart talk explicitly invites others to express their feelings and opinions about what is best for the company, the marriage, the progeny, or for keeping slugs out of a garden.

The EHJs of balanced communication

It takes two parts personal and one part logical to give our talking the best chance to be heard.

Let's use a balance scale to illustrate how feelings and the human factor are needed to balance judgment. The E and the H on the left side of the scale balance the J on the right side.

If all three are not included in some form, any attempt at communicating will be thrown off balance and the potential for misunderstanding will increase. Remember that we communicate the Emotion with stomach talk, the Human factor with heart talk, and the Judgment (thought) with head talk. *"I'm curious (E). Did you know (H) that this book is overdue (J)?"*

If the E drops off the scale, it will tip toward the J side. When the scale tips toward J, the judgment changes quality and assumes a judgmental quality and will likely draw a defense (attack). *"Did you know (H) that this book is overdue (J)?" "Of course. I'm not stupid (J)."*

Leaving out the H in our communicating also creates a "courtroom" quality and draws the usual defensive response. *"I'm annoyed (E). This book is overdue (J)." "So I'll pay the stupid fine (J)."*

This problem seems pervasive. Most of us grew up routinely learning to leave the E and the H out of our talking: *"This book is overdue (J)."* Such straightforward thoughts alone tend to call for defensive language. In life, such sentences often are modified or softened by the non-verbals: Tone of voice, context, smile. That said, we still spend a lot of time communicating courtroom style — J/D (Judgment and Defense).

Let's look at another example of courtroom J/D: J/, *"It's three o'clock and time to leave for the game."* /D, *"Don't bug me. I'm ready."* Had we included the E and the H, a balanced statement might have sounded like, *"I'm surprised (E). I just noticed the time and it's three o'clock (J). If you want to get there before it starts (H), it's time to leave for the game (J)."*

Let's look further at head talk (J) without any stomach talk (E) or heart talk (H): *"There is too much salt in the meatloaf (J)."* This simple thought without the personal parts, takes on the accusing tone that draws a defensive response, like: *"All you do is complain. You cook from now on (J)."*

It would be easier for the cook to hear that there is too much salt (J), if the talker includes E: *"I've come to like less salt since I cut down on it to lower my blood pressure."* And adds H: *"But that's just my taster. You probably followed the recipe..."* Adding the personal elements help balance the J and keep it from becoming accusatory.

On the other hand, if the J falls off the scale, then the balance shifts toward the personal side of the scale, *"I'm wondering (E) what you think (H) about government intervention in..."* This gives no hint about what the talker thinks about the intervention. The hearer has been asked to take a position without knowing what the talker thinks — feels like a set-up.

It's very much like when a talker says, *"I want to go out for dinner and a movie (E), whichever you're interested in... (H)."* No head talk turns

112

communication manipulative. It hands the talker's responsibility for input to the listener, makes the listener uncomfortable, and hands off responsibility if the food isn't good or the movie is a dud.

Stomach talk alone tilts the balance toward E and makes the hearer feel responsible for the talker's emotional state, *"I'm just so depressed. Nothing feels right. I feel worthless, and ready to collapse."* Or, *"I'm so excited about... I can't wait."* The talkers abdicate thinking about next steps.

Heart talk alone tips the balance toward H and leans on the hearer for decisions. Saying, *"Wherever you want to eat, just anywhere, whatever you think best,"* leaves it all up to someone else. The talker avoids any responsibility for participatory decisions.

Once again, a balanced statement includes all three components, *"The meatloaf tastes salty (J) to me (H). I've been worried about my blood pressure (E) so I've cut down on my salt intake and am used to a little less (J). You probably put in what the recipe called for...(H)"* (I went a little overboard here to make the point.)

Balanced statements are direct since they include opinions. They leave room for hearers and invite response. They are not too difficult to hear and certainly not judgmental because they are tempered with open ownership and an expression of our feelings.

When I'm facing a difficult encounter, I think first about what I want to say and then decide especially how to include the humanizing parts of communication into what I actually say. I'm amazed how often this really helps my connections with others. I encourage you to experiment with EHJs in your communication attempts and to observe others and how they do or don't use them.

However, even the best communication techniques can be misunderstood and argued by uptight, flat-brained, defensive folks. So, when you come through with a well thought out and balanced EHJ statement and your hearer turns defensive, what do you do?

What else? Turn the card in your mind, and get back to listening.

— ∞ —

How to Listen Better: Technique # 11

Sometimes if you *admit ignorance*, it will encourage your talker to help you understand what's going on with them, and it helps them understand themselves as well.

Admit ignorance

- *Briefly, tell talkers you don't understand what they are saying, don't know what's going on, or don't know what they should do about their situations. Then get on with using other listening techniques. This may be difficult for you. Many of us have terrible trouble admitting we don't know something. But if we are willing to be ignorant, we can provide better listening help.*

It helps me do this when I remember that ignorance is temporary. It just means I don't know yet, and that's fixable. Stupid means we can't learn and that's serious and permanent. (I know the latter is not your problem or you wouldn't have read this far.)

Admit ignorance works as a listening technique because it invites the talker to educate you. Even talkers who are upset will want to help you understand what's going on and fill you in. Try saying: *"I don't understand what you mean. Help me understand...?"* Or, *"Tell me that again, I didn't follow it...?"* Or, *"I just got here, and I don't know what happened...?"* (For more on admitting ignorance, check: **Technique # 20 – After a death**.)

When we risk admitting our ignorance, it keeps us from talking before we know what's really going on and this allows bothered talkers to "tell us all about it."

13

TLC — Talk Without...

WE'VE LOOKED AT WHAT to do when you're trying to communicate well. Let's look now at what not to do. Take a look at the list of **GOALS** and *Withouts* on the **TALKER** side of the card. Note the implicit style differences within them — sharing rather than accusing.

TALKER — Without accusing, attacking, labeling, or judging

Tracking the difference between sharing and accusing really makes a difference when you are talking. I call the keeping-track process "the finger method in communication" to help you remember it.

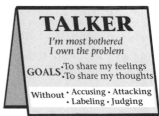

Here's how the finger method works for me: When I talk while pointing my finger at me, I'm describing my feelings and my thoughts, that is, I'm sharing what's going on inside me. When I talk, pointing my finger at you, I'm describing you, that is, I'm accusing, attacking, labeling, or judging you. Not helpful. Creates defensiveness.

Sharing instead of accusing keeps us out of the courtroom. When we are talking, arguments drop off dramatically when we simply shift from pointing at others to pointing at ourselves.

Using the finger method

When you're bothered with someone and want to share it without putting them on the defense, keep the finger method in mind. You can use it to keep clear whether you are sharing or accusing.

In a tense situation where you need to say what you think and feel, literally point your finger at yourself to remind you not to accuse, attack, label, or judge. You can do this without being obvious.

You can further refine this by:

- Pointing at your head and saying, *"I think ... or remember ... "*
- Pointing at your eyes or ears and saying, *"I saw ... or heard ... "*
- Pointing at your stomach and saying, *"I'm scared ... upset ... irritated ... excited ... "*

The finger method gets to the bottom of talking effectively in tense situations. For example: As your supervisor, I might point my finger at you and say, *"You didn't finish your assignment and left me hanging."* I judged your performance and accused you.

You might defend yourself: *"I gave you the necessary report."* Or, *"You didn't give me enough time to finish."* Or, *"You're never satisfied with what I do anyway."*

If I point at me and share my feelings it might sound like, *"I'm embarrassed at not getting my part to my boss on schedule, and I really caught it. I know you have a lot on your plate right now. I'd like to understand what's happening with your part of the project, so we can figure out how to handle it."*

If I'm not attacking you, it will be easier for you to hear my concerns. You might even be more cooperative in finishing the project quickly, so I can repair the damage with my boss.

The finger method with heat

Imagine it's morning. I'm not at my best. I stagger into the bathroom and step on a heap of wet towels. I point a finger at whoever is within earshot and shout, *"What inconsiderate clod left the wet towels on the floor? Why do you do this to me? You never pick up after yourself! You always ruin my mornings!"*

If you were the "shout-ee," would this approach create concern for my welfare? Would it foster a desire to pick up your towels next time in order to make my life more comfortable? Not likely, unless you are some kind of saint or a serious pleaser.

Such an attack would almost always draw a counterattack: *"What's the big deal? Everybody forgets and you leave your junk in my way too. Besides, I hardly ever leave wet towels on the floor."* I'll bet you could write the rest of this script.

Let's try finger method sharing. I could express the same frustration and anger without **accusing, attacking, labeling or judging**: *"I get so mad when I stagger into the bathroom and step on wet towels!!!! I want to do bodily harm!!! I don't like to start mornings off like this!! Oops, look at the time! I'd better get to work."*

Notice: By pointing my finger at me, I'm not attacking, accusing, labeling, or judging anyone. The reduction in exclamation points suggests that my emotional steam is being reduced with each statement and my brain is un-flattening.

Such comments describe and relieve what's going on inside the talker, without taking it out on the listener. It increases the odds of communicating. There is even some chance that the towel dropper, not needing to get defensive, might register how exasperated I get when I hop out of bed and step on wet towels first thing. After the next few showers the towel dropper might even think, *"Ah, the towels. Well, I do like the old guy. Might as well get his day off to a better start. Think I'll just put them in the hamper."*

So when we're talkers, let's not *attack* (win at any price), *accuse* (lay blame), **label** (call names), or **judge** (put others beneath us). No more taking out our anger by pointing at others. Okay?

Pointing at ourselves to share our feelings and thoughts has a better chance of improving our relationships than pointing at others and accusing them. And remember, long-term behavior changes come more out of *concern* than *coercion*.

How to Listen Better: Technique # 12

It helps talkers to know that their stories elicit human response in you. If they engaged you, they are not alone.

🖐 Own your own feelings

- *When a strong emotion pops up in you while listening, share it.*
  But keep it to a few words and get right back to the talker's story.

While sharing our feelings comes dangerously close to talking, it can be a useful listening technique as long as we refocus on the talker's story quick enough. I might say to you, *"I get excited, frustrated, scared, etc. when I hear you talk that way. Now back to what you were saying...?"*

Notice, I acknowledged my feelings, but returned immediately to your issues.

Sometimes when listening, talkers say things that flatten my brain enough to make it difficult to continue listening. I gulp and then reduce my emotional buildup by saying, *"Oops! That caught me off guard and shook me up. Now, you were saying...?"* This lets you know I'm engaged. It calms me down enough to go on listening. It lets me focus again on you and lets you know you're not alone.

"How's school?" "Fine."

How often have parents picked up youngsters after school and tried to start conversations with *"How's school?"* and gotten *"Fine."* as the first of many one-word answers.

The initial exchange is followed by:

"Well, didn't anything interesting happen in school today?" *"Nope."*

"Did you learn anything?" *"Nun-huh."*

"We pay huge taxes for schools and they're not teaching you anything worthwhile?" *"Right."*

"Is school a waste of time and money?" *"Yep."*

These one-word defensive dodges hurt (and young people don't understand why they're doing this either).

Can anything be done to improve these after-school conversations? Some years ago I went through the above frustrating conversation when

I picked up our youngest daughter from junior high. In the unpleasant silence that followed, I asked myself what I teach in my classes.

Then I remembered. People are cautious about sharing their feelings. Sharing is risky, an act of trust. This got me thinking of one of the principles I'd learned in leading groups. When I want others to share, I ask a feeling question, but then I share first. By opening up and sharing a feeling, I've established safety and they are willing to step in next to me and share at a similar level. I figured this applied to young people too.

The next day when my daughter hopped into the car, I said, *"As I was driving over here to pick you up, I was thinking about what I learned in seventh-grade social studies. I remember the teacher bringing a tiny rickshaw from China. All I remember learning about Chinese people was that they were really small, like maybe six inches tall. As I think back I'm really disappointed I didn't get anything useful from that class. I wondered if your social studies class is any better than mine was...?"*

Instead of one-word answers, she talked for thirty minutes about what she was learning and what it meant to her. We finished the conversation in the car, sitting in our driveway at home.

What happened? I started the dialog with **own your own feelings** before I asked her to share hers. This listening technique made it safe for her to share. I risked acknowledging that I had been *disappointed* with an educational experience and was *curious* about hers. I shared my feelings and thoughts and invited her to do the same. I treated her as though she had something to offer me (which she did). It gave her a chance to talk about her experience and to be valued by an adult who cared about her. It produced one of those wonderful connections that makes parenting worthwhile.

When you use this technique, when you keep your feeling sharing short, you let talkers know that you are emotionally responding to them, which makes it clear they are not alone. It also encourages your talkers to continue their self-discovery. And you may be touched and surprised with how engaging them this way deepens the relationship.

— ∞ —

14

TLC — What Does the Listener Do?

LEARNING TO LISTEN WELL encourages talkers to invite you into their lives. Listening like this cracks through facades, defenses, and dulled habits to the inner life of concerns, passions, hopes, and fears.

I hope your listening skills will grow so you can take your relationships to a different level, to make deeper human connections.

When people take on a tangled issue, they usually do it from opposite sides of a room, tossing jabs at each other. Now, imagine one person getting up, walking around the coffee table (or desk) between them, sitting next to the other, and saying, *"Let's look at the problem from your side first."*

In this image two people work together to figure out what one person is trying to say — two sets of eyes, experiences, memories, backgrounds, and problem-solving abilities focusing on one person's perspective, until they both clearly understand that developing point of view.

If they are a couple, they might touch each other or even hold hands. The concept works just as well in business, (but probably best skip the touching and hand-holding.)

Two heads better than one?

Two heads aren't better than one when they're each advocating for their own positions at the same time. Butting heads leaves little room for gaining from the other's insights. But two heads can create better solutions when together they take turns focusing on the view from one side of a table/desk at a time.

What do you do as the listener in this picture? You cross the room, temporarily leaving your view, to fully focus on the talker's concerns. Once both of you understand what the talker is trying to say, you both switch to the other side of the room. But, can we do that when we're invested in the outcome? You bet, but it helps to remember the talker is a person we care about when we're not arguing. It also helps to know that listening is not only selfless altruism.

Listeners act both out of self-interest and interest in the other person.

If we listen first, we help the other person gain clarity. And we're not caught in the fallout from their confusion. Since in this process we take turns, the other person soon comes to our side and helps us gain clarity in our views.

Such listening is a developmental process. It opens up creative possibilities beyond the painful compromises, silent cold wars, and grim resignations that we experience so often. As a bonus it builds bonds of trust and connection that support our endeavors.

FIRST LISTENER GOAL — To provide safety

The three goals on the TLC, *to provide safety, to understand, and to clarify*, focus our listening.

Talkers can't relax when they're in danger of being put down. For them to share freely and examine their feelings and thoughts they need safety. If we can listen without defending ourselves, it will provide the safety necessary for them to flourish.

Instead of pointing at themselves and sharing, flat-brained talkers tend to point at us and range through *accusing, attacking, labeling and judging.* How do we keep from defending ourselves as listeners?

We do the double-reverse-twist. In our imaginations we reach out, put the tip of our finger on theirs, carefully curve it back toward the talker, and say, *"You seem*

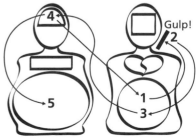

really upset and angry...? This must be tough for you...? Tell me what's going on with you...?"

Under the pressure of hurt and anger, talkers say some pretty awful things. As listeners, we'll need to watch ourselves. It's a temptation to bank what talkers say to use on them later: *"Well, you said you wanted out of this marriage."* Or, *"You said you wouldn't ever speak to me again."* Or, *"You said you were going to quit."* Remember, they meant what they said when they were flat-brained, but now that they've calmed down, they probably don't mean it anymore.

While it's difficult, let's cut talkers some slack and apply the three-day-return rule to communication here. Let's provide them an environment where they can calm down, think in safety, and be able to change their minds (and even grow).

Serious safety in a world of alligators

Our society has in place traditions that support the principle of providing safety. Miranda rights allow the accused to consult with a lawyer in confidence. Prisoners have the right to a priest who will hear their confession and not testify against them. States provide levels of confidentiality to various kinds of professional counselors. I believe people have a right to this kind of safety (except of course when someone reveals an intention to damage others).

As listeners we share some of this responsibility. Keeping confidences is crucial to being a safety provider. When we really listen, we don't use information shared in trust against talkers or others, then, or at a later time.

Providing safety empowers talkers. Folk philosophy says, *"When you're up to your ass in alligators, it's hard to remember your job is to clear the swamp."* When the world includes alligators that nip at our rears, defending ourselves takes so much energy we aren't free to reflect or learn. We get so busy protecting ourselves, we forget why we are there, and what we are trying to say or do. A good listener removes alligators and secures a setting where talkers can focus on clearing their swamps.

For example, I would need to feel safe with you before I'd risk letting you in on my issue with procrastination: *"I guess I really do procrastinate. I wonder if I learned it as a youngster. Or maybe I'm afraid that if I try something new, I'll fail publicly. A lot of things I put off are painful. Maybe I procrastinate to try avoiding the pain. Mmmm. I don't want to face the fact that pain is unavoidable. Come to think of it, procrastination just makes it last longer. I wonder if there's a better way for me to handle the painful tasks I avoid?"*

Imagine the same conversation but with an alligator nipping at my backside saying, *"You never get things done on time. When you don't come through the way you promised, I can't count on you. If you don't quit procrastinating, I won't ever be able to trust you."*

How can I deal more effectively with my procrastination, if I'm busy thinking up retorts, like: *"You're not all that punctual yourself! You talk a good game. I remember times when you didn't get your work done when I needed it. You've let me down, too."* We have trouble looking carefully at ourselves when we're under fire.

Safety enables us to assess ourselves, figure out what's important, move toward change, and put energy into creative living.

SECOND LISTENER GOAL — To understand

Effective listening helps the listener **understand** and the talker **clarify**. These are the second and third listener goals on the card. Both are accomplished by using the same techniques.

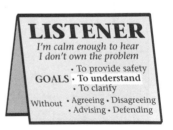

Sometimes listening seems like a chore. But listening benefits us too, because we begin **to understand** others. We glimpse life through their eyes, perspectives, and experiences. When we deeply understand another human being's motivation, perspectives, and intentions, our perceptions grow and change. Understanding other people's behavior increases our response options.

I find that the longer I listen to others, the more I learn about life (and me). I've avoided many mistakes because I learned from the experiences other people shared with me.

When we butt heads with others, more than likely we don't know what they really want or intend. As a result, helpful negotiations are tough to achieve.

As listeners, our lives become easier when we make the effort *to understand* where others are coming from, what concerns them, and why they do what they do.

Non-judgmental listening

Listening *to understand* requires a non-judgmental attitude that can go against what most of us were taught, that is, to listen for rights and wrongs. In our litigious culture judging other people or their perspectives comes easily, especially when we dislike them, their reactions, or how they see life. We may call them wrong, ignorant, or crazy.

Labeling people usually reveals more about us, the "describers," than the "describees."

People who represent various world religions and other points of view might well apply this thinking. How refreshing it would be if we *all* really listened *to understand* what made other folks tick, rather than jumped so quickly to judge their varied beliefs, practices, and behaviors.

I find that when I spend the extra time and energy required to understand another person's seemingly odd point of view, their behavior (which is based on their experience and understanding) makes more sense. And it does even though I might not agree with their opinions or choose that behavior myself.

When understanding dawns on me about what motivated another's "odd" behavior, then I say, *"Oooh, so that's why you acted that way!"* Adopting an attitude of curiosity about others can move us from saying, *"That was bizarre behavior."* To, *"I wonder what contributed to his/her acting that way?"*

Think of a youngster whose only family and protection have been his street gang. His fear of losing his safe haven among his peers and his desire to protect his friends causes him to stab an enemy gang member in a fight. Easy to judge him as a killer; harder *to understand* that his need for protection against the enemy resembles ours. Incarceration, of course, but hopefully someone will listen *to understand* what's going on inside him. That way he might find human connection outside the gang and other possible ways to live.

The Native American adage about not judging people until we've walked a mile in their moccasins fits here. With a curious, non-judgmental attitude we can understand behavior that we'd never condone. If we slip into condemning or condoning, we've stopped listening and started focusing on our own views rather than understanding the talker.

To understand means for listeners to become engaged in what talkers are trying to say — to see it, hear it, taste it, touch it, feel it, reflect it, and respect it. I want you to become a cohort with your talkers so you struggle together to learn what they are trying to share with you.

Listening: dangerous to our opinions

Listening is risky business. It may cost you some of your long-held points of view. When I listen to people who see life from other perspectives than mine, I imagine putting my beliefs, values, and points of view into the top drawer of my desk and carefully shutting it, so I'm free to get into their experiences. After walking through their lives with them, seeing the world from their vantage points, and feeling as much as I can through their senses, I return to the drawer to check on my beliefs, values, and views.

Some have changed, others evaporated, while yet others remain the same, or even grow stronger. Really listening means we might end up seeing things differently. This process unsettles me and benefits me, but then that's what learning and growing are all about.

THIRD LISTENER GOAL — To clarify

Listening *to clarify* helps talkers recognize their thinking and feeling. It enables them to better understand themselves and the interaction between their feelings, thoughts, behaviors, and world.

> **LISTENER**
> *I'm calm enough to hear*
> *I don't own the problem*
> • To provide safety
> GOALS • To understand
> • To clarify
> Without • Agreeing • Disagreeing
> • Advising • Defending

To clarify fine-tunes the talker's position and allows it to develop. It encourages talkers to move toward decisions that are fitting for them, not simply the first options that come to mind. Clarifying helps dive down through layers of meaning to uncover what the talker has only sensed might be there, but hasn't laid hands on yet.

125

People often discover what they think by talking out loud. Some figure it out inside their heads without talking, but most of us are "outside thinkers," that is, we benefit by hearing what we are saying. Because thinking and feeling develop as we talk, what we say early in a conversation may not resemble our conclusions after awhile.

In my marriage we learned that talking things over every few days helps us generate plans and steps for our relationship. One of us might suggest downsizing to Puget Sound, but we don't start packing. Over time, saying it enough times and analyzing the implications has made it clear we want to stay put.

It worked much like that when my last church planned phases of building. We'd talk about what we wanted, possible programs, the needs and desires of various age groups, directions in the community and world around us and again, over time, saying it aloud, good ideas surfaced, bum ideas fell away, directions clarified and when they did, we'd build the next phase.

No one said, *"But six months ago we were planning to build such and such."* We had agreed we'd talk and reflect until a plan formed we'd all buy into. A good listener realizes that this happens and doesn't hold a talker to what was said early on.

To clarify takes patience. Quick responses like, *"How can you think that?"* Or, *"That won't work."* Or, *"If that's the way you want it, I'm out of here,"* prevent talkers from thinking their way through to new conclusions. The listeners' job, over time, is to help talkers figure out what they mean. As you listen well, you'll help increase both your understanding and the talker's clarity.

For most of us, using listening techniques that do this is a learned skill. (And I hope you've been practicing.)

But will listening change anyone?

People who are impatient for change in others often ask irritably, *"But, can you change anyone's behavior by listening?"* The question masks a statement such as, *"Listening is a waste of time unless it gets people to agree with me or do what I want them to do."* To answer the surface question about whether listening helps people change, yes, often it does, but not necessarily or quickly. (For encouraging constructive change check *Chapter 21 – Listening Techniques for Moving On.*)

Now, back to the issue beneath the question. If our motivation for listening is to get someone to think or act our way, then we'll probably push (talk) more than listen.

Pushing produces resistance. While sometimes we can get people to knuckle under, it usually doesn't last. I love the phrase "vicious compliance." It describes what happens when someone gives up and goes along and makes it clear that "we'll pay for it in the end." People who "give in" usually find a way to pay us back (and win).

On the other hand, effective listening allows talkers to relax and reconsider their concerns, opinions, and actions. Talkers can think new thoughts and choose to act differently when they aren't too busy protecting themselves and their old ways. After having been heard, they'll be able to listen to us better. They might see us differently and develop new concern for us.

The best chance that others will change their behavior toward us grows out of their new understanding and caring for us, rather than from any pressure we might bring to bear.

When you show me where your back itches and I like you, I'll scratch your itch. Or if I realize how much something I do bothers you, I might make a change because I don't want to make you uncomfortable. Healthy humans try not to cause distress in others without good reason.

While we often change because of understanding and caring, at times we choose not to change in order to maintain our identity and/or integrity.

Sometimes listening doesn't work with problem people

Some talkers aren't interested in being heard and understood. They really want control. This becomes obvious when talkers say something like: *"I'm tired of just being heard. Knock off this listening crap and quit bugging me!"* Roughly translated this means, *"I'm not happy because you aren't giving in and I am not getting my way."* These talkers want control, not communication. In such situations good listening skills can keep us from getting hooked into their control needs, but won't often produce clarification or growth for them.

Sometimes highly experienced listeners can use the techniques so well that they can help controlling talkers recognize what they're doing, and move beyond it to cooperation. But that's a real challenge.

At other times it's best to think of high control-need people, not as folks with a problem to discuss, but as "problem people." They don't have much ability to engage in dialogue because they're locked into their own agendas (serious flat-brains).

A word of caution here for novice listeners — practice with people you trust. Problem people with heavy control needs can hurt you.

What can you do if listening does no good? Best be realistic here and move on with your life, that is, listen to people where doing it improves their lives and yours. You might say to the problem person (only if it looks right to you) something like, *"You seem bent on having your way. Guess you'll have to do that on your own. I'm not willing to continue in a relationship that does not include acknowledging two points of view and respectful conversation."* And when they *"Yes, but..."* say, *"Yes,"* and repeat back gently everything they said after the *"but,"* as you are going out the door. (For more on *"Yes, buts..."* check the **Chapter 17 – Avoiding Ten Communication Traps 7. *"Yes, but..."*)**

Listening into people's lives

At the beginning of this chapter I told you I wanted you to listen in a way that gently encourages talkers to invite you into their lives. If this works, it is a progressive process. They share, we accept, they trust more, they share more, and so on. People don't bare their souls up front. It takes gentleness, respect, and time.

The image this evokes in me when I'm counseling is of the talker's house. First, I'm invited onto their porch. If it goes well and I'm not a threat, I'm asked into the living room. We look around together and I get a sense for how they live and what's important to them. If I don't pry or push, we go to the kitchen for coffee and an understanding of their family relationships. If that works and they still feel safe, they offer me a piece of cake or pie.

When I trust them enough to eat something of theirs, they trust me to share a little deeper. Then they might show me into their hobby areas, or perhaps their junk rooms for a look at their eccentricities. As long as I operate in an accepting way we move on to see their cupboards, their closets, their cob-webbed hidden areas, and finally their dark places — under the stairs, the crawl spaces, and basements and all in their lives that goes with darkness.

Once they find that I accept and value all there is to know about them and respect them, they grow to accept themselves as well. Having shared their entire lives with me, they become relaxed and secure enough so they can join me, go out the front door, and risk seeing how I live and what I value in life. When they can comfortably walk through the house of my life, they increase in their ability to handle the lives and houses of their friends and others too.

This for me is what listening can do for others. And the gift for us as listeners? People share their sacred moments and life stories with us.

What a privilege.

— ∞ —

How to Listen Better: Technique # 13

When multiple feelings for your talker and/or you come into play and need sorting, assigning numbers to feelings often helps. This is so basic and practical I've already referred to it earlier in the book and will return to it in (*Chapter 22 – Listening through Making Decisions Together*).

👂 Number feelings

■ *Ask talkers to put numbers to their emotions so they can see how strong their feelings are and compare them.*

Use a zero to ten scale to understand how strong the talkers' feelings are. Ask: *"On a zero to ten scale, name and rank your feeling levels...?"*

A guy in turmoil over whether to get married and buy a house with his fiancé, might respond, *"Getting married frightens me a lot, about a ten, but I love her a twenty-seven.* (Some emotions pop off the chart and go way beyond ten. That can be illuminating!) *I don't have many feelings about buying. Nothing strong. A little anxiety, having never owned a home before, a four; and some excitement about finding a place that fits us, a seven. I guess I'm mostly torn between loving her and fear of making a mistake."*

Once he gets clear about his emotional energies, he'll notice that they are thirty-four pro and fourteen con. I'd say next, *"So you're not one hundred percent either way, but you're heavily leaning toward marriage and a home, about thirty-four to fourteen. How does that sound to you...?"*

As listeners, when we ask for numbers, we help talkers recognize their feelings and give them a way to describe them. We help make their decision-making a lot easier.

Special case: Guys and their feelings

Current folk-lore suggests that men don't know how they feel. Either they don't recognize their emotions or can't describe them. Does **number feelings** work for men?

It usually does. Most men like numbers. We (guys) can almost always attach a number to our emotional levels when asked. So when you want to know how bothered a guy is, ask: *"So you're not 'really bothered...?' How bothered are you...? Give me a number between zero and ten...?"* And he'll say without hesitation, *"Four."* Or, *"Six."*

Guys often know how we feel, but most of us don't know how to describe our feelings. Or we are put off by the word "feelings," and balk. Numbering them gets around this. To test this approach, try using numbers for preferences in a food conversation. You'll need a plus-ten to minus-ten though, because with food a negative dislike ranks below a no-feeling zero.

After a guy says, *"I don't really care what I eat. You decide."* Ask: *"So give me a plus-ten to minus-ten on your interest in pizza, chicken, and steak...?"* And he says, *"Oh, like I said, I don't really care, but, well, ah, pizza? Minus-five. Chicken? Plus-one. And steak? Plus-five."*

"I don't really care." Or, *"I don't really care that much,"* usually means less than a six, but noticeable enough to identify when asked clearly. And certainly, enough to get in the way of cooperative decision-making.

We can't make clean decisions if we actually care but think we don't.

After he'd said, *"I don't really care,"* if he'd found out the youngsters wanted pizza, he might have said, *"No way! I can't face another pizza."* And he "really" thought it didn't matter "that much" to him but it did. Pizza was a minus-five.

Often women in my communication workshops are skeptical about whether this works. So we test it. I ask the men to stand up and number their hunger, at that very moment, for an array of foods.

I've never had a guy who couldn't do it on the spot.

It works just as well when I ask them to put numbers to their interests in vacation options. The same men who would say to their wives: *"Oh, it really doesn't matter. Wherever you want to go as long as it doesn't cost too much,"* give immediate numbers for camping, cruises, fishing, Mexico, St. Petersburg, or Guam.

Low-level feelings

When my wife and I first started numbering our feelings, we discovered that her nine and a half excitement was comparable to my four and a half. If she was a little bothered, it was three, while mine was one and a half. We have friends who regularly get excited an eighteen, while they never become bothered less than a five.

Emotional ranges vary from person to person, so when you are listening you need to make allowances. Try to figure out whether one of you operates with a higher or lower range than the other.

When I indicate a two interest — discomfort, irritation, desire, or fear — she responds, *"Oh, low-level, hunh...?"* And compares it to about a four or five on her scale. This bit of short-hand works well for us in understanding ourselves and each other.

This simple *number feelings* tool makes our decision-making easier. I share this decision-making method in pre-marital counseling. Many of those couples came back years later and tell me that it was one of the most helpful things they learned from me. They say they use it every day of their lives.

As you listen and try to understand yourself and others, you may find numbering feelings very illuminating and useful. It will put a clear feeling-base under your decisions, and what's more important, help keep your relationships personal and connected.

15

TLC – Listen Without...

AGREEING, DISAGREEING, **advising, and defending** get in the way of good
listening. I listed these four **Withouts** on the **LISTENER** side of the card.
I'm going to describe them so that you can catch yourself when you use
any of them. While they may be fun, when we use them, talkers don't
get heard and we risk doing damage to our relationships.

LISTEN — Without agreeing

When I'm listening, it is my job to stay focused
on understanding you. If I am inwardly or out-
wardly *agreeing* with you, or even considering
whether I agree or not, then I'm milling around
in my thoughts, not yours.

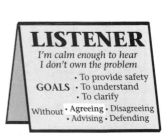

Agreeing is talking, not listening. To listeners the pressure to agree
is often strong. Talkers sometimes ask for agreement to counteract their
insecurity. While they may think *agreeing* is the support they want, if
we give in and give it, that is, if we stop listening and start talking, it
won't help and they'll likely get upset.

Even when they get what they want (agreement), it won't satisfy
them as well as being heard and understood. Example: A talker says,
"You know my husband is just awful..." and follows with a five-minute
litany of her husband's faults, ending with, *"You see why I'm so irritated
with him? I think I should leave him."*

If we agree we talk and say, *"I believe you're right. I've noticed what an inconsiderate clod you married. I don't know why you put up with him. He's every bit as bad as you say,"* she would feel unheard and likely defend her husband, *"Yes, but we've been together all these years. Most guys are worse. At least mine doesn't get drunk or beat me or cheat. And besides, you don't really know him very well."*

Somehow it's all right for people to criticize the turkeys they married, live with, are related to, or work with, but it's not okay for us to do it. If we agree with her and join her in attacking her husband, she'll jump right in to defend him against us — arguing with us, even though it was her idea in the first place.

What happened? We stopped listening. We focused on our thinking. We took time to decide whether or not we agreed and then, we told her what we thought. It's important to catch ourselves when we start evaluating so we can get back to listening. In this case, it meant helping her finish dealing with her situation.

Useful agreement

Agreement can be used as a legitimate listening tool, but briefly, and only if the listener quickly dives right back into the talker's story.

This works when talkers get locked in a rut, like blaming someone else for their problems. Sometimes when this happens I intentionally start agreeing: *"Your husband is completely responsible for your problems. You've been nothing but understanding and cooperative."*

This may surprise her into taking the other side and defending her husband by starting to talk about his good points. It may gently jolt her out of her accusing pattern. But don't forget to immediately hop back into her story and reflect what she is saying about her husband's good points: *"So you really appreciate your husband's stability and honesty...?"*

It's a tricky technique, but once in a great while, useful. If you try it, be excruciatingly honest with yourself about your intentions. Be careful not to use it to avoid listening, or worse, to play the "devil's advocate role" in a way that bullies your talker.

Agreement, a substitute for friendship?

A person pushing for agreement in effect says, *"You would agree with me if you cared about me. Not agreeing means you must not care, so we must not be friends."* When friendship is not established, then the need to agree becomes an important issue.

A person with a strong desire for agreement is often looking for it as a substitute for friendship. If you sense this, surface and deal with it by using good listening techniques.

Agreeing or disagreeing doesn't matter between friends.

Incidentally, good communicators enjoy and learn from each other even when their views differ widely, as opposing ideas are no threat to mature friendship.

(More on disagreeing between friends in **Technique # 24 – Reframe the rigidity.**)

LISTEN — Without disagreeing

Like *agreeing, disagreeing* is also talking instead of listening. *Disagreeing* is more quickly and ob-viously argumentative as it too shifts the focus from the talker's viewpoint to the listener's.

LISTENER
*I'm calm enough to hear
I don't own the problem*
• To provide safety
GOALS • To understand
• To clarify
Without • Agreeing • Disagreeing
• Advising • Defending

As a listener, try to keep from drifting away to your own thoughts. This gets especially challenging when we disagree with the talkers. If we go inside ourselves to think about how we are going to put our disagreement into words, we, in effect, leave the talkers alone to fend for themselves.

Disagreeing with the wife in the example above would sound like: *"When I worked with your husband, I found that he listens well and is under-standing. I don't know why you have trouble with him."* When the listener opposes the talker, listening stops, defensiveness sets in, and learning goes out the window. Disagreeing with her defends him and attacks her. Not helpful.

The problem with *disagreeing* escalates when we listen to someone close to us. A wife says, *"You're a jerk."* The pressure for the husband to disagree turns intense, and can easily distract him from listening.

However, neither *agreeing* nor *disagreeing* will help. If he agrees and says, *"You're right. I'm wrong,"* that blocks her and leaves her unheard and alone. *Agreeing* here is a defensive move because it shuts her up.

If he disagrees and says, *"You're wrong. I'm right,"* that won't help either, because *disagreeing* is talking when he should be listening.

LISTEN — Without advising

LISTENER
I'm calm enough to hear
I don't own the problem
GOALS
    • To provide safety
    • To understand
    • To clarify
Without
    • Agreeing • Disagreeing
    • Advising • Defending

The natural urge to help, which often produces advice, should be resisted until the talker is through talking and ready to listen. *Advising* too, is talking, not listening.

The situation with the five-minute litany about the husband's faults almost cried out for *advising.* If we did it, it might sound like, *"I think you ought to divorce the guy."* How would she have responded? She might have come off the floor, defended her husband, and cataloged reasons to stay married.

Or if we said, *"Divorce is destructive, cruel and you have children — go see your pastor,"* she might escalate her catalogue of his faults.

Why do people say that advice is cheap? Because it seldom is taken and rarely does any good. And why do we keep on giving it?

- We want to be helpful.
- To be honest, giving advice makes us feel important.
- Giving advice is much easier than listening all the way through someone's dilemma.

Many problems with advice come from poor timing, that is, *advising* before the other person is able to hear, before their brain can relax the pressure on their ears. When we give advice too quickly, the talker usually rejects it with displeasure, and often retorts: *"You never listen to me."* And, the talker is mostly right. We didn't listen long enough.

When talkers get frustrated, they'll ask for advice before they've finished doing their own sorting. Don't be suckered in to *advising.* It puts others down. It implies that they can't solve their problems as well as you can.

Do quick answers pay off?

Businesses usually foster competitive listening practices. They reward people for grasping issues and devising quick solutions. Being first may gain an advantage, but it may not produce the best ideas. A better plan might have been discovered had the listening lasted a little longer.

When a business-trained communicator comes home to a spouse who wants to discuss a problem, is it any wonder the spouse doesn't feel heard and gets irritated with quick and easy advice?

This is a recurring theme in traditional marriages — unhappy wives whose husbands try to give advice and fix problems without listening *to understand* and *clarify, "If you'd just be firm with Jarod, he would do what you tell him."* Husbands also complain that their wives give advice too quickly without hearing what the husbands are struggling to do in their work situations, *"Your work would be easier if you just fired your secretary."*

Incidentally, if the couples reverse working and stay-at-home roles, the patterns stay with the roles not the gender.

Advising or offering a quick solution may seem easier than helping someone sort out a painful issue, but when we don't join a spouse, a child, a co-worker, or a customer in their struggle for understanding, it may be costly in the long run for everyone.

When asked a question, ask a question

Ancient wisdom says that the young-but-not-yet-wise rabbi, when asked a question, can hardly wait to give an answer (advice). When asked a question, the older-but-wiser rabbi, instead, asks a question (keeps listening), recognizing that the talker isn't really asking a question.

The questioner is thinking through an issue (talking out loud): *"What do you think I should do with this dilemma?"* The wise rabbi might say, *"Mmmm, tough problem. What are your options...? Which are hardest...? And which easiest...?"* Rather than, *"You should do..."*

The wise rabbi's questions imply that the talker owns the problem and has the capability to think it out. *"You should do..."* suggests the advice-giver is more able to manage the other's life than the person whose life it is — a painful put-down.

When you do give advice

We all have ideas and relevant experience to share, but the trick is to "wait our turn" before we express them. After careful listening, when talkers feel heard and relaxed, it's our turn to share our ideas with them.

If we say, *"The only thing for you to do in this situation is..."* That's pushy, and won't give the hearer much room to breathe. If we sound like we have the absolute word and know better than they do, they'll most likely reject our suggestions. Whether the advice is good, or workable, won't matter.

Rather, include heart talk and say something like, *"You know, if I were in your spot, I think I might... How do you think that might work for you?"* Then switch back to listening. It's their decision to make.

LISTEN — Without defending

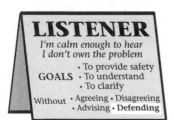

LISTENER
I'm calm enough to hear
I don't own the problem
GOALS • To provide safety
• To understand
• To clarify
Without • Agreeing • Disagreeing
• Advising • **Defending**

Defending is the most critical **Without** on the LISTENER side of the card. When we remove *defending* from our listening repertoire, we open up safe surroundings in which talkers can share with us and grow.

Sometimes couples ask, *"What's the quickest thing we can do to improve our relationship."* First, I acknowledge what they're saying under their question: *"Sounds like you're arguing too much and want help making your relationship more compatible...?"*

Second comes my answer: *"Stop defending yourselves."*

To stop *defending* doesn't mean to get quiet, swallow it, and hang around in a warzone. Rather, it means to replace *defending* with listening.

But this culture teaches us that we have a right to defend ourselves. Yes, true, if we're being verbally abused or physically assaulted. In such cases steps may need to be taken to get out of an unhealthy situation. For me, however, it's not true when we're just talking poor communication.

Defending equals attacking

In war, attacking and *defending* have identical effects. If we defend ourselves, we are really attacking the partner, spouse, employee, boss, co-worker, or kids and we damage those relationships. When we stop *defending* ourselves, our relationships have a chance to mend.

(Remember attack and defense being the same in **Chapter 6 The Flat-brain Tango?**)

I know that uptight talkers tend to lash out, pointing their fingers at us, tempting us to give in to the normal urge to strike back and defend ourselves. What I'm asking you to consider here is the "deviant" behavior described earlier.

(In **Chapter 7 Opting Out of the Flat-Brain Tango** - *Handling a "thud")*

That instead of automatically defending yourself, you listen to someone who is flat-brained and unloading on you.

Listening when the issue is close to home

Listening can get to be uncomfortable when the talker is wrestling with a problem that is a threat to you, but then, discomfort goes with the territory of being a listener. While you may absorb a few accusations and even face issues you'd rather not deal with, being attacked with words is unpleasant, but not damaging (unless of course it's relentless).

If you are not willing to endure some pain as a listener, then better not try to be one.

When you find yourself in a situation where you can't handle a difficult topic, don't get defensive. Just say: *"I'm not up to this now. I find it too painful. Let's pick it up on Saturday morning when I'm rested. I want to be able to listen without getting defensive. Okay?"* If that doesn't work, hang up the phone, leave the room, the house, or the office and take care of yourself.

Well-practiced listening techniques can come to your rescue at these difficult times.

Listening instead of *agreeing, disagreeing, advising, or defending,* focuses on your talkers in a way that helps them share their thinking and feeling and builds your relationships.

How to Listen Better: Technique # 14

How do you handle listening when your talker is on a roll and going on at a good clip? You don't want to *interrupt* because that seems impolite, but if you don't you'll forget and miss responding to important points the person is making.

🔊 Interrupt

> ■ *Don't be "polite" by waiting for the talker to finish covering "four-teen" points. Gently **interrupt**. Ask for clarification. Feed back small portions of what the talker is saying as the conversation develops.*

Most of us have been taught that interrupting is impolite, so we wait until people stop talking. When we do, we lose track of what they said earlier and can't feed it back.

As a listening technique, *interrupt* not only keeps us from forgetting what talkers said in their earlier comments, it lets them know we're paying attention. Talkers need to deal with their thoughts and feelings, but we can't help them later if we've forgotten what they said.

If we wait too long, talkers will not feel heard. Their anxiety will escalate. They'll feel more isolated and talk more and faster (or get quiet and distant). They'll lose their ability to gain insight from what they're saying. With more distress, their blaming and accusing will increase and their constructive problem-solving decrease.

Listening is not a time for unthinking politeness. It is time to act on behalf of talkers. You have my permission to *interrupt,* but do not use it to quit listening, to start talking, to take over the conversation, or to bully the talker.

So, gently *interrupt*: *"Wait a minute, back there, your third point, tell me more about that...?"* Or, *"I missed what you said about the fight. How did you feel about that...?"* Or, *"I don't want to miss what you said about the car...? I was confused and wondered what you meant by...?"*

Interrupt to clarify. Alternate feelings and thoughts, guess. Play detective. Para-feeling/para-thinking. Acknowledge and repeat accurately. Remember those? Use them when you interrupt, because if you don't, you'll forget and miss the clues that might help talkers resolve their issues. On top of that, your talkers will get the message you aren't listening and don't care. Listening takes hard work and engagement.

As a technique, ***interrupt*** reminds us that the Talker-Listener process is like a dance; we move back and forth with the other person. Interrupting is a reminder that there are two people involved in the process. It keeps talkers from skimming too fast through their own thoughts and gives them time to get clearer about them. Then they can make better decisions about their next moves.

16

When to Turn the Card...

I KNOW THAT WHEN I emphasize listening so much, some people get frustrated and worry that they'll never get a turn to talk, so they ask, *"How much longer do I have to listen?"* It depends on the situation, but think of it this way: Listening first earns us the right to speak and be heard.

Following are three situations to suggest how you decide when to turn the card, so the listener gets to talk and the talker takes a turn listening: A simple conversational loop, a complex, longer conversation, and a conversation where one person "talks all the time."

In short simple conversations: A loop

Think of one round of communication as a loop. A talker hands a listener a feeling or a thought, the listener reaches out, catches and acknowledges it, and then gently hands it back. When the talker responds and in effect says, *"Yes, that's what I was trying to say,"* or nods, confirming that the feedback is what the talker meant, the communication loop is completed and it's time to turn the card.

Talker-1: *"I'm hungry."*

Listener-1: *"Are you ready for lunch?"*

T-1: *"Yep. And I want to get out of the office."*

One loop: Turn the card.

Talker-2 (listener from above): *"I'm ready. Let's go for Chinese food."*

Listener-2: *"So you want out of here too. And you want Chinese."*

T-2: *"Un-hunh. There's a new buffet three blocks away. Let's try it."*

Another loop: Turn the card and T-2 becomes L-1 again, and so on.

Note the sequence — Says (talker), Acknowledges (listener), and Nods (talker):

Says: *"I'm pretty tired. I had a tough day at the office. I don't think I have the energy for a heavy movie tonight."*

Acknowledges: *"Sounds like you'd prefer light comedy and no cooking."*

Nods: *"You got it."*

One loop finished. The card can be turned.

Or it might have taken one more round to finish the loop:

Says: *"I guess after thinking about it. I'm too tired to go out at all. Think I'd prefer to stay home and read."*

Acknowledges: *"You wouldn't mind if I picked up a pizza so you could crash with your book?"*

Nods: *"Un-hunh, that works for me. Thanks."*

If the conversation is complex: Many loops and longer

Listening takes longer when issues are complex or loaded. Sometimes a talker needs to keep talking, that is, to get more out of their system or to gain more clarity. Then you need to use a wider variety of listening techniques to feed back a number of thoughts and feelings before turning the card.

This may take some time, perhaps anywhere from a few minutes to a whole evening. And it could mean many one-way loops. This can work, even when the talker is upset or angry with the you.

In one of these longer listening sessions, when it appears that the talker is winding down and feeling heard, it may be time to turn the card. Here's what you do as a listener when it seems time to switch talker and listener roles:

- Feed back the essence of what you heard.
- Ask if your understanding is accurate.
- Ask if the talker is ready to switch roles and be the listener.
- If not, listen more, then repeat these steps.

When the conversation is heavy, it helps for the listener to summarize what the talker said before turning the card: *"So you're worried the kids are watching too much TV, not finishing their homework, and too tired for school. If I heard you accurately, (talker nods) then let me take a turn and tell you how I see the situation. After you feed back my point of view and we both understand me, it'll be your turn to talk again. Okay?"*

This fits when we want others to listen to us. It helps to model listening behavior before asking others to listen. If they see it and experience it, they'll be better able to do it. Explaining the taking turns (fairness) process often helps, but be careful to share rather than lecture.

With people who talk all the time

By "talk all the time," I don't mean people who are so hurt and angry they need a lot of listening to clarify what's going on with them and calm down. I mean people who "just don't stop talking," who go from one topic to the next without taking a breath. It will be difficult (maybe impossible in our lifetime) for them to learn to communicate one loop at a time.

Carefully, set up the taking-turns process at the beginning of the conversation: *"I'm sure we both value our relationship and want to share our concerns with each other. And I'm sure we both want each other's undivided attention and want a turn to be heard. To make that satisfying for both of us, let's take turns (or try this Talker-Listener Card). You talk first, I'll listen and feed back what I hear you saying and when you feel like I understand your first couple of points, it'll be my turn to talk until you understand me. And incidentally, I'm suggesting that we go for understanding each other here, not agreement. After all, we are friends who respect each other's differing points of view. Sound okay to you...?"*

If you want this to work, be sure you both explicitly buy in before you start. Then say something like: *"I really want to understand how you see the situation and what you're feeling about it, so go for it, and I'll set my opinions aside until I've understood yours."*

So you listen and feed back what they are saying, you may need to interrupt here. When you have gained the nod (you've understood them correctly), and it has become your turn to talk, it will likely take more than gentle reminding: *"Wait a minute, remember we agreed to take turns. I took time to understand your concerns. Now it's your turn to listen to me. Can you feed back my concerns to me so I know you understand me? Okay?"* (nods)

If he/she interrupts and/or keeps talking, try saying with firmness: *"Hang on a second, it's my turn to talk. I listened to you, now it's your turn to listen to me. After I feel understood, then you'll get another turn. Can you do that or do we have to put this conversation off until you can take a turn at listening?"*

Your unwillingness to be bulldozed by a barrage of words may be needed before the other person sees the fairness of taking turns.

Some folks have so much pent-up emotion, they can't listen for more than a sentence or two, before their anxiety, insecurity, and anger flattens their brains and they start talking again. When I work with someone who can't listen well, I find that I need to listen twenty minutes and talk one, then listen twenty and talk two, etc.

If they really can't listen, don't continue talking, but say: *"Okay, repeat back what I've just said, then you can talk some more, but I'm not going to listen until you've fed back what I just said. Remember fairness. I want a turn to be heard too, and now it's my turn."*

Unless this is non-negotiable, you will likely get run over and not be heard. You'll be angry with the other person for ignoring your concerns and doubly angry with yourself for letting it happen to you (again).

The skill of turning the card supports your long-term friendships. If you don't develop it, you'll tire of one-way relationships, grow irritable with yourself for giving in, and gradually find ways to check out. So if you don't want your connections damaged, learn to *turn the card*. (Friendly suggestion: Practice on easier people first, before you take on the important toughies.)

There is a fairness in taking turns that cements a relationship into a good place. As we listen better and share more with each other, we learn to know ourselves with clarity. We grow closer, trust more, and connect at a deeper level of human spirit.

It simply improves our relationships.

—— ∞ ——

PART THREE:
Advanced Listening Techniques
& Philosophy

17

Avoiding Ten Communication Traps

AFTER DEFINING THE PROCESS of taking turns talking and listening, we're going to focus on more advanced and specialized listening skills and philosophy. But before we do, I'm going to highlight ten of my all-time-favorite communication traps. There are others of course, but these are common and routinely keep us from listening well. They get in the way of clean communication.

We humans seem to share a persistent under-the-radar tendency to want our own way, to stay in control (of others). This drive to win can surface both when it's our turn to talk and when we listen. Often when we think we're listening, we slip unknowingly into one of the win-based traps. When we do, although we think we're communicating clearly, mostly we're trying to get our way by manipulating the conversation.

Recognizing any one of these traps gives you the opportunity to shift into effective listening and relationship-building communication.

1. Ritual listening

Ritual listening looks like friendly listening, but it's not. While we're quiet and watching the speaker, what we're really doing is waiting for him/her to shut up or take a breath, so we can tell our story or make our point.

While others talk, ritual listeners prepare.

They marshal their thoughts, scout for errors, and decide how to refute arguments. Ritual listeners appear calm, but so do boxers who step back before landing a knockout punch. This struggle sabotages the safety people need in which to relax and experiment with new thoughts.

When you catch yourself **ritual listening**, shake it off and shift your focus toward understanding what the talker is trying to tell you. Hold what the talker says gently in your hands so it won't break. Then hand it back so your talker can see it better. You might say, *"Hold on a second, my thoughts just got in the way of hearing you...? You were saying...? Try it again and I'll stay focused...?*

When you treat the talker with respect, you turn the talker into a friend by being one yourself.

And the flip side for talkers, when you sense that your listener is not listening, say something like: *"I don't have a clue what you're hearing me say. Please feed it back, so I understand what is coming out of my mouth."*

2. Perry Masons

Be careful not to ask what I call **Perry Masons**. I named them in honor of the defense attorney on the forever-running TV drama series. When Perry asked, *"Where were you at 2am, Tuesday morning, the 18th of May, 1986?"* we knew that wasn't a question. He had the guilty party cold.

Grammatically, **Perry Masons** are confusing because they sound like they ask for information, but questions they're not. Wife to husband, *"Do you think I'm fat?"* On a date, *"Do you think she's cute?"* Or, *"When will I see you again?"* None of these are genuine questions and as a result, no answer will work without trouble. These **Perry Masons** are likely expressions of insecurity about weight, cuteness, and a possible next date.

A **Perry Mason** disguises statements or accusations with question marks. Don't be misled by that. A mild **Perry Mason** might be, *"Do you have a hair appointment scheduled?"* which could mask the statement, *"You look pretty scruffy. I think you need a haircut."*

As I was editing this section Sally reminded me I'd forgotten an appointment. As I hurried down the hall to get dressed I said, *"Were you going to fix breakfast?"* My question carried a manipulative twist, because the hidden statement *"I'm late and want breakfast"* and the request beneath it, *"Will you make it for me?"* weren't explicit.

She noticed my **Perry Mason** and replied as a listener, "Try that again?" I was caught and rephrased it as a statement with a clear request, *"Ah, I'm late! Would you mind fixing me two pieces of bacon and an egg?"* She happily said, *"Not at all."* My second attempt was straight-forward — a nice EHJ balanced communication blend.

When people use **Perry Masons**, you may observe that answers do no good. Why? Because answers work in response to questions and, again, **Perry Masons** are not questions.

The following illustrations start with emotionally charged **Perry Masons** that disguise accusations. Notice that the answers don't satisfy the askers:

- *"Were you looking at that blonde?"* *"No, I wasn't."* *"Yes, you were. I saw you."*
- Or husband to wife, *"Did you really need to buy another dress?"* *"Yes, it's for your office Halloween party."* *"You already have a closet full and besides, this is too expensive for a casual party."*
- Or parent to child, *"Do you have any homework?"* *"Well, yes, some."* *"Okay then, turn off the television and do it before dinner."*

No wonder children mumble or refuse to answer parental **Perry Masons.** They know they're not safe curiosity questions. They carry not-so-hidden agendas. They are usually precursors to orders and lectures.

If the three **Perry Mason** sayers above were more direct, they might have used EHJs and said:

- Wife: *"I felt hurt when it looked to me as though you were paying more attention to Alice than you were to me."*
- Husband: *"When you buy new clothes, I have an immediate hit of anxiety. I guess I'm really worried about our finances."*
- Parent: *"I'm worried that your teacher assigns more home-work than you have time to do. Is there any way I can help?"*

Some people raise **Perry Masons** to a high art form by using them in rapid-fire succession, like a battering ram, to wear down their opponents:

- *Where did you eat?*

- *Who did you eat with?*
- *Why did it take you so long?*
- *What did you do after lunch?*
- *Did anyone see you?"*
- *What time did you get home?*
- *And why wasn't dinner ready?*

When caught, they defend themselves by saying, *"I was just asking."* Baloney! They were bullying. This goes way past listening, beyond talking, to unmerciful attacking.

When you catch yourself using **Perry Mason**s, stop. Identify your purpose by asking yourself what you are trying to say, and then say it clearly. You'll probably need to follow it with listening to understand, not to win.

And the flip side, if someone uses one on you, shift into listening mode and use the techniques you've been learning. After all, when they use **Perry Masons** they've become talkers, not listeners.

3. "Why?"

Why? is a district attorney sort of question that carries a hidden agenda with an accusing tone. For example:

- When someone says: *"**Why** did you do that?"* It seems natural to respond defensively, *"I'll tell you **why**, because you..."*
- Or husband to wife: *"Honey, **why** did you pay this bill instead of that one?"* more than likely suggests, *"You paid the wrong one."*
- Or wife to husband: *"**Why** did you put the hinges on that side of the door?"* indicates, not too subtly, that he put them on the wrong side and would elicit this kind of exchange: *"If you don't like the way I'm doing it, then do it yourself."* She: *"That's not the way my father did it."* And he: *"Then get your father over here to do it. I'd rather watch television anyway."*
- In another setting he says, *"**Why** weren't you home in time for dinner?"* She responds, *"I was working."* And he says, *"Work is all that matters to you."*

What can you do when you catch yourself asking **why** questions and setting up arguments?

First, stop asking them. Then figure out if there is something you are curious, concerned, irritated, or angry about. If what you find is friendly curiosity, be aware that leaving out an expression of your curiosity turns your question into an accusation. Express your feeling before the **why** in your sentence: *"I'm really curious why..."* Or, *"I'm wondering why you did that...?"*

Second, if you are irritated with the other person, then say so: *"I'm uncomfortable (irritated or angry) with what you're doing and wonder why you're doing it that way."*

It takes both E (emotion) and H (human factor) to make questions personal and safe. If you leave out the E and/or the H, the **why** by itself takes on a judgmental tone and will routinely draw defensive responses.

And the flip side, if someone else throws a **why** at you, you'll feel that little thud in your belly, so shift into listening mode and find out what they are really telling you.

4. "Not?"

Listeners often try to guide talkers toward new insights or options by asking: *"**Don't** you want to try...?"* Questions that include the abbreviated form of **not** normally produce negative responses. Breaking up the contraction in the question above makes this clear: *"Do you **not** want to try...?"* Note that the question literally asks listeners to affirm that they do **not** want to try the suggestion. A grammatically correct answer might be: *"You're right. I do **not** want to try it."* Paradoxically, **not** questions encourage negative responses to the listeners' suggestions.

Not questions are a night-time ritual in many families. When parents want their youngsters to go to bed, they ask, *"Why **don't** you go to bed now?"* They combine the **why** and the **not** questions into a double whammy. They think they are making a friendly suggestion to produce a healthy move toward bed rest for the children they love. But, in fact, they are asking for a litany of all the reasons their youngsters can think of for not going to bed.

Literally: *"**Why** do you **not** go to bed now?"* draws versions of *"I do **not** want to go to bed now, because I'm not tired."* Or, *"I want to watch this TV program, play my electronic game, or (if all else fails) do my homework."*

The **not** question is not a question. Although couched in a question format, it's a statement: *"I'm worried about you getting enough rest to do well in school."* Or, *"I'm tired. I want you to go to bed so I can have some peace and quiet before I go to bed."*

Friends and counselors often ask **not** questions thinking that they are encouraging sensible solutions, like: *"Why don't you exercise more, take more time off, tell your spouse what you really think or how you feel, etc."* And have as much success as parents trying to get youngsters off to bed. Why? Because this is *advising* instead of listening.

So, what do you do when you find yourself asking **not** questions and getting into uncomfortable conflicts? Either think about what you want to say and then say it or go back to being a listener.

And the flip side, when a **not** hits you, as always, I suggest listening again.

5. *"I understand"*

When someone says, *"I just discovered I have cancer and I'm shaken to my toes,"* it often draws the seemingly empathetic response, *"I understand."* Why then so many defensive responses? Like, *"Excuse me? How can you possibly know how I feel? You have no idea what I'm going through. I'm just trying to figure it out myself."* Though, more often than not, the talker just stops talking, convinced that no one is listening.

Wonder why *I understand* so often kills communication? Because:

- We're talking, not listening. We started talking about our understanding, not their issue. It would have been better to listen and say: *"You're shaken to the core...?"* Or, if we want to let the person know we care, add: *"That shakes me too...? When did you find out...?"* Then shut up and listen to their experience.
- We really don't understand and that's the truth. We've not just been diagnosed with cancer, so the comment is presumptuous. Even if we have or had cancer, our experiences are different from theirs and they need at first to talk about theirs, not hear about ours.

Saying, *"I understand"* is often accompanied by an unconscious two-handed pushing away gesture. It suggests to the talker we don't know how to respond, we are uncomfortable with the topic, and/or we'd rather they didn't talk about it. The person with cancer senses this rejection, gets uncomfortable, and may shut down. If the pushing-away hand-movement is new to you, watch for it when someone replies, *I understand*, to emotional information sharing.

When I have the urge to say *"I understand,"* I grab my hands before they start the pushing-away movement. I roll them over to a palms-up position, as though ready to catch and hold whatever the talker shares. (I might even extend my hands into a hug which could be the best thing to do).

When you notice yourself saying, *"I understand,"* what can you do? Say: *"Wait a minute. I guess I really don't understand...? Tell me what's going on with you...?"*

When you sense the urge to say: *"I understand,"* bite your tongue and don't ever do it again. Then open your hands, be kind to your friends, and say something like: *"You must be surprised, shaken, upset, confused, shocked...? If it were me, I'd be a mess right now...? What's going on with you...?"*

And the flip side, when you start to share something painful and get hit with an *"I understand,"* listen and then ask in effect, *"Sounds like you may not want to know more about what is going on with me, or do you...?"*

6. Asking for one-word-answers

When you are listening and want your talker to continue thinking out loud with you, best not ask questions that can be answered with one word. They stop conversation. *"Did you do that?"* Or, *"Do you think you are wrong in this case?"* are really different from, *"What did you have in mind when you did what you did...?"* Or, *"How would you assess your own behavior in this situation...?"*

"Yes" or *"No"* would answer the first two questions, but stop the conversations. The second questions would tend to keep the talkers talking and thinking about what they did, why they did it, and how it might be perceived by others.

When parents ask, *"How are you doing with your homework?" "Fine."* The **asking for one-word-answers** communication trap turns up unwanted shut-downs.

For adults too (couples, family relations, business interactions, counseling sessions), when good listening, communication, and creative thinking are essential, **asking for one-word-answers** blows the process.

Let's say you haven't seen someone for a while who's been through a difficult time and you ask,

"How are you?" "Fine." Or, *"Are you getting along okay?" "Yes."*

Note that neither exchange includes the personal part of us, just head talk. So, many have learned to ask again, *"No, I mean, I care...? How are you really...?"* And having shared our feelings and asked for more than a one-word answer, we'll likely get the full story (unless they really don't want to talk about it).

Or we could listen by asking, *"I've been thinking about you lately and wondering what's going on with your writing (marriage, kids, job, etc.)...?"* They will likely fill us in, that is, go on talking.

At the beginning of a couples counseling session, I've made the mistake of asking, *"How's it going?"* and *"Fine"* shuts me down (briefly). Or, *"Are you getting along better now?"* And again, *"Yep."* Or, *"No!"* dumped me into a communication hole. I had to discard the trap and get back to better listening techniques.

Besides, a one-word answer like that is judgmental and the partner often jumps to a defense, *"What do you mean 'fine?' You haven't changed at all, you..."* And they are into an argument, instead of listening to each other. (Not what I had in mind.)

When my daughter got her first tryout for a newspaper reporting job on the east coast, fresh out of college, she finished an interview with the big editor and was in the outer office filling out the forms. Another editor was amazed and asked how she got the job since the big boss never hired anyone with fewer than five years of experience. Her answer, *"My dad taught me never to ask a question that could be answered with a 'Yes' or a 'No.' We kept talking until he decided to try me out."* *"Whew,"* he said, *"I'm going into my office and locking the door before you get my job."*

(For more on "Yes" or "No" answers, check **Technique # 26 - Asking for help** later in the book.)

And the flip side: What do you do when someone asks you one of those *one-word-answer questions*? If you want out of the conversation, give the one-worder. But if there is a chance for the two of you to go deeper by your sharing, then say something like: *"Well in one word, 'Fine,' but since you asked, it's not been easy, I've struggled with..."* Or, *"Yes, but there is more to it than that. Let me fill you in on what's really going on with me and how I'm handling it..."*

7. "Yes, but..."

Let's remember that **Yes, but...** usually means, No. When we use **Yes, buts...** as listeners, we've stopped listening and started talking.

While a **Yes, but...** may seem like we're hearing and agreeable, it really is argumentative. We know that what comes after the "but" is the truth, that is, what we really mean. People mostly hear what comes after it. For example, *"I love you, but when you don't call me to tell me you'll be late it steams me."* Or, *"I appreciate all the effort you made, but..."* Statements like these rarely communicate what we want them to.

Listening and remaining focused on talkers' views is difficult, especially when we don't agree. Almost without noticing, we'll slip in a **Yes, but...** to encourage people to change their thinking in our direction.

If it's any comfort, I have a tendency toward being a chronic **Yes, but...** offender. I often slip before realizing it, but then, when I do catch myself, I try to get back to listening. When you catch yourself using **Yes, buts...** on folks who need listeners, what can you do?

Apologize for *yes-but-ing*. Go back to listening until the talkers finish their turns. Then and only then have you earned your turn (right) to talk.

Take a breath and join me on a useful sidetrack: While **Yes, but...** normally subverts our *listening* attempts, it can be an effective *talking* technique. Assertiveness training consultants recommend using **Yes, but...** as a means of holding your own against unpleasant and pushy people.

For example at a car dealership, say: *"Yes* (repeat what the salesperson said so it is clear you heard it), *we'd look just great driving down the* *street in this affordable new car, **but*** (express feelings only, no thoughts the salesperson can argue), *we don't want to spend that much. We want the car for $3,000 less."*

When the sales rep comes up with more arguments, repeat the ***Yes, but...*** process: *"**Yes** (repeat here all the new reasons), **but** [repeat your feelings above).* Continue the process until the rep wears down, that is, knows he or she has been heard and knows clearly what you want or don't want. It works with most pushy people.

When at cross-purposes with insistent kids, it can be used to hold the line and benefit you and your children: *"**Yes**, you really want that $2,800 dirt bike. You're the only one on the block without one. You'll be embarrassed riding up the trail on your old one, **but**, I want to save money for your college expenses."* A repetitive and consistent use of this method helps youngsters feel heard and makes it a little easier for adults to carry out their parental responsibilities.

And the flip side: When someone ***Yes, buts...*** you, since they are talking, feed back what's on both sides of the "yes, but" with the emphasis on what comes after the "but." Because that is what they mostly mean. Listening response to an above statement: *"So while you love me, you want me to hear that you really get fried when I don't call you to let you know I'm going to be late...?"*

8. *"You're not listening to me!"*

Deep into an escalating conversation we might get around to a "righteous" accusation, *"You're not listening to me!"* That's what we say when our partners (children, co-workers, etc.) score high enough on the feeling scale to be more interested in what they think and feel than in what we're saying. In truth — they *aren't* listening to us.

So, how did that happen? Well, you know. We told them slowly and carefully what we wanted them to understand. Then we said it again and came up with super illustrations. When that didn't work, we demanded more time to say it one more time, logically. Surely, we thought, that would help. Perhaps we even raised our voices to get the message across. Failing that time too, we doggedly spelled it out for them, again and again.

And what were they doing while we were making this gigantic communication effort for "the good of our relationship?" Why, they were getting fidgety, even irritated and defensive, maybe trying to hold on to themselves to keep from shedding tears or breaking a vase.

That's when we put the accusing capper on it, "You're not listening to me! I just want to be understood!" And we're right. They're too busy defending themselves against our convincing efforts to listen to us. For the Talker-Listener process to work, it requires that someone be able to listen, but once a heated conversation starts, it's tough to stop even though we're barreling down a wrong road.

I'm sure you've never done this yourself, but for your friends or counselees who get into this jam, the sooner they decide to turn around the better. It makes no sense to waste breath trying to get folks to understand when their brains are too flat to hear. So, when you think about saying, "You're not listening to me," let that be your clue that it's time for you to go back to listening. Maybe you can take enough pressure off their ears so they can hear you again.

And the flip side: When they say it to you (and they are right), decide whether you are too flat-brained to listen (and need a break) or get serious again about listening: *"So you figure I'm not listening to you...? And you just want to be understood...? What is it that I'm missing that you'd like me to understand...?"* And keep on listening because they are really upset.

9. Fixing it — "I want a consultant, not a husband (or wife)"

I've saved the most common communication trap people use on each other for near the end of the list — the desire to help others by fixing their problems or at least giving advice. So, how do we shake loose from this communication killer?

I know, I know. I've already talked about *advising* (in *Chapter 15 – Listen without advising*) being a "No! No!" and how important it is for a listener to keep track of *who owns the problem* (in *Chapter 11 — Who Owns the Problem?*).

But most of us keep trying anyway. Fixing is a dominant and dangerous inclination. It damages listening by wrenching the problem away from talkers, cutting into their confidence.

We guys read the male handbook that says, *"Your forefathers protected their wives from being carried off by marauding tribes, bagged game to feed the family, and fought off lions and tigers. The least you can do is fix your wives' problems."*

So with the genes, it came naturally. We want to take care of and fix the problems our partners face. Nice motivation, but when we try, it doesn't work and we get criticized, *"You never listen to me! All I wanted was to talk it over."*

And it's not only guys afflicted with the fixit gene. In my counseling experience I've found it shared about equally between the sexes. I expect most gals read the mother handbook that says, *"You are responsible to bring your youngsters up well (whatever age, including husbands) and that means not letting them suffer, keeping them from harm, tying their shoes, fixing their meals, and their problems."*

Few of us (male or female) like it when someone treats us as children (like we can't manage our own lives) by taking over and trying to solve our problems.

Truth shows up in strange places. A novelty store placard says, *"Sometimes people do not want the answer, they want a friend."* That brings to mind a computer guru buddy, who describes his trouble with problem-solving and listening in his first marriage this way: *"I struggle with this. I like to solve problems. It's so ingrained in me that I think that way all the time. What is it? Is it working? Can I make it work better? If not, why not? Can I fix it? If not, try anyway. That's how I see the universe… makes it hard on a relationship."*

In his second marriage it took him eight years to learn to do this instead:

1. *"Listen;*
2. *"Validate her feelings no matter what I think;*
3. *"Listen more;*
4. *"Validate more;*
5. *"Is she still talking? … Keep listening;*
6. *"Need more validation? No, okay, but keep listening;*
7. *"NO! STOP! She did not ask you to fix it… Keep listening;*
8. *Is she still talking? Keep listening…"*

And here's a clue about the flip side: Couples often get into trouble when one wants to talk things over and the other wants to be helpful. Asking your partner to think through an issue with you can stir up immediate conflict.

My spouse/partner, Sally, taught me how to handle this one. She discovered that when she walked into my office at home with an issue she needed to think through, I would quickly forget what I teach and leap into action, giving advice.

That of course frustrated her, but made me feel really smart and important, that is, for the short time before she got mad and considered not ever placing her problems in the hands of this rotten listener again.

Fortunately for us, she figured out a way to get me off the guy problem-solver-thing and into a useful mode of listening. For years now when she walks into my office, she first asks, *"Is this a convenient time to talk?"* And when it is or we set a time for later, she says, *"I have an issue I want to talk over with you. I need a consultant not a husband. Can you handle that?"*

Whew, bumps me right out of my groove and off my advice pillar. I know how to do that. I grab the Talker-Listener Card and slide into listening mode. The TLC reminds me it is her problem. I'm to work at understanding and clarifying, no advice, no agreement or disagreement and especially no defending. I don't try to solve her problem. She gets heard, sorts out her issues (I stay out of trouble) and we both feel better.

10. Screens of all sizes

Since the first edition of the book, *screens of all sizes* have waded into the middle of our communication and can't be ignored. As with most things in life we can use our electronic screens either to benefit or to damage our relationships.

Telephones morphed communication into therapeutic listening, phone therapy, distance coaching, and now those phones are enriched by screens with Skype, Facetime, etc. We don't have to be geographically close to connect personally, face-to-face.

My laptop screen bailed me out of a counseling session with a young hearing impaired couple. The two had cochlear implants and used the oral method of speaking that sounds to me a little like a foreign dialect. And dialects challenge my high range hearing loss. We struggled, attempting to understand each other, trying to sort out their marital issue. Finally, I asked (mimed), *"Do you type?"* They did. I sat between them with my laptop so we could all see the screen. We passed the computer back and forth, handled the counseling session on the screen until we'd resolved the issue. I printed the file and they took it with them. Wonderful!

However, do note that I've included *screens of all sizes* in the section on communication traps, figuring that if we don't keep an eye on them, they will take over our relationships and wipe out face-to-face interactions. They also seem to possess addictive qualities and are now showing up on lists of troublesome personal issues. Most of us have felt ignored and unheard at times when others seem lost in their screens. And we've probably done it "unto" others as well.

One Fourth of July weekend, seven family members from three generations gathered around a crackling campfire in the Wallowa Mountains in northeastern Oregon. Stomach full and happy, I looked around. Only two of us were *not* fiddling with screens of one size or another. And the other non-fiddler was reading a book.

In a playful way I kidded about how *modern* we were. *Acknowledging* what we might be saying by our behavior in a non-judgmental way touched off a little group embarrassment at being caught using electronics in the midst of all that outdoor beauty and amongst relatives. It also opened an interesting conversation about what we were doing, why we were there, and what we had to share with each other.

A recent TV commercial for a diamond pictured a well-dressed couple at a corner table in a classy restaurant, champagne poured, both peering down into their smart phones. The guy texts the gal, *"Look up."* She does. He hands her an engagement ring. She happily accepts. Funny, scary, and something more than puzzling.

If we assume "screening behavior" (watching computer, pad, T.V. & smart phone screens) is talker body language, then we can listen by asking, *"Are you interruptible...?"* or *"Is this a convenient time to talk...?"* or

"Looks like you have something going...?" when we'd like to communicate with someone engaged with a screen.

How can you handle smart phone interruptions in groups? Or what about the "smartphone effect," when one person pulls out a phone and everyone else does too? You could agree that the person, who pulls theirs out first buys the drinks or washes the dishes.

Some people leave their cell phones home when the event is nearby and safety is not an issue. Others civilize their friendly dinners by playing the "phone stack game." After ordering, they pile their phones face down in the center of the table and ignore the rings and beeps. The first person unable to resist their phone's siren song and who picks it up also picks up the check.

It puts the question front and center, *"What is that text message worth?"* It also may focus the evening on sharing, just like acknowledging screens did around the campfire.

When you put the people with you ahead of those beckoning from across the ether, you open the door to deepening your immediate relationships. With fear and trepidation some families risk setting unplugged meals, evenings, drives, events, or weekends — no screens of any size. And then you make reconnection possible (though still challenging).

The issues: How to make the most of our lives in an age of electronic screens, how to handle the demands of immediate connectivity, and how to apply common courtesy (love) in this new world will fill many books. But, it's too soon and too much for these pages.

However, don't get me wrong. In our home we love our **screens of all sizes.** They bring the resources of the world to us anywhere, though we try not to let them run our lives. Our goal is to master our tools, not to be mastered by them.

What if a talker or listener uses one of the ten traps on us?

When someone tries a communication trap on you, keep this in mind: They probably don't realize what they're doing. They think they're listening or talking in a helpful way. So, what can you do?

- Because they aren't listening, switch from talking to listening and clarify what they were trying to say beneath the trap. Then after they've been heard, get back to your turn again.

- Or, you can remind them that it is your turn to talk. You can ask them to set aside their views for the moment and listen until you've been heard and understood. You can make it clear that after you've been heard, you'll take time to listen to their concerns.

These communication traps are so common we hardly see ourselves using them. You may have noticed I admitted to using several myself. If you remember them, you can catch yourself and others using them. Then re-say what you intend to say or listen and find out what they were trying to say. Frequent trap use pushes away the very people we want close to us.

Paying attention to these traps will keep you out of unnecessary skirmishes and strengthen your connections with people.

18

A Few Essential Listening Modes and Attitudes

As I JUST SAID ABOUT the screens in our lives, most things in life can be used for either good or evil. So too with listening techniques. They can enrich communication, connection, and growth. Or they can be used to take advantage of someone, to get our way, and to bully. Underneath the words are attitudes and ways of treating people that make a difference. I'll share some options in the next three listening techniques.

How to Listen Better: Technique # 15

Is there a way to listen when you don't agree with the talker, when you have figured out already what the talker should think or do, or when you don't expect the talker to have much worthwhile to offer?

Allow space

■ *Make space in your mind for insight and surprises to emerge from talkers' reflections and comments.*

Be aware that while others are talking, we tend to decide whether they are right or wrong and what they should do about their situations. Sometimes we even make up our minds before our conversations get started. Such prejudgments can prevent us from understanding what's going on or helping them come up with options that fit them. They also can keep us from thinking new thoughts.

To **allow space** means opening our minds to possibilities beyond what we've already thought. This goes deeper than technique — to an attitude change. It means appreciating someone who thinks differently than we do and whom we may not even like.

Remember? Listening is dangerous to our pre-formed opinions. Real listening requires getting inside other people's thought processes, which may cause us to discard a few of our old thoughts and replace them with new ones. Seeing through someone else's eyes and experience may transform us. (Scary.)

To **allow space** means letting talkers' thoughts emerge and valuing them. We might say to a talker: *"I'm having trouble hearing since our views are so different...? But I'm going to set mine aside so I can understand yours...? How does what you think about this issue feel to you on the inside...?"* Or, *"Let me catch my breath while I set my thoughts aside. I want to understand yours...? You've apparently been struggling with this for some time...? Tell me what you've been thinking, what you've considered, and what you've tried...?"*

When we suspend our views to **allow space** for other people's concerns, it's like temporarily locking them in a safe. This frees us to engage in their thinking processes with them. Such good listening can produce growth in listeners, as well as it does in talkers.

An **allow space** attitude suggests listening more in general. It means opening ourselves to people we normally "pass by on the other side." It doesn't take a lot of extra time, but does take concentrated effort. Those few minutes at the water cooler, on a commuter train, waiting for meetings to start, or lunches together present opportunities to deepen connections that make working together more effective (and it enriches our lives).

Listening to co-workers, family members, or strangers with genuine interest, being fully present without an agenda, hearing their passions (children, art, sports, books, etc.) and finding commonalities — these simple things benefit them and us.

When I do listening skill training for businesses and participants are getting sold on its value in their work, I stop, ask them to take a breather from work, and suggest that surprisingly all these techniques work at home as well (and it comes as a surprise to some). I encourage them to think about their partner, spouse, and/or family on their commute home, then walk in the door ready to listen, and to make their day, rather than expecting to be looked after (and likely disappointed.)

To **allow space** broadly in relationships initiates the possibility of deeper connections with others and ourselves and of staying on a growing edge.

∞

How to Listen Better: Technique # 16

How can you handle listening when you get impatient with the speed at which they are moving through their issues? When it's their turn to talk, your desire to move them faster is not only irrelevant, but gets in the way. It's more effective to match pace.

✎ Match pace

■ *Reflect the pace of the talker.*

Many of us have trouble with this. Television taught us that problems can be solved in thirty minutes less time out for commercials. We prefer keeping things moving on our schedules, after all, "time is of the essence." We want talkers to get to their insights soon, that is, at our pace. But, it means that we shoot our empathetic demeanor in the foot — the talker has no sense that we are with them. And in fact, we are out ahead of them (and maybe in the wrong direction).

In these situations, if we push, they resist by slowing down even more. Not helpful. So, respect your talkers' speeds of self-discovery.

Remember, like midwives, we listeners help talkers give birth to new understandings. This process depends on the internal clocks of the mother and the baby. Allowing a talker to move through an issue is a similarly delicate and time-consuming process as birthing. It requires slowing down our drive to move fast, for them not to feel criticized and left behind.

Generally, it's essential for us to move slowly, unless the talkers happen to be unusually fast-paced. If we let ourselves get bored with the processing others do, we may not be focusing well enough on them (because we're more focused on ourselves?) and we may be missing too much to help. If you simply can't give the time and attention now, then carefully make an appointment to finish the conversation when you can.

When you ***match pace*** with your talkers, it will help them feel a change in how seriously you are listening to them. It will allow them to take more time to think things through. They will be better able to assess their situations so that new directions can surface.

How to Listen Better: Technique # 17

Sometimes "calmness" comes across to talkers as lack of interest, zero caring, and looks mechanical and unfeeling. It is possible to use good listening techniques and stay unengaged, leaving the talker alone and feeling (and maybe being) worked over. How do you both get engaged and come across as engaged?

Meet intensity

- *Ramp up your emotional intensity to within two points of the talker's. That doesn't mean matching a specific emotion like anger, but rather keeping your emotional engagement level near the talker's.*

I'll illustrate this first with the women who complain that when they're upset, their husbands become infuriatingly calm and logical. Many men mistakenly believe that when their wives are shaken, all they have to do to help is flatten out emotionally and their wives will calm down. (This behavior at times also fits wives, friendly listeners, and counselors with their clients.)

Logic Man's approach leaves women alone in their emotional plight. For women, that's akin to hanging out on the end of a high, creaky limb, all alone. This helplessness often gives way to a sense of hopelessness and anger.

Let's number feelings: A woman hovering near eight could easily jump to fifteen in the presence of a man who meanders between zero and one. If the man were to listen by stirring up some emotional intensity (within two points of hers) and use a few other listening techniques, she would feel heard, less alone, drop a few emotional points on her scale, and figure there is hope. If he moves toward her intensity, it would allow them to move ahead together without her shutting down or getting angry.

How might a guy get his energy level to reflect hers so she doesn't feel alone? This has both a personal and technical side. It takes both caring and the appearance of caring.

First, regarding caring, better think about what's important and ramp up your concern for the talker. (No fair pretending until you gather info you want and then checking out.) Examine your own motives and go for understanding (supporting) not replying or winning.

Some folks have reported that they tried the Talker-Listener Card with their spouses, but that "it" caused disruption rather than connection. I'm suspicious and suspect that they approached the techniques in a bloodless, emotionally flat way, gaining one more indicator that they "tried everything" and it didn't work. Sometimes people who "try" are trying to get their partners to agree with them rather than, trying to understand their partners. Motives do matter.

Second, work on technique. Perhaps own your own feelings by saying, *"This is tough for me to hear, but I care about you and want to stay with you through this…? Tell me what's going on…?"* The listener could also increase **meet intensity** by putting the paper or book down, turning off all electronic screens, turning toward the talker, leaning forward, making eye contact, (slightly) raising the pitch or tone of voice, using a little more dramatic language, and focusing exclusively on the talker's concerns and point of view. If they're a couple, it might help if they went to another room, to a restaurant, for a walk, or away from the children.

At times men feel alone in what matters to them too — work future, financial responsibility, politics, relationships, sex, sports, hobbies, etc. The intense and undivided listening described above makes a real difference to them as well.

People not only need to be heard, but to feel heard as well. So get engaged and listen as though your life depends on it.

19

Special Circumstance Listening Techniques

There are a variety of common situations we'll encounter when we listen to people. It has helped me to have ways to think about them and sound methods for handling them.

How to Listen Better: Technique # 18

Older (and sometimes younger) people tend to tell the same stories over, and over, and over again. They do until their families, friends, counselors, and care-givers glaze over and politely go into hiding or run for cover.

Old folks and "boring" stories

- *When older talkers start re-telling those boring, surface-level stories, ask what they learned from their experience, what it meant to them, and how their lives were affected by it.*

Ironically, the old stories are boring to the tellers as well. You'll note that their expressions are flat and tones unengaged. The stories seem stuck in their throats as if they have to keep telling them to get them out of their systems. And those of us within earshot get embarrassed when our children, who echo our boredom, express it out loud.

When we try to ignore the storytellers, nothing changes. They keep telling the stories. No one benefits.

Years ago I went to a meaning formation workshop where the professor taught us to look at stories, life experiences, and situations we'd observed and then draw meaning from them. I found that unpacking a truth from a story or experience created excitement and energy. I found this mining-for-meaning process immensely helpful in my teaching, counseling, and preaching career. When I visited folks in nursing homes and encountered the recurring stories, I figured there must be some better way to deal with them than rolling my eyes and ignoring them. So I experimented with listening and searching for their meaning. I found that using this method stirred energy in the old-timers (and made visiting them more fun for me).

I came to believe that their repetitious stories were not finished enough to be left in the past. To complete them, they needed to appropriate their meaning. My experience taught me that if they glean meaning from them, they could leave the stories behind and move on.

So what do you do to help the weary storytellers?

When folks start cranking up their familiar old saws, use a few listening techniques so they clearly get into their stories and you let them know you're in the story with them. Then ask: *"What did you learn from that experience...?"* Or, *"What did that mean to you...?"* Or, *"Sounds like there was a life principle in that...? What was it...?"* Or, *"How did that affect your life...?"* Or, *"How did you use what you learned in the rest of your life...?"*

The questions go roughly in this sequence:
- *"What happened...? Describe it...?"*
- *"What did you learn from it (meaning, life-principle)...?"*
- *"How did you use it in your life...?"*
- *"What difference has it made to you...?"*

These questions often help people connect with something beneath the surface of their life history. Something the story pointed to. Watch them come alive, light up, relax, and get excited. They feel better after they've been heard and usually don't have as much need to bring up the stories again.

Using **old folks and boring stories** benefits you, the listener, since you learn a lot about how people became who they are and what makes them tick. Just before I started to re-write this section, I received an email saying wistfully, *"I wish I had read this section this morning, before I had lunch with my mother!"*

One of my readers noted this works well with children as a way to help them learn from their experiences. In fact, if we ask these questions of ourselves (and perhaps our families to enliven holiday dinners), we'll enjoy discovering more of who we are, too.

Using these listening questions will stir up the sunshine in another person's life, enlighten yours, and even enrich dull lunch conversations.

─── ∞ ───

How to Listen Better: Technique # 19

When we notice *tears* forming in people's eyes or they start to cry, many of us get nervous and run for cover.

Tears

■ *When your talker starts crying, don't let tears stop you from listening. Find out what the tears are about.*

If we get tongue-tied and don't know what to do around tears, we leave talkers alone with their rising emotions. We stop conversations about what might be painful and yet important to them. If *tears* set off a nervous thud feeling in us, it may suggest we don't want to deal with whatever is causing them, but let's do it anyway. People need to be heard and have their concerns valued in spite of *their* tears and *our* fears.

A common mistake in dealing with *tears* is to ask questions that invite talkers into the courtroom by making accusations: *"What's wrong?"* Or, *"What's the matter?"* Such questions draw judgments such as: *"What's wrong is that you let me down."* Or, *"You forgot to call me."* Or, *"You didn't listen to me when I needed you…"*

If we ask for accusations, we usually get them. But, some people will choke up instead and reply, *"Oh, nothing,"* because they don't want to blame us.

Sometimes, as listeners, we feel guilty and ask for accusations: *"What did I do wrong?"* When talkers answer such questions, arguments ensue or they clam up, sensing that if they answer, they'll touch off WWIII.

Few people already weeping would recognize *"What did I do wrong?"* as a talker statement, switch to listening, and respond appropriately: *"Sounds like you think you did something to cause my tears...? Is that right...?"*

Tears may well up from happiness, sadness, irritation, anger, frustration, excitement, or the tension involved in a situation that is deeply personal and touching. They can surface when a person feels passionate about something, anything. Sometimes folks tear up when they feel heard, because, sadly for them, being really listened to happens way too seldom. In such situations being heard can be so meaningful that it stirs up deeper feelings of intimacy and connection.

When someone verges on crying, I often say something like: *"I notice your eyes seem to be getting watery. What's going on...?"* Or, *"This conversation seems pretty painful for you...?"* Or, *"You seem upset...? What's bothering you...?"* Or, *"I'm concerned. You seem to be tearing up...?"* Or, *"I'm okay with tears...? I assume you want to continue talking...? This must matter to you...?"* Or, *"You seem touched...?"* Or, *"This must be very important to you...?"* And then depending on their responses, I continue listening in other ways.

However, some people use **tears** to avoid dealing with painful issues or situations. In the past they learned that tears got them off the hook because so many people were afraid of them.

If I'm suspicious that someone is using **tears** to avoid, I listen by saying: *"Looks like you are pretty uncomfortable...? Do the tears mean you're having trouble discussing this...? What's getting to you...?"* Or, *"Can you handle talking through the tears or would you really rather talk about it tomorrow morning when you're calmer...?"* Or for serious tears, *"Do your tears mean you want to avoid this topic altogether, or do they mean something else...? What do you have in mind...?"*

These acknowledgements and questions allow talkers to take responsibility for whether they want to talk further or not. As a listener, be careful not to stop conversations because of your fear of crying. If you do you're deciding for talkers and taking control of their timing in dealing with their problems.

As listeners when we give the timing control back to the talkers, we both let *tears* surface important issues and be a part of their healing.

How to Listen Better: Technique # 20

Many people are reluctant to visit bereaved friends because they don't know all the details, don't have a lasagna in hand, or aren't sure what reassuring (religious) thing to say.

After a death

- *What matters is that you get there now, listen, and then listen regularly over the next months, and even years.*

Knowing the details

Some of us are slow to visit *after a death* because we want to know all the details first to increase our confidence, and it takes time to gather the info. The fear of looking foolish, of not knowing everything, ought not keep us from comforting others.

Actually, it can be better if we don't know much. Our ignorance of details makes questioning more natural. When we admit we don't know what happened, the grievers will retell the story to help us. Asking what happened allows the grieving person to share and begin to assimilate the loss. Ask your friends to visit too and suggest they each ask for a retelling — the more times through it the better.

(For more on not knowing what to say, go back to **Technique # 11 – Admit ignorance.**)

The lasagna

Others hesitate to visit *after a death* because they worry about intruding, about not having professional skills, or not being an especially close friend. They think they need to be more than they are or do something extra, like "bringing a lasagna." Somehow we're not worthy of visiting unless we have a dish of food in hand.

But times have changed. We think we should prepare something, but with busy schedules we don't get around to it and besides, who cooks like that anymore? So it takes awhile to admit that and decide to buy take-out. The whole process takes too much time and leaves our grieving person alone. Let the people who don't know how to listen, bring the casserole or cookies (and there will be plenty).

We don't realize how much our personal presence alone is a support to a person with a loss. Sad. We all lose — some by not comforting and others by not being comforted.

People need people even more when they experience a loss. No one should go through grief alone.

Knowing that someone cares enough to be present in a painful situation provides real support for the grief-stricken person. So get there fast and say: *"I heard that John (or Jane) died...?"* Or, *"What happened...?"* Then, bite your tongue and let them tell you. That will help them and give you clues about what to do next.

And please, don't waste your breath asking what you can do for them. They're in shock, confused, and thoroughly flat-brained. They usually don't have a clue what they need. Look around and do whatever needs doing, but mostly let them talk.

The six-and-a-half-week rule

In our culture an unwritten rule suggests that people feel okay discussing losses for about six and a half weeks. After that, those who suffered the loss think they shouldn't burden their friends by talking about it any longer. And their friends don't bring it up, because they're afraid that doing so would re-open sore wounds.

In reality the grief process takes a minimum of eighteen months — with serious losses it can last a life-time. Because of the six-and-a-half-week rule, most people are left alone with their grief after those first few weeks.

Please don't let that happen. It is a terrible thing to do to your friends. People simply get healthy quicker when they don't have to carry their grief alone.

Besides, going through it with others will stir up issues for you and while painful, they are real. You can learn from them and they will build your grief-handling muscles for times when you are going through it yourself.

If people really don't want to talk about it

I never ask, *"Do you want to talk about it?"* because people often say, *"No."* They don't want to burden us with their pain. I encourage you not to ask either. Don't let their culture-bred inhibitions get in the way of accepting the listening help they need. They may think their concerns are unworthy of your time or even feel embarrassed to admit they can't handle everything on their own.

Once in a great while, someone really doesn't want to talk about their loss (or other hurt-filled situation, like discovering cancer). If so, they'll let you know, usually by changing the subject. People have well-developed avoidance skills. They may ask about your family or job, the latest sports event. They'll do it so fast it'll astound you.

For me, I ask about their loss, acknowledge their pain, and let their behavior tell me if they want me to listen through their grief with them. This may or may not be the time for them to start talking it through. If they aren't ready, I go with their rapid change of topic. But, I'm there for them when they need me, whether they know they need support or not.

So I plow in gently with a listening response to what their body is saying and ask: *"I heard that John (or Jane) died...? What happened...?"* Or: *"You seem confused, what's going on...?"* Or, *"You look like you just got bad news, what's happening...?"* Or, *"If that just happened to me, I'd be shaken, what are you doing to handle it...?"* Or, *"It seems like you're angry with me, what's that about...?"* (Notice how all the questions are open-ended and can't be answered with a conversation stopping "Yes" or "No.")

In any case, come back later, every month or two (for years), and give them a follow-up question: *"I've been thinking about you and wondering how you are doing with the death of your spouse (loved one, etc.)...?"*

Again, ask and listen. Let them talk or change the subject.

Reassuring (religious) things to say?

Death often raises spiritual issues. Some folks avoid going to visit *after a death* because they think they need to know the proper religious things to say. The implications here are that there are correct answers to give and that the grieving person can hear them.

Keep in mind that folks with losses are so fat-bellied and flat-brained they can't hear what you say anyway. What they need are listeners, not talkers. Bereaved people need to sort out what they believe. Reflective listening is the best way to help *them* do that.

When people are struggling with faith after a loss, listen first (your faith understandings, lack of them, and/or beliefs are irrelevant here). Ask what their attitudes and feelings are about death, what it means to them, what their faith tradition says about it, whether they feel abandoned by God, and where they find their strength.

When I visit someone after a death, I assume anger will be there, because it grows out of painful losses. Ask them specifically, what expectations were shattered by the death. Ask what is bothering them, what they might be angry about, or if they figure anyone let them down. They may have trouble acknowledging their anger, but it will likely be there and focused in some direction. They might be angry with you for not getting there sooner, with themselves for things they didn't do, with the doctors for not finding a cure, with the smoker who died of lung cancer, or even at God, who they might think let it happen.

Anger is irrational. It springs out of pain. Wherever people's anger points, acknowledge it. You may feel like defending someone against their anger. Don't. Not even if they are attacking God. God doesn't need defending. (My guess is that God doesn't want defense either, because then you'd be attacking someone whom God loves.)

And again about "reassuring (religious) things to say," grieving people are the ones who need to be heard and understood by you (you may be God's stand-in). Bite your tongue if you feel the urge to fix their pain or preach. Accept their responses and they will begin to sense they are not alone and healing will begin. A long while down the road of their healing, they may be ready for a shared conversation with you about your faith journeys.

I encourage you to be there with people as they go through the pain of their losses and grief. When you do that, they are not alone. How can you communicate anything more important, loving, and spiritual than that?

How to Listen Better: Technique # 21

So, how do we respond to a child or adult who has suffered a *horrific loss?* To a child who's afraid to go to school? To someone who's lost a loved one when a building blew up? To folks in the aftermath of a tornado or a tsunami? To parents who fear that schools are unsafe? To anyone impacted by a crisis in their family or community? To those still alive after indiscriminate shootings? To those frightened by political upheaval?

Horrific loss

> ■ *So, what do you say to folks on the heels of disaster? Nothing. Instead, listen and make a safe place for people to talk out their disruption and heal.*

Tough questions float in the air around calamities. When people cry out, *"Why did this happen? Will it happen again?"* We get anxious, because we don't have answers and fear that there is nothing we can say that will help. And we're right. Our talking statements won't do it no matter how true they are:

- *"Percentages tell us that schools are safe,"*
- *"We'll buy you another dog,"*
- *"You're young yet and you'll find another love,"*
- *"We're Americans and we'll survive, in spite of everything."*

Such assurances (even religious ones) on the heels of crisis are glib, damaging, and at best, useless.

Why don't such reassurances work? It's because these come too soon and they are talking responses. The anguished need listening. They are not asking questions for information and they are not ready to listen, even though they might think they are. If you produce answers, you'll find out because you'll get resistance.

They are in truth talking and saying something like: *"I'm frightened! I'm shaken to my toes and angry at this unfair world and the God who allowed this to happen!"* Their agony cries out to be heard, not to be told stuff.

Now you may have some really practical and helpful information to share with survivors, but bite your tongue and hold it until people have had their hurts and fears acknowledged, been heard and know that they are understood — until their upsets have calmed and their ears start working again.

My rule in a crisis is: "Listen First — Talk Second." If you *acknowledge* people's fears, pain, losses, hurts, confusion, anger, etc. first, then they may calm enough to hear your thoughtful reassurances. (Once you have listened more, you may learn that your first answers wouldn't have fit anyway.) And you'll have the information and time to come up with something to say that might actually be helpful.

How to Listen Better: Technique # 22

Dealing with *anger* requires an understanding of where *anger* comes from as well as solid and determined listening skills. *Anger* masks both hurt and caring and it tends to put listeners off. Don't let it do that to you.

Expectations and anger

■ *Four listening skills for when your talker is angry:*
1. *Help identify the talker's anger and acknowledge it.*
2. *Help identify the hurt under the anger and acknowledge it.*
3. *Help identify the caring under the hurt and acknowledge it.*
4. *Help identify the gap between his/her expectations and reality.*

People get *angry* when an unmet *expectation* produces a loss, resulting in hurt. And they don't get hurt unless they care. So when someone is *angry,* you will find hurt and caring there under the *anger.*

Realizing that they hurt and care, encourages me to risk diving down through the unpleasantness. When I help couples get beneath their **anger**, they reconnect and sometimes in tears say, *"All I saw was your **anger** and disappointment with me. I didn't know you still really cared about me."*

Anger is proportional to the gap between what people *expect* and what happens (reality). Big gap — big anger. Little gap — little anger (irritation, disappointment, resentment, loneliness, etc.).

When our *expectations* aren't met, we get hurt first. Then the hurt turns into anger. And while anger is a secondary emotion, it often is what we and others notice first.

So start by acknowledging the *anger* you hear on the surface: *"You sound really angry with your husband...?"* Or, *"So you are somewhat angry with me...?"* Or, *"How angry are you...?"* *"Mmmm. That angry...?"* Or, *"On a zero to ten scale, your anger is...?"*

Continue the process by surfacing the *expectations* that set up the hurt and *anger*: *"You're angry because your husband didn't remember your anniversary...?"* Or, *"What did you expect from me that I didn't do...?"* Or, *"You were disappointed that I didn't get home in time for the special dinner you planned...?"* Or, *"So you were hurt that I didn't care enough to come see you, and then you got angry...?"* Or, *"You felt really lonely after Dad died and expected me to spend more time with you...? So you're hurt and angry with me for not visiting more often...?"*

In effect you are asking what they were before they got *angry. Anger,* being secondary, follows on the heals of disappointment, resentment, loneliness, sadness, irritation, etc. Helping them acknowledge that lets some of its hurt/energy go.

Keep in mind that these folks would not have been hurt had they not cared. So acknowledge that too: *"I'm touched...? Sounds like you fixed this special meal because you care about me...? That must have made my being late even more hurtful...?"* Or, *"I guess from what you're saying, you were pretty disappointed I wasn't there after your dad's death...? I must matter a lot to you...?"* Or, *"Sounds like being angry with your wife grew out of feeling lonely and irritated when she spent so much time on her project...? You must care a lot for her and want to spend time with her...?"*

Rather than avoiding folks because they are *angry*, I encourage you to acknowledge their *expectations, anger, hurt, and caring.* You can do this for people whether they are angry about the way life treated them, a significant death, their youngster's report card, a job disappointment, an election, or you.

Such listening allows people to get clearer about what's going on with them, reduce the heat in their anger, salve their hurt, and bring their caring to the surface.

Altogether? A healthy process.

How to Listen Better: Technique # 23

When a person is ferociously angry, using the image of a *bullfighter* can help you listen more effectively. Think first of the bull, coming into a ring — unfamiliar setting, too much noise, too many frantic people, frightened, and then angry. A classic flat-brain-producing situation for the bull and you too, when the bull (talker) approaches.

Persistent anger and bullfighters

■ *When your talker is "really" angry and persistent about it, visualize yourself as a bullfighter, facing a talker who is charging at you like a bull. For your cape, use lots of listening techniques. Keep it up and let the angry energy dissipate by charging past you, not hurting anyone. If we faced a bull in the ring, it would look scary. The powerful body, substantial weight, strong arched neck, head down, snorting, feet pawing the ground, eyes squinting, charging. It feels the same when some folks come at us — really mad.*

Our fear of an angry onslaught makes us quickly conscious of two options — grab the bull by the horns and break its neck or get gored to death. Fight or knuckle under. Neither sounds appealing.

If we confront an angry person head-on, grabbing the bull by the horns, someone is going to get hurt. (Not to mention that trying to explain a few of the reasons the bull should not be angry just isn't going to work.)

The *bullfighter* chooses a third option — waves the cape, watches the bull charge, steps aside, sucking in his/her gut so as not to get gored, lets the bull blast past to expend some energy, and says with body language, *"Oh, you're angry...? You must be more than annoyed...?"*

The bull shakes himself off, realizes he is still angry, snorts, and charges: *"Don't give me that psychology crap! You let me down and we both know it!"* Let's do the **bullfighter** thing again: *"You're not a little angry. You're furious with me. You figure I let you down...?"*

And the bull expends more energy with another run at you, *"Well, wouldn't you, if you were me?"* Acknowledge the talker beginning to calm by saying: *"You were powerfully hurt that I didn't come through for you the way you expected. Really bugged...?"*

"More than bugged, you don't care about me." Don't get in the way of the bull by becoming argumentative. The bull isn't ready to let it go yet, so ask: *"What was it that got to you the most...?"*

"Well, I guess it was..." It's working. The bull is being heard. Emotion is abating. Thinking is clearing.

If you were really in a bull ring, the bull would finally have tired, relaxed, gotten over his fear, and quit charging. But then some jackass on a horse comes along and sticks a spear in the bull's rump to hurt, frighten, and anger him enough to charge again. At this stage in the calming process, talking, giving advice, or arguing can have the same effect as a picador's spear.

Experiment with picturing an angry person coming at you as a raging bull and try to get yourself into the **bullfighter** mode. And remember, the **bullfighter** respects the bull.

When you listen rather than defend, no one gets hurt. While some people prefer to stay angry, the **bullfighter** technique can allow ferocious bulls (customers, spouses, bosses, counselees, people with opposing viewpoints, and young people) to become friends.

Practicing this one will often produce miracles.

How to Listen Better: Technique # 24

When your talker uses loaded pressure words like should, ought, have to, must, need, the only way, always, or never, they are masking embedded values. Those words have noticeable feelings lurking beneath them. They sound like absolute requirements that come from some authority on a mountain top, when in fact (as I see it), they are their points of view, ramped up with passion and anxiety.

During my forty years as a pastor, I ran into this a lot, people who thought they knew "the truth" about religion or waterless cooking. They all assumed that since they were "right" I should agree with them. While I felt judged and like kicking them in the shins, I figured my job was to listen in a loving way. I expect you run into them at parties, on the bus, in your families, in the counseling office. So I decided I best not duck this important issue here, even though it's difficult, too important not to share what I learned.

As I see it, talkers' flat-brains may confuse their point of view with "the truth for all people" and turn rigid. I suggest that flies in the face of the respect, acceptance, love, and openness to others that is the essence of this book. If you agree, you may want to help loosen their rigidities. Let's take a look at how to do it.

When someone says, *"That's the only way to do it,"* what they're saying is: *"This is the way I see it* (H). *I really want you* (E) *to see it that way too. And I'm anxious* (E) *that you might not see it the way I do and I'll lose face* (J)."

People wanting others to think or act a certain way, doesn't make them rigid. Adding anxiety about *needing* them to does. If they simply want something a certain way, they can still listen to your suggestions. When they're anxious about not getting you to think or act their way, then they're not open to your views. This makes working or living with them difficult.

Anxiety turns desire into rigidity.

And where does the anxiety and insecurity about being right come from? Them (us), their parents, or guilt perhaps? It could be worth figuring out.

👂 Reframe the rigidity

■ *When people take absolutist positions, gently slip some stomach talk (E) and heart talk (H) into your feedback. It acknowledges what*

> *the talkers haven't said and reduces the pushy quality of their language. It helps them discover the passion beneath their comments and see that no matter how strongly they feel about them, what they are saying is still their point of view, not necessarily the truth.*

When we listen in this way, it helps **reframe the rigidity.** We help identify the essence of their point of view and concerns. Doing this often allows talkers to relax a little and recognize that *their* views are their views, that their strong feelings are *their* strong feelings, and that others may differ and have strong feelings as well.

Most of us know that new converts to *anything* are difficult to have around. Conversion isn't just a religious issue, it's a process. People can be converted to anything, like a new diet, a political view, an environmental concern, a sports team, a child-rearing approach, how to load a dishwasher, a place to live, or how to stop an addiction. Think of the people you've met who've just discovered "the truth" about anything. They tend to fit one of my favorite sayings that nutshells rigidity: *"There is no one more righteous than a newly-converted sinner."*

So let's look at dealing with new converts to diet methods and then to religious or political positions.

Reframing the rigidity of dieters

Remember, leaving out the E and the H makes language pushy and reduces its hear-ability. For example, a reduce-the-fat-talker says, *"The only way to lose weight is to cut the fat from your diet."* You can include the H by reflecting, *"So it seems to you that excluding fat is the best way to lose weight...?"*

He might respond to your heart talk by moving toward it himself: *"That's the only thing that worked for me."* And then you say: *"The way that worked for you was to quit eating fat...?"*

Now you add some E. *"So you're pretty excited about the way that worked for you...?"* And he says, *"Mmmm, yes, I'm pleased and relieved (E) to have given up eating fats, because this is the first time I've ever dieted successfully (H)."*

The high-protein-low-carb-talker rigidly disagrees: *"But low-fat foods have high carbs, which make you crave more sugar, and eventually, your body stores more fat. The only way to lose weight is to eat more meat and fewer carbs."*

Listen by inserting heart talk: *"Mmmm, You found that increasing pro-tein and fat, while reducing carbs helped you lose weight...?"* And she says, *"No, that's the only way to lose weight."*

And you say gently, *"So you believe what worked for you will likely work for others...?"* Softening the hard line by adding H, she says, *"Well yes, it worked for me and I expect it would work for others. Well, maybe not everyone, but it did work for me and I'm excited about it."*

Reframing the rigidity of conservatives and progressives

You do not need to believe the same as your talker to be a good listener (or counselor). Just apply the TLC and do the *understanding* and *clarify-ing* it calls for.

Conservatives and progressives stand at the edges of thinking in various religions, politics and a myriad of other points of view. But be-ing rigid is a different issue from where we fall on any particular range. Any point of view can be rigid or flexible.

Neither being conservative nor progressive makes us open or closed-minded. Either can value others and gain from their diverse thinking or devalue others and shake off any possible gain from their beliefs with glacier-like rigidity.

However, (we) religious folk have a tendency to confuse how we see things with "how it is with the Almighty." That inclination stirs up a special religious case of rigidity. Though again, in my experience, anyone at any point in the range can be rigid in their thinking and judgmental in their relationships or open and accepting of others and their varied faiths.

When you are listening to someone at the other end of a range, what you believe is not the issue, because your job as a listener is to fo-cus on their point of view *with them* (this has implications for listening to those with different values and behaviors as well).

Remember the TLC — your goal is *understanding and clarifying,* not arguing. I buy the saying, that *"When two people argue religion, both are wrong."* Because, when we argue, we are battling to win over each other, not to understand, to love, and to support each other.

(Incidentally, some folks you deal with may be too threatened to allow you to be who you are. They may not respect your right to think, believe and behave as you do. Keep in mind: That is *their* problem, not *yours*. You may be able to help them with theirs by listening. However, if over time they can't respect you, you may want to decide how much time to spend with them.)

Some regular people (and counselors) struggle to deal with people who think very differently than they do. I find that we can maintain our integrity, our own belief systems, and that we don't have to agree with others to listen to what their belief does for them, how it effects them in positive or negative ways, what it means to them, and what it calls them to do and be in the world.

Just as you would mine a thought or an incident for insight, mine their beliefs to find out how they are impacted by them and what you (and they) can learn from them. Then return to your own possibly-modified, but held-with-integrity beliefs.

~ ∞ ~

How to Listen Better: Technique # 25

Sometimes people you are listening to have *dreams* that are significant to them. They ask you what the dreams mean. Well, it feels good to be asked, but a little scary, because no one really knows, do they?

I hope by this time you recognize the trap, *the temptation to quit listening and start talking.* While they asked for your opinion, you could share some authority's theory (or your best guess). But you would be talking when it is your turn to listen. Yep, this question about dreams is not a real question. It is your clue to help the "asker" figure out what the dream means to him/her.

𝄞 Dreams

■ *Ask your talker if they'd like to explore their dream. If so, ask them to pull their dream into the present, as though they are in it right now and then ask them to role-play several people and parts in the dream, starting with themselves. Have a conversation with them as they "get into" the various roles. Ask them to*

> describe what they see, how it is to be the person or part, what they
> feel. Use whatever listening techniques help you both focus on their
> dream and how they might see themselves in experiencing each
> role. Listen for significant descriptions that might help them
> understand aspects of themselves that they may or may not
> have recognized.

Role-play gets the actor into a part in a way that can get past the conscious into the subconscious. When I would role-play a Biblical character as a sermon with the congregation asking me questions, what came out often surprised me. I found thoughts and feelings in me I didn't know were there. In my experience the same process can help when talkers share their dreams.

But it doesn't work when they just recount the dreams, because that keeps it in the past. You are just hearing their reflections and guesses, probably not much better than yours might be.

Role-playing each part in the present helps them to slip by their conscious intellectualizing. Start by asking them to say, *"I am me (name) and right now I am seeing... and am frightened of..."* Or, *"I am the dog, (big and cuddly) I'm following my master through the woods...? I would fight to protect him...? I am grateful that he is good to me..."* Or, *"I am an overflowing river, afraid I'll destroy the home in my path..."*

And you listen by following and going deep into their experience, how they feel, how they see themselves as the parts they are playing and also themselves as the dreamer. This will be new to them and they will bounce out of the present into talking about the past, which is easier and safer, but not useful. When they do, remind them to go back into the dream and talk with you as though they are in it right now.

To listen further you might ask, *"So, how scared are you right now...?"* Or, *"What's it like to be a big cuddly dog...?"* And later, "So how does being 'big and cuddly' fit you...?" And, *"Are you the kind of person (dog) who is grateful and would protect your master and others..."* Or, *"So sometimes you are powerful and gush out of control, but are afraid you might damage things and people...? How does that fit you...?"*

I learned this method from Fritz Perlz many years ago. He would say, *"YOU ARE YOUR DREAM!"* with his deep raspy European accent, almost catching me up into suspending my sense of reality and thinking I was my dream, but I caught myself and figured, *"I am not my dream."* But when I slide into the dream and role-play its parts in the present, I find it to be a pretty effective way of getting past my conscious mind into that unknown area.

And since it's my dream that I'm role-playing, I get to decide what fits me and what doesn't. (This is the safety valve for your talkers, different from you deciding for someone else and judging them and their dream.)

When a psychological type wants to tell me what my dreams mean, I'm offended. After all, they are my dreams. I'd be happier if they helped me focus on *my* dreams or shared what *their* dreams mean to *them*. I've always been bothered by the concept of dream interpretation. I didn't understand why, until I discovered that they promoted talking when they should have encouraged listening.

Yes, I know there are great theories about particular words, symbols, and archetypes, but when I share a dream, I'm not finished talking (investigating) and want a listener to help me find *my* meaning in it.

I experimented by trying this listening/dialogue method on one of my recurring dreams, one that I couldn't finish and that always left me afraid and feeling small and powerless.

I walked through the process and what follows is a shortened version of it. *"I am me, Jamie, nine years old living on a farm. I'm climbing on the pig-pen fence. I'm having fun. I like looking at the pigs wallowing in the farm-smelling muck. All of a sudden the pigs turn into wild boars, like the ones I've seen in Buck Rogers comic books. I'm scared. They start after me, knocking down the fence. I'm running toward the back door of our house. My steps are getting slower and harder. The boars are snorting and screeching. I'm getting more frightened by the second. When I reach the three steps up into the screen door and safety, I can't make it. I fall on the stairs, exhausted, can't move, and I wake up."*

I applied this listening process to my dream. Since you know all the listening skills now, I'll just share the results:

- As little Jamie, I'm feeling vulnerable, powerless, and frightened that what sometimes appears to be safe and familiar can turn mean.
- As the pigs, I like to wallow in safety and the familiar and don't look scary.
- Sometimes I can be like a wild boar, strong with powerful back muscles and have within me power to knock down fences and frighten people.
- As the fence, sometimes under pressure I just fall down and don't do my job.
- As the distance between the pen and the back door, I can only watch sometimes when frightening things are happening and I don't like it. (Like watching the Middle-East.)
- As the steps, I can be formidable and people don't find it easy to walk over me.
- As the farm house, I yearn to take frightened folks in, but tend to stand back and let them come to me.

The aftermath of this listening-to-myself process, which included a couple of sessions with Sally in the listening role, was that I finished the dream and stopped having it. Instead of redoing that dream and always feeling small and powerless, now I have other parts of me that I recognize from the dream. I garnered a number of feelings and learnings about myself that I hadn't seen before. It gave me some clues about changes I wanted to make in my life, ministry and relationships. (For example: As the house, instead of being concerned and waiting for others in trouble to come to me, I now take more initiative in going to people to act on my concerns for them.)

If you try the process, remember to ask the talker to play various parts of the dream, not just the fearful ones and then to enter the dream with them in a conversational way. Here are some listening questions; you can fill in the responses: *"So when you are the monster, what do you want to do…? Do you feel capable of lifting the tree trunk off the child…? Now back in this room, right now, does the monster's strength you just described reside in you too…? How could you apply that energy in your life…?"*

So keep an eye on yourself and be careful not to take over someone else's dream (and turn to talk), even if they ask.

How to Listen Better: Technique # 26

Sometimes we want a talker to keep on looking for solutions to *our* problems and to provide *us* some help, but they seem to want to settle for a simple negative answer: *"No. You (or I) can't do that."* Or, *"No. The rule-book (system, the government, or law) doesn't allow it."*

🎧 Asking for help

■ *There are three steps:*
  1. *Describe your situation.*
  2. *Acknowledge their expertise in the system.*
  3. *Ask how they might help you accomplish your goal (not whether they can help).*

Say we want to apply for a loan, a zoning variance, a permit, an extension of time, or an exception to a rule. We are going to run into people who have the power to help or to turn us down. If we want to keep them sorting through their systems to help us, the key is not to ask a question that they can answer with a *"No."*

Questions like: *"Can I do this?"* make it easy for them to hit us with their rule-books and stop being talkers who own the problem and might be able to fix it. Once they slip behind the rules, all thinking about how to help comes to a complete stop. Our *"Can I...?"* is quickly and efficiently answered with a *"No."*

These folks work in "customer no-service departments."

I'm not against rules. But people can use rule-books in different ways. Some will let you do only what is specifically allowed, while others will let you do anything that is not specifically disallowed. When we are lucky enough to get the latter, we usually sail through our tasks — missions accomplished.

But things get tricky when we run into the first group. Human beings tend to be attracted to the easiest paths. Our minds get lazy and will do their darnedest to avoid creativity, because it's hard work.

How do we approach these folks when what we want is for their brains to keep on thinking and generating creative solutions? In talker-listener terms, you want to stay in the listener role and keep them in the talker role. Then they keep ownership of the problem and continue working on it.

To use a**sking for help**, first describe your situation: *"I'd really like to be able to get a loan on this uncompleted house. I understand that's not normally done. I'm baffled by the real estate mortgaging system."*

Second, acknowledge their expertise or understanding of the system: *"You've been working a long time in the mortgage business. I expect you know a lot about how it works."*

Third, ask for their help in accomplishing your goal: *"How can you help me through this complicated system, so I can move my family into this home...?"* Notice that the question was not, *"Can you help me or can I get a mortgage on this house?"* which could easily have elicited negative responses. *"How can you help...?"* invites them to hold onto the problem a little longer and think toward a helpful solution.

Here, you give the talkers clear information, that you don't have a clue how to accomplish what you want and that they likely know the system well enough to figure it out. You challenge them to wake up and step up to a tricky task, which you believe they can do, a direct compliment. You also ask them to act on their best inclinations to be helpful.

I believe that most people want to be helpful, but often don't know how. When you ask them how they can contribute, it offers them a chance to think about how they can. More often than not, you will make it possible for them to rise to the occasion and be their best. And you become the kind of person around whom good things happen.

20

What About the Heaviest Listening Situation?

SOME OF THE RELATIONSHIP issues and listening examples I've described may seem heavier than you want to handle. However, if people sense that you are a relaxed, safe, and accepting listener, they may choose to talk with you about their deeper struggles.

Certainly, you can choose when you want to respond and when you don't. But, there are crises in people's lives when you are on the spot, when there is no safe or easy way out, and no referral available. These are heavy.

How to Listen Better: Technique # 27

My experience says that most everyone runs into a suicidal person at least once, and when that happens, what you do may be critical. Even though these situations are scary, when there is no referral available, I'd like you to be prepared to listen well. Listening techniques are pretty much the same in both light and heavy situations. If you stay focused on what the other is saying and not on your fear or your need to solve the problem, you can often help them calm down, think more clearly, feel less alone, and be more ready for you to guide them to a professional.

Suicide hints

- *Someone hints or tells you he/she is considering suicide. Own your own feelings that you are shaken to hear it. Set aside your own stuff and get into theirs. Use listening techniques with directness and acceptance. Make an appointment for them to see a professional, or if that fails, for lunch with you.*

Some of the listening examples I've been using may seem intrusive. You might suspect some of the questions could even stir up unpleasant options they hadn't considered. However, especially in the illustration following, most likely they've already thought of everything that scares you, and people are better off not being alone with those fears. Sharing them and exposing them to the light of day usually takes an edge off the fright and negativity involved.

Keep in mind that as the listener you are the responder not the initiator. A good gauge for what may feel like probing is to let what they are saying and how they're reacting be your guide. When you reflect back what you hear them saying, the talker decides whether the reflection fits. Safety lies in the talker determining the depth of the sharing.

It encourages me to remember that people have an infinite ability to avoid subjects they don't want to talk about. If they don't want to talk any longer or go deeper, they won't. They'll change the subject, stop talking, or head for the refrigerator.

First a disclaimer

If you are not a professional, I strongly urge you to get people with problems of this magnitude to professional help. I am not writing this to advise you how to handle suicidal people. However, when you are the only option in an emergency, I'd like you to be able to listen well, that is, to be as helpful as possible. I'm sharing what has worked for me.

No one I counseled has yet committed suicide, though a few attempted it. I know it could happen and I'm clear that I've been lucky. If it does happen sometime, I want to know that I did everything I could to prevent it. I'm fully aware that there are no guarantees and that the only person I can keep from committing suicide is me. I assume the same applies to you.

With the risks clear, let's say you are in a social setting, relaxed, and a friend says offhandedly or more seriously, *"Life is a mess. Nobody would miss me if I were gone."* Or, *"The world would be better off without me."* Or,

"I've been thinking a lot about suicide lately." Or, *"School is starting, but I won't be around to notice."*

Comments like these leave us dangling and make us uneasy — the thud experience. We'd be suspicious about what the person means, but suicide is so frightening many of us would be afraid to say the word out loud, just in case they hadn't thought of it yet.

While it's natural to feel an urge to change the subject, head for the punch bowl, or argue, take the comments seriously. If you ignore them, play them down, or argue, you'll likely strengthen their resolve to act, not lessen it.

Poor listeners often react by saying: *"Oh, you don't really mean that."* Or, *"But you have three wonderful girls, how could you even think that?"* Or, *"I don't know why you'd say that. You are so talented and have so much to offer."* Or, *"Oh no, you're wrong, we'd all miss you."*

Such responses are talking not listening. They are argumentative and grow out of our anxiety. If the people didn't know whether they were understood before, now there'd be no question. They aren't. And we would have left them alone in their depression. All those responses rebuffed the talkers. Let's look at some possible Talker-Listener responses:

➲ Talker: *"Life is a mess. Nobody would miss me if I weren't here."*

Listener: *"So life is a mess and you figure no one would miss you, if you weren't here...?"*

Talker: *"Right, not even my husband would miss me."*

Listener: *"Mmmm, that must feel pretty bad. Sounds like you two aren't getting along and you're really lonesome...?"*

Talker: *"Yes, really alone. Nobody understands how bad I feel."*

Listener: *"So no one really understands you...? It must be awful to feel so alone...?"*

Talker: *"Well, maybe you understand...(and I'm not feeling quite so alone now.)"*

➲ Or, talker: *"The world would be better off without me."*

Listener: *"So the world would be better off without you...?"*

Talker: *"Yes, it would. I don't have anything to offer."*

Listener: *"Nothing to offer...?"*

Talker: *"No, nothing at all. I don't have the gifts other people do."*

Listener: *"So you're not talented the way other people are...? You sound pretty down...?"*

Talker: *"I am. I can hardly get up in the morning."*

Listener: *"No energy at all...?"*

Talker: *"Well, I did finally get up and make it to this party."*

Listener: *"So you did want to be here. What was important to you about the party...?"*

Talker: *"My friends are here. I hoped someone might care about what's going on with me."*

⮩ Or, Talker: *"I've been thinking a lot about suicide lately."*

Listener: *"So you've been thinking about suicide lately...? What's got you thinking about it...?"* Or, *"What have you been thinking about suicide...?"* Or, *"Does it appeal to you some days...?"* Or, *"So suicide sounds like a relief to you...?"*

⮩ Or, talker: *"School is starting, but I won't be around to notice."*

Listener: *"So school is starting soon, but you won't be around...? Are you talking 'permanent not around' or what are you saying...?"*

Talker: *"Oh, just not around."*

Listener: *"I'm feeling uneasy about what you mean by not around...? This sounds serious...?"*

Talker: *"Well, yes it is, but no matter."*

Listener: *"So you don't figure it will matter if you're not around...?"*

Talker: *"No, I don't think anybody would care."* Please, don't argue here. Keep listening. *"So, you really don't think I'd care if you jumped off a bridge...?"* I haven't said much about tone of voice, but for this to be helpful it would have to come through as caring, honest, and reflective, not at all condescending or sarcastic.

Talker: *"Well, maybe you would, but most people wouldn't."*

Listener: *"Sounds like there are people who matter to you, but you don't think they care about you...?"*

Talker: *"Well, yes...."*

And a ways into the conversation, if suicide seems to be a consideration, listen by saying, *"How seriously are you considering suicide...?"*

Talker: *"Not very. It just sounds like a relief to not have to face tomorrow."* Or, *"I've given it some serious thought..."*

Listener: *"What options are you considering...?"*

Scary to ask, but they could be thinking about it and it is important to clarify the seriousness of their intentions. If they have a gun in the car, pills in a purse, or some other plan in mind, you may need to do something, such as calling the police or driving them to an emergency ward.

Usually, they will feel understood, less alone, and have some sense of hope if we take the time to use a variety of listening skills and provide a safe setting for them to talk about what's going on with them.

That won't happen if we explain to them how much they have to live for, because that makes it clear we're not listening. They won't believe we understand their pain.

When they calm down and are able to hear, then it's our turn to talk about specific options, such as finding a counselor, their professional religious person, a hospital, or asking them to promise not to kill themselves until you talk again, or at the least, making an appointment to get together for lunch. (This may sound simplistic, but people seldom jump off bridges when someone understands their pain and has a lunch date scheduled with them. These actions indicate that there may be hope and a future.)

However, there are no guarantees. Every situation is different and circumstances vary. I advise you to seek individual and independent advice from a professional and to get such professional help for people who are considering suicide. You might call a suicide hot-line or a hospital for options or resources.

These situations are frightening and dangerous. We can't tell what someone else will do. If they won't make any kind of positive commitment, then it's time to call the police (dial 911) and get them to a hospital, where they will have a psychiatric evaluation to determine next steps.

When you encounter someone who is seriously depressed, if you listen to them in a way that lets them know they are not alone, they may be able to take your hand and crawl a little ways out of their depression hole with you.

21

Listening Techniques for Moving On

AH-HAH! MANY OF YOU readers may have been anxiously waiting for "what's next?" How to help your talkers move on to decision-making and action. And if you are like me, you've been dying to get your oar in, waiting for your time to talk, make suggestions, wrap it up, get them to take a forward (positive) step, speed them up, put some starch in their backbones, etc.

For starters, bite your tongue, as this is mostly our impatience, not a response to their readiness to move on. Notice too how these motivations all lead to talking not listening. Our goal here is to help talkers figure out where *they* are and what *they* want to do about *their* situations. Let's look at some options for doing that, when they are ready.

How to Listen Better: Technique # 28

Often after wives bring up bothersome issues, their husbands never mention them again, as though the conversations never happened. (This does happen in reverse too.) And it happens for friends and counselees whom we listen to and who trust us enough to share something really sensitive. And then later, if we don't bring it up again, it leaves them hanging with it alone.

For the person who brought up the painful issue, it would be like tossing a *pebble in a pond* and having it make no rings. When you think about it, it might seem unnatural for a significant conversation never to come up again, while the pebble is still there, lying on the bottom of both people's minds.

It was hard enough for the talker to bring it up the first time. For most people bringing it up again is too much. It is up to the listener the second and deeper time.

🎧 Pebble in the pond

> ■ *A talker shared a serious concern with you in an earlier conversation and doesn't return to the subject and the result, no decision or action. After you've thought about it for a while, bring it up again and listen further.*

Listening by bringing it up again later creates rings on the pond. It makes it clear we heard what was said and that we have been thinking about it. We're taking what the talker said seriously, rather than letting it fall on deaf ears and hard hearts.

A silent husband might not bring up a troubling issue again, thinking that he didn't want his wife to go through the pain again. Or, he might be uncomfortable dealing with the issue or emotions himself. Whatever the reason, silence leaves her alone with it. Over time too many of these experiences will fill the pond with pebbles — not a healthy ecosystem.

It's even harder for us to listen when a spouse (partner, friend, counselee) is upset with us. We'd likely not want to open the issue again for fear of being criticized. Most of us don't like parental lectures and have trouble voluntarily opening up discussions where we might be chewed out and feel like youngsters again. Yet, by not initiating a return to the issue, we run the risk of abandoning people close to us and of getting cut off from intimacy and acceptance ourselves.

Here's how *pebble in the pond* might work: A wife talked to her husband about something he had done that upset her. (Because he just might have read this book, he didn't get defensive.) He sensed the thud and shifted into listening mode. She was able to share her concern with him in the safe situation he provided (or he blew it, which is all the more reason to come back later).

Over the next couple of days he thought about their conversation. He generated some ideas about what might be troubling her. Later, he came back to her and said, *"Honey, I was thinking about our conversation on Thursday and wondered if this might be what you were bothered about...?"* Her painfully pitched pebble had made rings.

What a great way to reopen an unfinished conversation and continue with helpful listening. It lets her know he's in it with her. Supportive behavior like this can't happen too often. There are few things that endear us more to our significant others.

He might also have switched to talking and said, *"I've been thinking about what you said was bothering you. I wonder if it might be easier for you if I...?"* Taking the time to think about her concerns and risking bringing them up again expresses immeasurable caring. She'd likely be both surprised and touched.

Pebble in the pond for planning

Pebble in the pond works well for couples who come up with ideas, goals, activities, solutions, and plans together. Rather than one-shot decision-making sessions, they have ongoing discussions, letting the last conversation feed the process for the next ones. They check in with each other and ask what their partner is thinking about a particular issue now. Over time, they generate next steps that satisfy them both. The trick is not hurrying the process by pinning down answers too soon.

So when those at home, in a volunteer organization, or at work bring up painful topics or new ideas, let's not let their interests hit the pond without making rings.

When we come back and make rings around the pebble, we'll surround a talker's concerns with caring. We'll help by moving with them into deeper, clearer thinking and relationships.

How to Listen Better: Technique # 29

Sometimes fear of possible outcomes and consequences block a talker's decision-making and action. To help them move on through the fear barrier, some communication specialists suggest asking ***worst-case conditions*** questions.

✋ Worst-case conditions

> ■ *Ask what the worst thing is that could happen and acknowledge it. Ask what he/she would do next if the worst did happen. Then repeat the pattern of acknowledging their answer and asking what he/she'd do next.*

When possibilities seem really bad to people, they might talk right up to the edge of a crisis, get frightened, freeze, and then back off to a seemingly safe, but anxious place. They don't want to look at what might happen — the worst possible outcome.

For example, when I listened to one woman's struggles with her marriage, she shared freely right up to a decision point. Then she shut down, almost paralyzed. I could see it in her body language, her eyes wide, her fear palpable. She said, *"But, if I talked to him about it...he might...he might...I can't even think about it."* She seemed unwilling to face the possibility that her husband might divorce her.

First, I used *para-feeling*, *"When you think about talking with him you get frightened to death about what he might do...?"*

She responded, *"I can't even think about it."*

I repeated accurately, *"You can't even think about it...?"* After acknowledging her feelings and thoughts and allowing her to let off a little steam, I began asking about ***worst-case conditions***, *"So if you talked about it with him, he might get really upset...? What is the absolute worst thing that you can imagine happening...?"*

"Ah, he might leave, ah, divorce, I suppose, but I can't even think about it..." I repeated accurately, *"So you can't even think about him leaving, ah, that is, divorcing you...?"*

"No, I can't." I used *para-thought* and *para-feeling*: *"So divorce is the worst thing that could happen, and that absolutely frightens you...?"*

"Right," she replied.

I acknowledged and asked what she'd do if it did happen, *"So, let's say the worst thing happened and he decided to leave you, what would you do then...?"*

"I'd just collapse."

"Un-huh, so after he left, you'd just collapse...? And how long would you stay collapsed before you went back to work...?"

"I couldn't work right away, but, ah, I suppose two or three weeks."

"So, you couldn't work right away, but you'd go back in two or three weeks...?"

"Well, if I didn't go back to work, I'd lose my job."

"You'd go back to work so you'd have an income. Then what would you do...?"

"Well, I guess I'd have to get a lawyer."

"Mmmm. So you'd get a lawyer, and what then...?"

"Well, I'd need to figure out if I could afford to stay in the house with the kids or whether we'd have to move into an apartment."

"You'd figure out where you could afford to live, and what would you do next...?"

You get the point. Notice how I acknowledged the block. I did not belittle it. Then we moved past it and started considering what she would do if her fear of the worst happened.

In dealing with **worst-case conditions** you treat folks as though they will be around to fight another battle after the worst is over. It helps them move through their fear of disaster.

When you ask, *"And then what would you do...?"* they begin to stop letting their fear immobilize them. The question assumes there is life beyond their present predicament.

By guiding people through their fear barriers, in a subtle way you offer hope without talking. It's a bit like **Technique # 31 – Lead the witness.** So even if the worst happens, people realize they can still make choices. They'll begin to believe that life goes on, and that they will too.

How to Listen Better: Technique # 30

After quite a bit of attentive listening, when talkers appear to be calmer, more focused, and ready to begin thinking ahead, try *explore the future*, *sometimes called **nexting**.* However, if you run into resistance, go back to listening and wait for *their* readiness not *yours*.

🕉 Explore the future (nexting)

■ *Late in the listening process, ask your talker about next possible steps, decisions, and likely consequences. This may be towards the end of a short and easy conversation, or after an hour, an evening, or weeks and even months.*

Current communication literature calls questions like: *"What's next...?"* or *"Now what..."*? *"**nexting**."* It supports the collaborative effort of moving on through communicating and connecting.

When the time seems right, try *explore the future*, by saying: *"Sounds like you have a pretty good grasp of your situation...? What options occur to you...?"*

Off the wall options and beginning steps

Often people worry about suggesting any alternatives since they might not be perfect. Help them loosen their thinking by asking, *"Without thinking about consequences, what off-the-wall options occur to you...?"* After stretching their minds with a few odd-ball ideas, they may begin to come up with some more realistic ones. Here you could toss in a few of your own, but then ask for one or two more of theirs, to surround yours with theirs.

Then play with the following: *"Which of the alternatives look most appealing to you...?"* Or, *"What consequences do you see for the options you like best...?"* Or, *"Which would likely produce the most gain and the least loss...?"* At this point whether they pick one of theirs or one of yours, it will belong to them because they chose it.

Other possibilities to encourage small beginning steps: *"Any options you can discard to get them off your mind...?"* Or, *"Is there anything you can do that might give you a little relief from the stress...?"* Or, *"Are there any steps you might take today that would move you off dead center...?"* Or, *"If you don't take a step now, what does that mean for your future, your values, for others...?"*

And beyond this listening conversation, *"Is there any other informa-tion you need to have before you can make a decision...? Or, "Is there anyone else you should be talking with...?"*

Handling stuck, going nowhere conversations

When your talker seems stuck and the conversation seems to be go-ing nowhere *repeat accurately* (until the cows come home) is my tech-nique of choice. However, sometimes in a long-term conversation (counseling or with your friends), talkers take "stuck" to a fine art and make no changes. Each session repeats earlier ones. No progress is made. It's frustrating and to be honest, boring (and probably bor-ing for them too).

I am happily willing to spend significant time with people who will make decisions, change their behavior, and take action. But as I've got-ten older I'm less willing to spend my (limited) time with folks satisfied with marking time in their messes.

So, I have said *(own your own feelings)* to some of those with whom I had a solid relationship, *"I realized over our last few sessions that I'm bored and I wonder if you are too...? Seems to me that you are re-telling the same story, over and over...? Not willing to make changes in your behavior...? Am I missing something or does that fit you...? Do you see yourself as stuck, not wanting to take any action that would change anything in your life...?"* This challenging kind of interchange will call on you right away to use many other listening techniques.

Even in calmer situations the give and take of the ***explore the fu-ture (nexting)*** process may need more time, additional sessions. You could say, *"I'd like to continue our conversation...? Let's set a time for us to get together...?"* And decidedly not, *"Do you want to get together and talk about it some more?"* That's like asking someone if they'd like their teeth drilled.

Again, if talkers get defensive, run, don't walk, back to the basic lis-tening techniques. They aren't ready for this step. When they are ready, these questions will encourage them to focus on next steps.

When you ask the ***nexting*** questions, you instill confidence in your talkers. You hint that talkers have decent brains and enough ability to make decisions and to act on them. And you subtly suggest they have hope and a future. (And in a crisis they may be worried about that.)

How could you be more helpful?

How to Listen Better: Technique # 31

Sometimes your talkers (youngsters, friends, partners, or counselees) lean toward negative or damaging options. You can *lead the witness* toward a healthier direction.

Lead the witness

- *After acknowledging destructive option(s) your talker is considering, ask how such actions would help them, other people, or the situation. But be careful, it would be easy to slip into manipulating here.*

Leading the witness is not appropriate often, because it usually means that listeners are slipping into talking, that is, shoving their points of view into talkers' air-time. We gain the right to use this technique only if our brains are not flat and we have nothing at stake in the decision.

When folks are depressed, angry, blaming, or have poor self-images, they tend to focus on negative things to do. They might be hooked in an unhealthy way to quitting a job prematurely, making a threat, punching someone, destroying something, getting drunk, or divorcing without careful thinking. Again after *acknowledging* what's going on with them, *lead the witness* can awaken them to a more sensible and fitting reality.

Leading the witness might sound like: *"How would that help...?"* Or, *"Would that make things better for you or anyone else...?"* Or, *"Which option might be most helpful in your situation...?"* Or, *"How would you be better off if you put your current thinking into action...?"* Or, *"What small thing could you do, that might improve your life a bit...?"* Or, *"Anything you could do that would make the company more effective...?"*

When we lead witnesses (talkers) this way, it subtly suggests that they can do something *positive* to impact their lives. It's a tricky form of the previous **Technique # 30 – Explore the future (nexting***)*. Sometimes as listeners we can gently nudge them toward constructive options. This helps because people often feel powerless, as though they can do nothing that would make a difference.

However, this does not mean to lead them by their noses, that is, start pushing our solutions on them when it's theirs to decide.

You might also try *own your own feelings* along with **lead the witness** by saying, *"I'm worried that what you are talking about doing might not fit you (your values, faith, beliefs, style, relationship with God)...? How might you make your plans fit those...?"* Or, *"I wonder about what you are considering...? Do you think you would look back and be proud of it in five years...?"*

If at some point they get defensive, go back immediately to using other listening techniques until they calm down enough to consider positive options. When it works and they come up with a more constructive solution, then say, *"So, you've come up with an option... that might help, what do you think about it...?"*

Parental responsibility

There are times when empathetic, non-judgmental listening is a good start, but falls short of what's needed. Consider situations where teenagers need to be guided away from destructive behaviors. Listen first (and long), until they calm down, feel heard, and clarify their options.

Then, if their direction is not constructive or they're "stuck," **leading the witness** can help guide them toward non-destructive behaviors or ones that do not go against your family's values: *"You're so mad, you want to key (scratch) the principal's new car...? How will that help you get out of high school and into the college you've chosen...?"*

How do we create an atmosphere in which children can hear us?

You have a good chance of being heard, if you modeled listening for them and they experienced its benefits. Your chance increases if your kids have played *Listening through a Mealtime Game* in Chapter 23 and if taking turns listening has become a family pattern. Young people understand taking turns and fairness, though they may need reminding: *"I took time to understand how you think and feel about this issue, remember you said... Is that accurate...? So now it's your turn to try to understand how I see it. Does that seem fair...?"*

With this preparation parents can share their thoughts about choices and consequences with some hope of being heard. Teens and others are more prone to consider respectful, non-judgmental suggestions than pushy or dogmatic directives.

Parents usually have to do several rounds of lengthy listening, interspersed between their (short) attempts at talking, before teens can really hear.

Sometimes, parents need to take a stronger stand and say, *"You may still want to do something destructive, but that's not acceptable. In this case, I'm deciding for you. You may not like my decision or that I'm deciding for you, but this decision is my responsibility as a parent. Your responsibility as a young person under this roof is to go along with it."*

If you need more help here, best check out some books, programs on parental discipline, and/or counselors.

Keep in mind that to **lead the witness** requires lots of other listening techniques before the talker is ready to think ahead toward positive options. All these moving on techniques come way late in the listening process. If they raise your talker's hackles, likely you're on your own schedule for *nexting,* not theirs.

Hearing and unloading the resentments, disappointments, and angers come first, giving you a chance to **lead the witness** toward more constructive behaviors, second.

— ∞ —

How to Listen Better: Technique # 32

Sometimes folks don't decide and move on because they can't find the right answers. The listening technique, ***problems or predicaments,*** can help your talker because it suggests there might not be a "right answer" and, that is okay.

𝕊 Problems or predicaments?

- *The talker is struggling with a dilemma that may not have a specific solution. Share the difference between problems and predicaments. Then ask which they face.*

What's the difference between a *problem* and a *predicament*? **Problems** have right and wrong answers, for example: Two plus two equals four and does not equal five. **Predicaments** have options with positive and/ or negative consequences. (Note that I'm using "problem" here with a mathematical twist as opposed to "problem" on the TLC, which might better be translated "issue.")

We can get blocked in decision-making because we think we should be able to find "the one right answer" — when there is none. This happens often as most decisions aren't related to **problems,** but rather, to **predicaments.** Continuing to look for single solutions to **predicaments** can leave us stuck indefinitely.

When we realize that there is no "right" answer, we can be free to choose an option that fits "reasonably" well. A simple example is deciding what smart phone to buy. There is no correct one, though some people think so and spend tons of time trying to get it right. And then to compound their frustration, after weighing all the options, they make the decision and the purchase, only to find out a few days later, that a different one added a new feature that would have changed the balance.

A more difficult example is deciding what to do with elderly parents who rely on you for moral or physical support. Whose decision is it at this step? Is it time for assisted living? Is it the right time to sell their house? Should they move in with you? Will home health options be enough? When is hospice care the right move? We don't want to get it wrong and struggle to get it right when there are no "rights."

When listening to someone struggling to make a right decision, you might help them decide that it is not a **problem,** but rather a **predicament.** That clears the way to look for possibilities with the most pluses and the least minuses and can move them along —another example of *"nexting."*

Ask: *"What are your options in this situation...?"* And then after reflecting them back, ask: *"And which of these have the most desirable and least objectionable consequences, assuming none of them is perfect...?"* Again, after reflecting back, ask: *"And which makes most sense to you...?"* Or, *"Which would fit you the best...?"*

Another great question businesses use to facilitate decision-making is: *"Which option is good enough...?" "Good enough"* saves immense amounts of wasted time and moves a company (and a person) along nicely.

When you help yourself and others get clear about whether you're dealing with a *problem* or a *predicament*, you'll have discovered and shared a great sanity-producing skill and the increased likelihood of moving on.

How to Listen Better: Technique # 33

Sometimes we can't make decisions and move on because of the lack of clarity about motivation levels. We get hung up among (1) what we want to do, (2) what we want done, and (3) what we think we should, ought, or have to do. We can help ourselves and/or our talkers by sorting out these three *motivation levels,* so we can use them to act on what is important to us. It will give us the ability to use our motivations to drive behavior changes that we want and open the door to new approaches to life.

Motivation levels?

- *Describe the primary, secondary and tertiary motivation levels and then ask your talkers to examine theirs in regard to their past behaviors or the decisions they are facing (works for you too).*

Similar to the technique in *problems and predicaments,* highlighting the three levels of motivation can open the door for your talker to find which emotional energies lie beneath their past decisions or the ones they face now. These playful concepts provide clarity that can free them to put more energy into what matters and to avoid more of what doesn't.

Primary motivation yields enjoyment

Primary motivation is *where we do what we want to do.* And the pay-off? **Enjoyment.** Enjoying what we do puts us in the flow and is a powerful motivator. As the pleasure-pain principle suggests, we tend to move toward pleasure and away from pain.

Doing work we enjoy is not at all the same as working only to put food on the table *(secondary)* or to keep from goofing or looking like failures *(tertiary).* Doing things we enjoy builds energy back into us. It doesn't wear us down. Time passes quickly, often without us noticing it. Again, the pay-off of doing what we like to do, that is, *primary motivation,* is **enjoyment.**

Sometimes, I fish because I enjoy fishing.

Secondary motivation yields satisfaction

Secondary motivation is where *we do things because we want them done,* not because we want to do them. We want the results. The pay-off? **Satisfaction.**

When we are clear that we want the results of doing something we may not enjoy, we have good, smooth-running energy to apply to it. We might say, *"While I don't want to do this (primary motivation), I do it because I want it done. (secondary motivation)."*

For most of us, saving money is not much fun, but we save because we want money invested for retirement and emergencies (delayed gratification) and find that *satisfying.* I can't remember ever washing dishes because I enjoyed the process. I'm a *secondary motivation* dishwashing guy. I do it because I want to find clean dishes when it's time to eat, don't like mold, and don't want the health inspector to shut us down. My preference would be to have someone around who likes to wash dishes *(primary motivation).*

Satisfaction is a moderate motivator, but does not build as much energy back into us as **enjoyment** does. Doing all *secondary motivation* activity, brings to mind a version of the old saying, "all work and no play makes Jack and Jill effective, but a little dull."

To keep our operating energies in peak mode, a management expert said that sixty percent of our time should be spent on *primary motivation* activities. So if you work at a job only for the paycheck and security, you'll need to play a lot of golf, fish, or read (substitute what you like to do) to balance it and keep your energy up. Again, the pay-off for doing what we want done *(secondary motivation)* is **satisfaction.**

Sometimes, I fish because I want smoked salmon for a party, meat in the freezer, or to get away from the office.

Tertiary or anxiety motivation yields relief

(Oh what fun! How often do you get to use a word like tertiary? Oops, back to work...) *Tertiary motivation* resembles *secondary motivation*. It goes for the result of doing something. But it implies that someone or something else is forcing our behavior, *"I did it because I had to."* (Sounds like I'm not in control so therefore not responsible. Ugh.)

Phrases like, *"I should...,"* *"I ought to...,"* *"I need to...,"* or *"I have to..."* suggest that not doing a particular thing makes us unacceptable. Saying: *"We have to clean the house, pay our taxes, fix the washing machine, call mother, get the report into the boss,"* implies that we're not doing them because we want to or want the result. We're doing them to prove ourselves, to look good, to not look the fool to others or ourselves, or to please someone else.

This *anxiety motivation* gets us muddling around inside ourselves, confusing self-worth with accomplishing a task. It splits our energy between doing something and proving ourselves. In high school my insecurity showed up on the basketball court. I was torn between handling the ball and checking the coach to see how I was doing. It didn't work. You can't effectively watch two directions at once on a basketball court (or in life). It dissipates the energy (and I missed too many shots).

Healthy anxiety

The proper function of *anxiety* is to raise questions for us about who we are, what our purpose is, and where we fit in the universe. When we answer these questions, we come out healthier, more directed, and clear about our value and place in the world.

If we've done that, when we consider a task, we can simply decide how much *we want to do the task* or whether *we want the task done* enough to do it. That's a clean decision, not muddied with anxiety.

If we haven't settled the anxiety questions above, then we remain anxious about our worth and sense a need to prove ourselves to ourselves, to others, and to the universe in whatever we set out to do. So when we take on a task, whether we do it well or not, it becomes an issue of pass or fail as humans. If the steaks we grill aren't perfect or our opinion gets voted down, we are not okay. That's a lot of pressure hanging on such routine activities.

When we rush around to clean house to look good, to prove our-selves because mother is coming to visit *(anxiety motivation)*, what we get is relief. *"Whew, got through that one."* No **enjoyment** and no **satisfaction.** Just an energy drain.

When life batters my self-esteem, my fishing partner is catching and I'm not, or I haven't caught one for awhile, then whether I catch a big fish seems directly connected to my manhood. Takes the heart *(enjoyment and satisfaction)* out of fishing.

Sometimes, I fish to prove myself and catching just gives me **relief.** (And relief is what we ought to get from Rolaids.)

Checking out the motivation levels

Asking your talkers whether their motivation was/is, *primary, secondary,* or *tertiary,* or some mix of the three, gives them a chance to move more of their behavior up a level or two.

When we help our talkers focus on what they actually did or plan to do, and realize that it is their motivation that drives their behavior, then clarity develops about what is important. This makes real change possible. When I don't need to prove anything to anyone, then I can back off that dragging behavior and do *what I want to do* or *what I want done* (shifting from **anxiety** to **satisfaction** and/or **enjoyment** motivation).

Here's an example about how that learning worked for me. I transitioned from being a reluctant term paper writer who didn't want to fail *(anxiety motivation)* to a teacher who wanted his ideas written to share in book form *(secondary)*. But I knew I didn't enjoy writing enough *(primary)* to ever take the time off from ministry, being with people and fishing to get a book written, so I decided to use my motivations to help me.

I signed up for a doctoral program because I wanted to get the book written and out there for people *(secondary)*. I paid a lot of money and was too cheap to waste it *(secondary)*. I told everyone so I'd be too embarrassed not to finish the dissertation/book *(anxiety)*. And after that life-changing experience (over 300 pages of putting my teaching into print) and writing the next thirty years, I have become an author who simply enjoys writing *(primary)*.

I have to admit that sometimes it takes *wanting it done* and *anxiety motivation* to get me back to the laptop, but when I get there, *enjoyment* takes over. This has been one big life change for me! Sally, friends of mine (and I) did a lot of listening to help me clarify my motivations, to keep me writing.

And so?

When we listen to folks and help them clarify and move their motivations for doing something away from *proving* themselves and more toward *wanting to do it* and *wanting it done,* the less they get into that parent-child bind, that gets them (and us) to resist.

You can help your talkers drive life changes by clarifying their motivations and recognizing that what they are actually doing is what they want most to do.

It will give them the ability to use their motivations to drive behavior changes that they want and open the door to new approaches to life with more **satisfaction** and **enjoyment.**

22

Listening through Making Decisions Together

I TELL YOUNG COUPLES who are getting married that they will make decisions more than anything else they will do together. This holds true for people who work together as well. Good listening enhances cooperative decision-making.

When it works well, everyday decision-making includes three steps — sharing, negotiating, and closing.

1. Sharing

The Talker-Listener process supports all three, but is indispensable in the first. If you each take a turn *sharing* your feeling/thinking and take a turn listening, then you will have gathered the information necessary for making realistic proposals.

Here's an example of mishandling step one. I walk into the house, greet my wife, and ask, *"What do you want to do tonight?"*

She responds, *"Oh nothing. Thought I'd stay home and read."* Now I'm stuck. I was interested in going to a movie, but didn't say that. I was being "nice," that is, first asking what she wanted. Doesn't work. Need a better method.

In fact my question put her in the talker role when she hadn't been thinking about it. So under pressure she treated me as a listener by answering. I got what I asked for, but not what I wanted. What would normally happen next? Not feeling heard, I would mention the movie I wanted to see and note that we hardly ever go to movies. She would feel manipulated. We'd argue over how often we go to movies, and end up with an unpleasant evening no matter what we did.

The first rule in decision-making: *The person who brings it up, shares (talks) first.* If I had talked, I would have said, *"I drove by the movie theater just now and noticed a film I'd like to see. Are you interested in going with me tonight?"*

Then she would have listened and said, *"Really? What movie…? Tell me about it…?"*

I would have told her and she might have asked what appealed to me about the movie and for a number on the zero-to-ten scale. Then we both would have been clear about my inclinations. I would have felt heard and understood whether we went to the movie or not.

When I first asked: *"What do you want to do tonight?"* she might have noticed a small thud in her belly and that I was making a fumbling attempt at talking. Then she would have gone into listener mode and said, *"Oh, it sounds like you have something in mind…?"* (Often she bails me out like that.)

Then I would have said, *"Oops, you're right. I was thinking about going to a movie and would like to have you go with me."*

After I'd admitted I wanted to see a movie, she'd continue listening: *"So, what movie did you have in mind…? What time is it playing, where…?"*

"It's that thriller I've wanted to see." I might also have said, *"I'd like to see the movie and have a little time to visit with you. We've been busy this week and haven't had much time to catch up with each other."*

And she'd listen asking, *"Oh, you'd also like to spend some time with me, hunh…?"*

"Yes. I like you and miss you when we get so busy." (Here's where we hug each other.)

Then we'd switch roles and I'd ask what she's interested in. It would be her time to talk: *"Well, now that I've had time to think about it, I'd like some time with you too, but I'm too tired to handle one of your action movies. I'd rather rest and read."*

Both of us needed to finish *sharing* before moving to step two or what we didn't say would come back to bite us. If she had gone to the movie without saying where she was with it, the decision would have been unbalanced. The movie would have been mine. If it turned out to be bad, the popcorn stale, or her foot stuck to the gum on the floor, that all would have been my fault.

But when the decision is really joint, then bad movies, stale popcorn and foot-sticking gum are just that, no one's fault.

2. Negotiating

In this case, we fed back what each other had said. We felt heard and understood each other. So we could constructively move on to step two. If *sharing* works, then *negotiating* is usually pretty simple.

I proposed: *"Let's take two cars, have a quick dinner, and catch up with each other. Then I'll take in the movie and you head home and dive into your book. Okay...?"*

She either makes a slight counter proposal or says, *"Works for me."*

3. Closing

It looks as if we've made a decision, but the process isn't complete. It takes one more step.

Closing includes all the reporter questions: Who, what, when, where, and how. So we settle on what time we leave, where we eat, who pays, what time we head our separate ways. Now we've made a decision based on what we actually feel and think and it includes the details necessary for action.

You can use this three-step method for making decisions about car purchases, vacations, investments, paint colors, carpets, job changes, or whatever you need to work out with another person.

You can also use it to help folks you're listening to sort out their decision-making quirks and foibles. It also easily expands to help committees and businesses.

Why didn't we do anything?

Incidentally, the lack of closing wipes out more committees and work groups than you can imagine. Folks get together, share their concerns, struggle to make sensible proposals and counter-proposals, and then negotiate an agreement. They heave a sigh of relief, because they think they've made a tough decision.

But the next time they get together, nothing has happened. Why? Because they didn't *close.* No one asked what seems like nagging questions, that is, who would do what, by when, what resources would be gathered by whom, and who the heck would do the publicity and reserve the room?

So, a busy couple *shares* that they both want a break and a chance to feel sand between their toes. They *negotiate* a weekend trip to the beach to relax and reconnect. But when the season passes and the rain sets in, they discover they haven't gone and subtly blame each other for not having cared enough to arrange it. But mostly, they didn't go because they hadn't *closed* their decision-making process. They didn't sync a weekend date into their smartphones. They hadn't decided whether they would camp or motel it, roast hot dogs on the beach or hit the bookstores, or who would handle which arrangements.

If someone knows how and is willing to ask the closing questions before the above conversation ends or a meeting adjourns, it can turn a well-intentioned non-productive bunch into a happy-get-it-done gang.

Understanding these steps can allow you to have a positive impact on your life and the lives of those around you. Keeping the three steps in mind will help you make sense of so many of the mix-ups we get ourselves into and give you a direction to go to help you, the couples, and the groups you work with get along better.

Making decisions when couples get together

When people get married or move in together, they bring their past experiences (baggage) with them. They usually know how, when, and with whom to open Christmas gifts among many other disparate patterns. Whether they are first-marriage-young or heavily-experienced, they may confuse *their* ways with the *right* ways to do chores, carry out family customs, and manage their new partnership matters.

On the day I married a couple of older retired friends, we talked about the challenges faced in second marriages by fully-formed folks.

She nut-shelled it by saying: *"He has his truth in the kitchen. And I have my truth in the kitchen. And they are not the same truths."*

She was clear in her kidding that they had a lot of past experiences and resultant conclusions to revisit, discuss, and negotiate in their new marriage.

They both did a lot of listening by saying, *"Oh, so you did it that way, what did you like (dislike) or get out of that...?"* Or, *"My experience went this way ... how did yours go...?"* And, *"What would pick up the best (most meaningful) part of yours and mine to make a fit for us...?"*

Often in marriage counseling, after I listened a lot and helped a couple listen and understand each other better, in effect I would say versions of the following (when it was my turn to talk): *"There is no right way to pay bills, invest and save, celebrate holidays or anniversaries, load the dishwasher, divide the chores, rear the children, decide on where to live, vacation, or spend Saturdays. Instead, there is how you two will work it out and adjust it over and over again to fit as you grow and change...?"*

"So what do you each bring to this specific concern...? What do you get out of it...? What matters most to you...? What parts of the past would you like to discard...? What would make your lives easier and more pleasant...? Which tasks can each of you do that would make life easier for your partner...? What would you simply agree to disagree on...? And what makes sense in managing your lives together...?"

Life-planning (on-going decision-ing)

Sally is the better planner in our marriage. Due to her lead, the basis for our joint planning became a special out of town, two to three day year-end trip. We review our past year to figure out what worked, what we're happy about, what we want more or less of, what we want to leave in the past, and what we want to carry into the next year. We do this with a flip chart to spread our lives, our calendar, our current issues on paper so we can see them. This visual picture makes it easier to see what we're thinking, what information we need, and what we'd like to discuss. (This is the *sharing* part of decision-making.)

One of those review sessions made it clear that we'd been traveling one out of three nights the prior year. No wonder we'd fallen behind on our home and writing projects. So we cut the travel back to do more of what we wanted. Another year, we added more travel back in to our plans to spice our lives.

We take turns a lot, listening to each other. We've planned vacations, writing travel, house remodels, finances, job changes, who does which tasks around the house, what we do with our families, and how we manage our retirements.

Now that we are (semi-) retired, we carry this process through the year by going out for breakfast on Monday mornings. (We had to shoehorn in these periodic reviews when we both worked.) We eat, review the past week to see what we got done, what we didn't, how the week went (including our writing), what's left over and what issues we're facing. We plan the upcoming week (and months) and agree on who does which of the follow-up details (*closing*).

The saying, *"The unexamined life is not worth living,"* seems to be one of our themes. But with examining our goals, we do occasionally encounter different *"truths in the kitchen."* We then go to work listening into each other's *truths* until we know what they mean and can figure out what we are going to do with them.

Decision-making-balance-scales

However, sometimes folks have trouble deciding and acting because they don't know how to measure the weight of the factors and feelings involved in a complicated decision. I've devised a system that works to decide either a "Yes or No" or a "This or That" kind of choice. I use this on myself and in my counseling. At first glance it looks complicated, but bear with me, I think you'll find it simple and useful.

I'll share an example from when I made the decision to take up fishing. After I'd been a pastor about ten years I noticed a mismatch between the time I spent talking about fishing and the amount I actually fished. While I told myself that I *really* wanted to fish, I observed little fishing (a clue).

So I started by drawing an equal arm balance scale. (Remember the EHJ scales?) I put *Fish* and *No-Fish* on either end of the scale. I placed **for** and **against** factors on there.

FACTORS

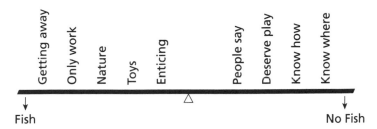

Above you'll see that I put **getting away** from the office to relax and having **only work** in my life as the first two factors on the *Fish* side. Also I added getting into **nature**, playing with the **toys** (equipment) involved in fishing and **enticing** the fish to bite.

On the *No-Fish* side I put what **people** (might) **say** when I fish instead of work and whether I think I **deserve play** time. I also added two other factors because I didn't **know how** or **know where** to fish.

Notice that there are five facts on the *Fish* side and four on the *No-Fish* side. Could be twenty factors to one on the *Fish* side and I still might not spend much time fishing. A fact doesn't weigh anything, but the emotion related to it does and it has measurable weight.

Now I'll incorporate my emotions related to the factors on a second scale, measure their intensity, and then weigh them. The feelings will be connected to the factors from the earlier scale. I use a zero to ten scale (but note: That's the basic range. Some feelings go off the chart and carry tremendous decision-making weight, which you'll see later).

FEELINGS

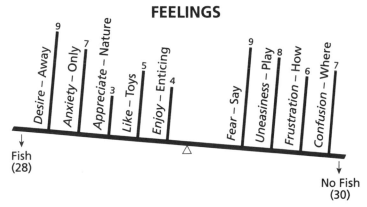

Above note that on the *Fish* side, I scored my **desire** for getting **away** from the office for stress relief 9 and the **anxiety** over having **only** work in my life 7. I added the fact that I **appreciate** nature 3, I **like** toys 5, and I **enjoy** enticing fish 4. Those feelings bumped the total weight to 28 on the side of becoming a fisherman. Seems like a lot so why wasn't I fishing more?

On the *No-Fish* side I put the emotions related to what **people** (might) **say**, a **fear** of criticism 9, and my **uneasiness** over whether I worked hard enough to **deserve play** time 8. And when I added to the scale my **frustration** over meager fishing **know how** 6 and **confusion** over the **know where** to fish question 7.

When I did the numbers, *No-Fish* won over *Fish* 30 to 28. While I thought I *really wanted* to fish, I *wanted not* to fish even more. Both listeners and talkers get pretty good clues when they try this process.

FACTORS & FEELINGS REVISTED

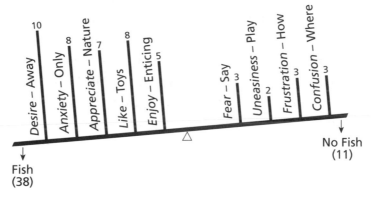

After adding up the sides, it's time to compare, review and discuss. Having a listener helps. So, my listener and I went over the scale more closely and added the magic. The serious examination of the factors that *interested* me about fishing grew those interests from 28 to 38. Expressing and sharing feelings often changes them either up or down, sometimes in surprising ways.

With this further reflection, it turned out I wanted a whole lot more than I thought to have more in my life than work and I really enjoyed the fishing toys and trying to outsmart a fish in a gorgeous rushing river.

I considered again the factors on the *No-Fish* side. My listener asked, *"Do you really want your time-off controlled by your fear of what others might say...?"*

After pondering that question out loud, my *fear* of what **people** might say dropped to 3 since I *didn't want* to let other people's attitudes control my life. I even reviewed my work output compared to other ministers and decided I was more than earning my paycheck and did in fact, **deserve play** time. My *uneasiness* dropped to 2.

Then I went to work on the other two factors, the **know how** and the **know where** questions. I took them seriously, decided to buy some books and subscribe to a couple of fishing magazines to learn. I decided that instead of talking to fishing friends about going with them "sometime," I would use the closing method I teach and ask, *"When would work for you...?"* We'd set a date and I'd learn to fish from people who knew where and how. My *frustration* and *confusion* each dropped to 3s.

A little adding put *Fish* over *No-Fish* by 38 to 11. That's when I made the move from talking to fishing. (Sure, fishers talk and possibly even exaggerate a little, but you get the point of the story.) I also learned I could add weight to the *Fish* side by inviting someone ahead of time. Then at the last minute when I was tired and considered bailing, I had a 20 *embarrassment* to keep me on track. (They are my emotions, why not use them to help me do what is important to me?)

Our values, principles, faithfulness, beliefs can factor onto our balance scales — even upset them at times. Weighted with feeling numbers, they can be powerful influencers over our decisions and behavior.

Here's a fishing example: I had saved a fall date in the middle of September, a high-energy church program time, to get away to fly-fish the famous Deschutes River in Eastern Oregon. The Go side was high. I planned to fish with a good friend and it was the only time we could pull it off, bumping it even higher on the scale.

A member friend from my first church called and said, *"We know you are too busy with your church to break away, drive to the beach at the last minute, and do Aunty's memorial service, but she really would have loved for you to do it."* And guess what? The service was on my Tuesday fishing date. My friend gave me every excuse I needed. All I had to do was say, *"Ohhhh…"* and I would have still been fishing. Instead I said, *"Tell me the time and I'll be there."*

Now let's be clear. This was not about being responsible, the calling, etc. It boiled down to this. Those people mattered a lot to me 25+ and that tipped my scale. While I was disappointed not to fish, I *chose* to do what I *wanted most* to do. No resentment, clean decision.

Over the years this way of thinking kept me from wishing I could fish when I was at work and from thinking I ought to be working when I fish. The balance scale makes it clear that what I am doing is what I want *most* to do, that is what is most important to me at the time — *what tips my scale.*

23

Listening through a Mealtime Game

THE LISTENING GAME CAN help you practice and teach good listening skills in your family. The game is a fun way to learn the Talker-Listener Card process and to improve your relationships. As you hear each other better, you'll deepen your understanding of each other and grow to care more as well.

People grow in healthy, cooperative settings. Your family can be a source and center of strength for all its members and everything else you each do in your lives will go better.

This is especially true for young children. This loving, listening environment will support their learning to work with others. And they can easily participate because they already understand taking turns and fairness.

It's best to get agreement from your spouse before you try it. Incidentally, the game works as well for a gathering of housemates, friends, or co-workers at lunch as it does for families, and of course, buy-in is necessary for it to work.

In the game everyone gets a turn to talk and no one else can spoil it by interrupting, arguing, changing the subject, or lecturing. (When a friend of mine read this part she said, *"But what else is there for a parent to do?"*) Youngsters love to catch their parents or siblings breaking rules. It may be harder for parents to play this game than for youngsters.

Start the game by telling your family that you've discovered a table game that's fun for ages 5 to 105. Show them the Talker-Listener Card and point out the Talker on one side and the Listener on the other.

Explain that everyone will get a turn to talk. They get to talk about anything that is going on with them and that everyone else has to listen to them. In this game children, young people, and adults are to graciously signal that they've caught a rule-breaker, someone who quit their listening turn and started talking, by simply turning the card around. No accusing, no attacking, just turning the card.

The rules of engagement

1. Anyone may say, *"Pass,"* and have a second chance after everyone else has their turn. Each person gets a turn to talk about whatever he or she wants to, while everyone else gives their undivided attention.

2. Listeners play by using one of the approaches below. Ask all questions with kind, friendly curiosity. Nothing pushy or unpleasant. Review this example together before you start so all listeners are on the same page. The first talker looks at his plate and says, *"But, I don't like anchovies on my pizza."*
   - ***Repeat as accurately as you can what you heard the talker say:*** *"So you don't like anchovies on your pizza...?"* or,
   - ***Put in your own words what you heard:*** *"So, you think you'll throw up if you have to eat any of that fishy stuff on your pizza...?"* or,
   - ***Ask a question so you understand better:*** *"I didn't understand. Did you mean you aren't going to eat the pizza because it has anchovies, or that you will take the anchovies off so you can enjoy the pizza...?"* or,
   - ***Ask a question for further information:*** *"What would you like to have on your pizza instead of anchovies...?"*

3. Begin by placing the card in front of the first talker with the Talker side facing him or her. Everyone else sits on the LISTENER side of the card. This continually reminds everyone whose turn it is to talk and whose turn it is to listen.

It may take a little practice to learn to tell the difference between talking and listening. That's part of the fun. (Gently catching someone breaking into another's talking time is a way of learning the difference and respecting each other.)

4. The first talker begins. When someone else interrupts and talks out of turn, anyone can turn the card around so the TALKER side faces the rule-breaker.

5. The culprit who's been caught has to turn the Talker side of the card back toward the one whose turn it was and say, *"Oops, goofed. It was your turn to talk. What were you saying...?"* Or, *"Sorry, it was your turn. You were saying you don't like anchovies, please go on...?"*

6. You may have to ask the talkers whether they are understood. (And notice, that's *understood,* not *agreed.* Understanding is the basis of good communication.) The talker's turn is finished when the talker says, *"Yes, you understand me."* Or, *"You got it."* Or, nods and mumbles, *"Un-huh."*

7. When a talker is understood, continue until each person has had a turn to be heard.

One family's example

Dad gets the game rolling with the kindergartner (Youngest goes first in this group). *"Okay Sammy, it's always your turn to be the talker first. What do you want to talk about...?"*

"Well, Jason took my crayons and my teacher didn't do anything about it."

Junior high Jeremy says, *"I hope you didn't go crying to the teacher. Nobody likes a crybaby. You should have punched him."*

Dad turns the card around to face Jeremy, who then says, *"Whoops, I'm caught. Sam, it was your turn. What happened...?"* Or, *"Sounds like it bugs you when Jason steals your stuff and the teacher doesn't believe you...?"*

Sammy sighs, *"Yeah. That's right."*

Mom says, *"So it wasn't much of a fun day...?"*

"No, but I liked lunch and recess. We got to play wall ball."

And Jeremy says, *"Is that your favorite game...?"*

"Yeah!" And that ends Sammy's turn to be the talker. To be sure, someone can ask, *"Have we understood you...?"* (When the talker nods and says, *"Yeah,"* or some clear indication he or she has been heard, turn the TALKER side to the next older person. This keeps one person from monopolizing the conversation.)

So now it's Jeremy's turn, *"I don't like it when you turn my music down."*

Dad says, *"You call that racket music!?"*

Sam catches Dad, and with a big smile turns the talker side of the card on Dad, who sheepishly says, *"You caught me. That's right, let's see, it was your turn, Jeremy. Let me try it again. So you don't like it when we turn down your music...?"*

"You bet I don't! It makes me mad. It's my music and I like it."

Dad, nearly choking: *"It's your turn, aaah, what do you like about your music...?"* And Jeremy gets to talk and be heard about his music, something that matters to him. When he is understood, his turn is complete.

Sometimes it helps to finish a turn if someone summarizes what the talker said before asking, *"Have we understood you...?"*

Then the TALKER side goes in front of Mom. The kids say, *"It's your turn, Mom. What happened in your day that you want to talk about...?"*

"Nice of you to ask. I had a tough day. My boss wants me to do something I think is unethical."

Sammy, *"Does that mean he wants you to do something wrong...?"*

"Yes. And if I don't do it, I might get fired."

Jeremy, *"Boy, it sounds tough to be an adult. What are you going to do...?"*

When she has been fully understood, Dad gets a turn. The kids ask, *"Dad, what is going on with you...?"*

"When I come home from work, I'm so tired of people that I'd like a few minutes of quiet time."

Sammy, *"You mean you don't want us to bug you when you come in the door...?"*

Jeremy, *"What would you like...?"*

Dad, *"I guess what I'd like is a hug from each of you. Then I'd like to go to the basement for twenty minutes to putter. After that, I think I'd be ready to help with dinner, help with your homework, play catch,* or something."

Mom, *"So you need a break to unhook from a tough day at work...?"*

Dad says, *"Yep, that's it. You got it."* He feels understood. Game over.

Talk about miracles! What teenager ever asked a kindergartner about his frustrations at school? What father ever asked a teenager to explain the nuances in his music? What youngsters ever asked their parents about what's important to them?

(An informal historical search suggests that questions like these have been asked only seventeen times in recorded history. This simple mealtime game could possibly change the nature of civilization as we know it.)

Having a safe place to share and sort out our issues, where we are heard and acknowledged, makes for healthier and happier lives. You could add a wrinkle to this game by using it to discuss a family outing, party, work project, or misunderstanding.

When we play games that teach us to really listen and understand each other, our relationships can deepen as family interactions become more pleasant and meaningful.

The TLC with game rules can help a family crisis

When a family has learned these skills by playing the listening game, think what they can do when there's a crisis. The kindergartner comes home crying, *"Zeke threw rocks at me."*

Mom, instead of responding with standard "parent talk" and saying, *"I'll go call his mother,"* listens by asking, *"Were you scared...? What happened...?"*

"Yeah, he almost hit me. We got into a fight over his bicycle. He wouldn't let me use it, so I took it."

"So you took it...? What happened then...?"

Eventually, in her role as a listener, she could ask, *"What could you do that might help...?"*

"Well, I guess I could take his bike back and tell him I'm sorry."

This approach would hear Sammy and encourage him to figure out what to do about his situation. He would sense his mother's confidence in his ability to resolve his own conflict and likely calm down enough to think more clearly about his options.

Or, Dad meets Jeremy at the front door at 2 o'clock in the morning a few years later, *"You're late with the car!! You're grounded!!"*

"Wow, Dad, you sound angry. You must have been really worried about me...?"

Dad, *"You bet I'm angry, you're grounded!"*

Jeremy, *"Were you scared something awful happened to me or are you more mad because I didn't get the car back when you told me to...?"*

"Well, Jeremy, I was mostly scared, but I'm also upset you didn't do what I asked you to do. We love you and we don't want anything to happen to you. So what did happen...?"

When a crisis erupts, the calmest family member gets the TLC, and sets it on the table. And the family caught by awareness, says, *"Oh, that's right. Let's see who talks first and who listens. We can get through this. Everyone gets a turn to talk, everyone listens, and that's fair. That's how we play the game and get along together."*

At one level, life is a game and when we learn to play by the rules of taking turns and really hearing each other, then everyone has a safe place to sort through their issues and handle their lives more constructively.

At a deeper level life is not a game at all. It is real. All the more reason why we need all the help we can get to live in this challenging and complex world. Learning together to listen to and support each other can make that world less scary and more possible for us to navigate wisely.

Best wishes as you consciously choose to learn together how to care more and support each other better.

(You can order a free PDF version of this chapter from the website to print copies.)

24

Listening through Difficult Discussions

WHEN YOU WANT TO discuss a sensitive topic in a group or build a model for group cooperation, the Talker-Listener Card can help prevent, or at least, reduce the level of conflict.

So often when discussing difficult issues, participants don't feel heard, understood, or valued. And that hurts. The hurt produces anger, voices get raised, discussion turns to argument, thinking gets fuzzy and defensive, and behavior becomes aggressive. Then arguments escalate into name calling, questioning motives, straining working relationships, and ending friendships.

If a group wants to discuss a tough topic cooperatively, introduce the TLC process. This method is similar to the Native American "talking stick" tradition. While one person holds the talking stick, the others listen and wait in silence to show respect for the person, their time, and their comments.

The Talker-Listener process adds two steps:
- *Listening responses make it clear to the talker that he/she has been heard and understood.*
- *Listening responses also help the talker clarify and develop his/her opinion.*

This is a collaborative process where the goal is to learn from each other and support everyone's growth. It works best with an unbiased participant taking leadership by monitoring the process to be sure that everyone gets to speak and be heard.

Put the Talker-Listener Card in front of the person who wants to speak first. Remind the group to focus on understanding one person at a time. When one person is talking, everyone else listens. (You can print and share copies of the four questions in the Listening Game as a quick model for listening.)

Before the second "wannabee" talker gets a turn, he/she must first earn the privilege by summarizing, to the first talker's satisfaction, what the first person intended to say.

Thereafter, listeners repeat or paraphrase the views of prior speakers before they get to talk. As you monitor the process, see that no one gets away with talking unless they first hear and acknowledge the prior speaker.

Again, this does not mean agreement. It means understanding. When this works, everyone gets heard and fireworks start less frequently.

Differing opinions don't necessarily generate heat, except for people who are insecure and have trouble realizing that others can legitimately see the world differently. For them "listen first, talk second" won't cure their upset, but if you carefully guide the process, it should reduce it substantially. More importantly, it also should prevent them from killing a productive discussion for the others.

Heated arguments often arise out of the hurt people feel when their opinions are not heard and respected. The "listen first, talk second" model wipes out this heat source by hearing and respecting people's views.

So, *no* to arguments; *yes* to discussing differing opinions and learning from each other.

For example: A second speaker says, *"So what you said was...and it matters a great deal to you. Right...?"* First speaker, *"Yes, that's what I meant to say."* The nod or agreement about being understood ends the first speaker's turn.

Second speaker's turn, *"So I differ from you in this way..."* Third speaker to the second speaker, *"So your opinion is as follows... Is that the way you see it...?"* Second speaker, *"Yep, you got it. It feels good that you took the time to understand me even when I know you don't agree with me."*

Sometimes, I call these gatherings *"I see it — You see it"* groups. The first person begins by saying, *"I see it this way...and how do you see it?"* The second responds by saying, *"So the way you see it is...is that right?"* And if it is, then the second takes a turn as a speaker saying, *"And the way I see it is...and how do you see it?"*

The *"I see it – You see it"* language in this method makes it clear that having divergent points of view is the norm, and as such, more than acceptable.

During the 1991 Gulf War, I invited a group to discuss their reactions to America's involvement. We began by establishing ground rules. I would monitor the process. Everyone would get a chance to talk and be heard.

Each person had to earn speaking time by first understanding someone else to his/her satisfaction.

Because views were strongly held, we would not try to convince anyone, but simply share our opinions, respect others, try to learn from each other, and come out of the discussion as friends.

While we can't accurately categorize any viewpoint, for the sake of simplicity, I'm going to refer to the divergent views as "hawks" and "doves." A dove began and shared her view. The hawk jumped ahead to his response before hearing her out. *"So you go for peace at any price. But someone has to protect this country."*

I asked the first talker whether she felt understood. *"Not at all,"* she said. So I said to the listener, *"Okay, try again and repeat back what she was trying to say."* He couldn't. I asked her to say it again, but he still couldn't repeat it. He was too busy thinking about what he wanted to say. He finally was able to repeat it back on the third try: *"So what you said was, you want to use every possible means of diplomacy before resorting to violence, that is, military intervention...? Is that what you meant...?"* And she said, *"Yes. That's it exactly. Thanks for hearing me."*

The doves were no better at listening than the hawks. When a dove had to feed back what a "military brat" thought, the dove could hardly choke out the words: *"So you grew up believing the military is primarily interested in making a more just and safer world...? And that's what you see America doing in the Gulf...?"*

They struggled, but spent the evening carefully listening to each other. They gained understanding about how the others felt and what they believed. They felt heard in a way they had not before. The evening ended with folks saying to each other, in effect: *"I had no idea you felt that way. I didn't understand what your experience was. No wonder you think the way you do. We certainly don't agree, but at least now I understand your position and respect you."*

The "listen-first-and-talk-second" model works whether the group takes turns systematically going around the room or irregularly moving to the person who wants to talk next.

Regardless of the order, the critical issue is the same. *Before anyone gets to talk, that person must earn the right by feeding back what the previous talker said to their satisfaction.*

This works best when someone moderates the process and sees that everyone gets heard and understood. A group can self-monitor, but that requires that members understand the method and be willing to speak up and see that no one gets away with talking without first listening.

The next week, I was to be out of town and the group decided to meet and continue the discussion. I urged them to use the ground rules and monitor the process. At the meeting they decided that since "they were friends and understood each other now, they wouldn't need to." You can guess what happened. The discussion turned into a heated debate, punctuated with misunderstandings and hurt feelings.

If you are going to lead or participate in an emotionally loaded discussion, it helps to know that either the group will discuss without a plan, relying on current cultural patterns (which likely means everyone focusing on their own views and disregarding others) or the group will proceed with a plan. I encourage you to introduce this system to allow everyone to earn their right to speak by listening first.

Taking turns respects and values each member of the group. You have the tools available to help disparate folks with divergent, strongly held opinions build community. Good luck. The world sorely needs what you can do.

(You can order a free PDF version of this chapter from the website so you can print copies.)

25

Listening through Couple Conversations

OFTEN IN COUPLES' COUNSELING I interrupt one partner and ask what the other just said. They stammer: *"Well, ah, she/he was, ah, wrong...ah, well, I don't know exactly."*

It takes practice to learn to focus on one person's point of view at a time. That's where the ability to moderate two-party conversations can be helpful.

When you care enough about people who want to communicate better, you can offer to moderate their discussion, using the Talker-Listener Card process. It's risky though. They may not want any help and you might lose friends, but if they ask, or if it is important enough to you, the TLC can be a great tool. (And this method is useful too, if you are a pro.)

I'm going to walk through a marriage counseling session so you can observe what I think about it and how I apply the Talker-Listener Card. You can think about how you might apply the method, that is, use the TLC in circumstances you might try to moderate. Between parent and child, boss and employee, Democrat and Republican, co-workers, relatives, you name it.

Communication is usually the critical issue in marriage counseling. If couples were communicating well, they wouldn't need a counselor. They'd resolve their issues on their own. Sometimes the communication goes awry because over time their poor methods allow distance and misunderstanding to develop. Their brains go flat slowly until they hit crisis level and they no longer can hear each other accurately.

At other times, pressure situations arise where emotions overload, brains go flat, and all their communicating and relating functions go south. In either case they need help unloading without damaging each other, listening without defending, and rebuilding their ability to communicate and connect with each other.

After awhile they kid each other about getting flat-brained and become more able to listen, knowing that they can help the others' flat-brain relax and function better. It gives them a way to understand themselves and each other and reduces the pressure in their situation. Naming their upsets gives them some control over them.

Early on we take time to acknowledge that they want to get along better and that the way they presently communicate isn't working. I explain taking turns, what is listed on the card, and the first few listening techniques so they have a basic idea about how to listen and elicit what the other thinks and feels.

I tell them that if they learn to use the TLC, the foldable third person, they won't need me to moderate their discussions. Somewhere in the process where it seems appropriate I quickly sketch the flat-brain syndrome to them so they understand that what they are going through is common and understandable. People usually relax realizing that being flat-brained is okay and not permanent. The language is accepting and it gives them a common language to take home with them along with the TLC.

They often ask whether listening will make any difference. My answer: *"When you help your spouse figure out what they are trying to say and then fully understand it, two things happen. First, when you understand what your spouse is going through, you will care more, and as a result, make willing behavior changes to make their life easier. And second, when the talking partner gets clearer about what's really going on in themselves, they'll make better decisions."*

The benefits double when the card is turned and understanding goes both ways. Improved communication goes deeper than just exchanging accurate information. When couples "reconnect" with how their partners feel, like them more, and want to act on their behalf, then the relationship changes.

But to listen this deeply means each will have to let go of how they see the past and set aside how they currently understand their partners. If they hang on to how bad it's been, they won't be able to hear what their partners are struggling with or see how they are changing. For this to happen, hurts, anger, and expectations need to be identified and released. We start with a lot of listening to unload the baggage that could get in the way. It often helps to ask what baggage they carried in with them.

It's important to open their minds to their spouses so they can hear them in a fresh way. I ask them to pretend they just met each other in a setting that would be comfortable for them. I want them each to hear as though the problems being described are with some "other" spouse.

I tell them we're going to move in and out of the Talker-Listener process. We'll use the TLC to discuss one of their issues, and then switch out of the discussion to observe what is going on. We might talk about what's working and what's not, look at how they could communicate better, clear any roadblocks to understanding each other, or I might suggest or model listening techniques.

Then we switch back into the Talker-Listener process. This switching in and out of the process helps keep the discussion from getting out of control.

For example, I might stop them in the middle of an emotionally charged discussion of their sex life. We look at the card to be clear who's talking and who's listening or who's started accusing or defending. We could note that Caroline feels heard, and it's time to turn the card so Jeff can talk. While we observe the process, heat and pain around the issue subside.

Switching back and forth between process and observation is a model I want them to learn to do on their own. I tell them to try this kind of exchange at home and to let me know how it works. When they shift between discussing and observing, they are cooperating. They are working to keep the heat low in their conversations and moving with each other toward new understandings.

Now it's time to use the Talker-Listener Card. We figure out which of them is most bothered, that is, who will have the most difficulty listening well. In this illustration Caroline is angrier than Jeff, so I say, *"Okay Caroline, you talk first. I'll roll my chair over next to Jeff and help him listen to you. You begin by describing what is going on with you and do as little accusing as possible. Okay?"*

Then, sitting next to the listener, I say, *"Jeff, I'm going to help you listen to Caroline, so she can describe what is troubling her. You and I are going to try to understand how she sees it and how upset she is about it."* And he says, *"But her view is all screwed up on this one."*

I interrupt and say, *"Hang on a minute. Remember the process? You're the listener. Your job is to focus on what she says, her point of view, not yours. This is her turn. Your job is to set your opinion aside until it's your turn to talk. Okay?"* And he says, *"Okay, but this is going to be hard."*

Then I say, *"So, this looks hard already...?"* He nods. And I go on, *"I never said it was going to be easy. But you'll get along better, if you work at it. All I'm asking you to do is reverse forty-five years of bad habits. [They chuckle uncomfortably.] You know how to communicate the way you've been doing it, which incidentally isn't working, or you wouldn't be here. So let's try it again...?"*

Sometimes, I go on to tell them that when people decide to improve their relationships, they usually try harder. Unfortunately, they each try at times when the other isn't receptive, and what's worse, the methods they try are the ones they were already using, which weren't working. So, when they try harder using non-working patterns, what happens? Things get worse.

While it's a good idea for couples to focus on their relationships, it helps more if they use better listening skills.

Back to the couple, *"Jeff, are you ready to find out what's bothering Caroline?"* And he says, *"Well, yes, okay. So honey, what's troubling you this time?"*

And I say, *"Very good, except drop the 'this time,' that was a bit of a shot."* Sheepishly he says, *"Oh, aah, yes I guess it was. So, what is troubling you? I'll really try to understand this time."*

I suggest a few listening techniques for him to try: *Repeat accurately, acknowledge, ask for more information.* When he gets stuck for what to say next, I model ways to listen. He gets to observe his wife being heard, to see how she relaxes and shares when she is not worried about being contradicted, ignored, or attacked.

I remind him that he and I are, in effect, counseling her. If he slips out of listening into giving advice, arguing, or correcting her, I stop him. We leave the conversation and observe again. We acknowledge what happened. He can see how it shut her down. He could almost see her brain flatten and her ears close. I ask him to say, *"Guess I slipped from listening to talking. It was your turn, wasn't it? You were saying...?"*

I use a little of what I learned that dark and stormy night. I repeat to him the deep feelings of sadness, loss, hurt, and love, she is trying to communicate to him. When he is not busy defending himself, he can hear — translated through me — what she is trying to tell him. Now he is touched and begins to develop a deeper concern for her and her feelings. Healing happens and the relationship begins to improve.

After she figures out and describes some of what is bugging her and he hears it in a way that makes it clear she has been heard, we turn the card and give Jeff a chance to describe his concerns and feelings to Caroline.

I roll my chair near Caroline and say to her, *"Okay Caroline, now it's your turn to set your views aside and try to understand what's going on with Jeff."* And immediately, she says, *"Oh, I know what's going on with Jeff. He's just mad because he's not getting any sex."*

Then I say something like: *"Well, you can check that out, but you'll have to ask him and then take his word for it. Now it's his time to talk not yours. You and I are going to try to understand where he is coming from, without imposing your thinking on him. Okay...?"* So, she asks him, *"Is it just the sex that bugs you?"*

I interrupt and say, *"Whoops, Caroline, drop out the 'just the sex,' that's a little shot from your point of view and it puts Jeff down. Now really try to understand him. Okay...?"* Reluctantly she offers, *"Well okay. Jeff, is it the sex that bugs you...?"*

And he responds, *"Of course I miss sex, but that's only part of it. We used to be close, you know, able to talk about anything. Now whenever I try to talk about my work, the kids, or whatever, you get mad and tell me I'm not considerate."* And she, *"Well, you aren't considerate."*

I interrupt again: *"Wait a minute, Caroline. Looks like you quit listening and went back to accusing again. What's he telling you?"* Caroline, *"Well, I guess I have a lot on my mind and I don't listen so well."*

"Hold on a minute, you're still focused on yourself. Your job is to find out what he's trying to say to you." She tries again: *"I forgot. I'm sorry. What did you say...?"*

He repeats it and she asks, *"So, you want to talk with me about your work, the kids, and whatever...? Are you saying, you used to enjoy talking with me...?"*

And he, *"Of course I did and I miss it. I don't know what happened. We seemed to get busy and somewhere along the line got really picky with each other."* She paraphrases: *"You miss talking things over and it isn't just that I get picky, but we both have gotten argumentative...? Is that what you are saying...?"*

"Well, yes, I guess that's true. I guess I got into arguing most of the time, but at least it was talking with you." She asks, *"You mean arguing with me is better than not talking at all...?"*

And I mention: *"I noticed that you didn't feed back what he said about missing sex with you. Try that."* She counters with her bias: *"So you always want sex...?"*

"No, I don't all the time. I'm too tense when we're fighting. But sometimes when we're relaxed and getting along...?" She defends: *"We're not ever getting along, we're just not fighting. You always want sex. I want you to talk about your feelings."*

I interrupt: *"Whoops, his turn. Remember? You're telling him what he thinks, not asking. You're back into your agenda. You tell him you want him to talk about feelings, but when he did you didn't hear him. Ask him again."* Her, *"Oh, that's right, so what were you saying, Jeff...?"*

He's beginning to feel heard and goes on more calmly: *"When we're not fighting for a little while, I relax and remember I love you. I get to think-*

ing about being close to you and I don't know any other way to do that." Her, *"Really? You mean sex is the only way you know how to get close to me...?"*

"Yeah, after we have sex I feel about as intimate and close to you as I ever do. And besides, I still find you attractive and I do enjoy sex with you." She says, *"So you like sex and you feel intimate afterwards...?"*

Here, I point out that when we listen, we often filter out nice, warm, and personal feelings. For example, Caroline missed feeding back two of them: He finds her attractive, and he enjoys sex with her with an emphasis on "with her." She goes on with a little smile, *"This is hard to say, but it's not just the sex. You still find me attractive and you enjoy sex and feeling intimate with me...? Is that right...?"*

He says quietly with a bit of a relaxed smile: *"Yeah. That's right."*

They both feel closer to each other than they have for quite awhile. There is much more to deal with, but they've moved along in the reconnecting process. If they have the energy, we could turn the card or, better yet, quit on this hopeful note.

I encourage them to practice using the TLC over dinner at a restaurant, where they leave their bad habits at home. No arguing. (They don't need to practice that.)

I suggest using the TLC on any skirmishes that surface and if any turn into arguments, to stop, put them on a list, and bring them along to our next meeting. We'll practice working through their difficult ones so they begin to build new patterns that treat each other with respect.

I hope you can glean something from this lengthy illustration and the tools in the book to use in helping others communicate and connect in a way that builds people and relationships.

26

Concluding Philosophy

I SAID EARLY IN THE book that the word communication derives from the root "to commune," which suggests that people connect with each other and with whatever is basic to our humanity at a level deeper than thought, bringing to mind the adage — "you can't be human alone." There is something in community that has the power to make us whole. Many approaches to psychology affirm this with different language by suggesting that the unconditional acceptance of a therapist supports and empowers the growth of the counselee.

I have been touched and grown both by real people who listened to me with unconditional acceptance and by my listening to others similarly. In writing this book I've hoped that you would join me in a continuing journey of self-discovery and growth.

For me, and I trust for you, when we listen well to others, we meet something of ourselves in them and so treat each other better. I've said this before: Real changes in relationships do not come from knuckling under to another's wishes or demands, but through hearing, understanding, and deepening our caring for the other person and his/her concerns.

In listening deeply we also encounter some of the inner resources of life, though we describe them differently. Some say they pay attention to the rumble of the universe, others describe connecting to the ground of being, while yet others figure they tap in to whatever is deepest inside us or to God. A Psalmist drew a word picture of God inclining an ear to us, literally leaning over, paying attention to us. And for me in listening we return the favor.

Varying points of view

My intent has been to make the book accessible to people inside the church and outside, to folks of any religion and no religion. Tricky. In dealing with relationships and growth we get to the heart of much of life. I've tried to describe what I see as truth or reality in both religious and secular language.

I remember picture boxes as a child. A scene was set in the middle of the box with four viewing windows cut into the sides. Each showed a different view of the same reality. For adults the windows could be labeled religious, non-religious, psychological, sociological, economic, political, serious, humorous, and whatever more you can come up with. Four windows won't cover them, but you can choose which you use to describe reality.

The scene in the center is the same, the descriptive language, the viewpoints and the accuracy of our eyes vary. I find that I can hear echoes of the same truth I see when others from varying perspectives and points of view share their insights with me.

Scholarly lingo?

I've had criticism from a few readers that my book language and concepts sound simple and not terribly scholarly (not enough multisyllabic words). I did include a great Table of Contents, but no proper footnotes. (Horrors!) I intentionally used language that I saw as accessible and memorable, the language I use in teaching. I didn't want to put the folks in my classes to sleep and I wanted them to remember the concepts (who can forget the flat-brain?).

I also wanted readers from all across the academic board to find practical help in relating. (And to be honest, I can't be serious for long, so I included humor to make it easier for me to write and hopefully easier for you to read and practice.)

Listening is an act of love

My second favorite psychiatrist said that listening is an act of love, which fit one of the two counseling ideas I learned in seminary. A professor described a counseling session as "structured agape." Agape being a first century Greek word Biblical writers used to describe what they saw as the fully accepting, life-giving, non-judgmental love of God, which struck me as the spiritual equivalent of the psychologists' "unconditional acceptance" (think picture box).

That grabbed me well over fifty years ago and has formed the basis for my thinking, counseling, and teaching ever since. It meant to me that when I entered a counseling session or started listening to someone on a bus that God's love (or relationship reality) was organized around that person, so he/she could relax in that safety, sense the acceptance, and come more alive, taking a step toward becoming the best they could be.

For me I never feel alone when working with people. For those who don't buy the spiritual side of that, but who can go with "unconditional acceptance," then there is still a power in the structure of how the human community operates that supports growth (again for me, same thing, different words). And I learned from my favorite psychiatrist that one person's healthy brain can send signals electronically to another person's when it has been damaged. We have processes going on when we're with people that we don't fully understand yet. Nice and encouraging.

When you or I listen or counsel, we become a community with another person and in that community more is happening than passing facts back and forth — communication that produces growth at a deeper level.

That is a long way around to say to you that I believe learning to listen and communicate really well will enhance your relationships (especially those with a close life-mate) and offer the greatest possibilities available for human beings to gain significant maturity and joy.

That is why I struggled to write, hoping to encourage you, no matter what your belief structure, to surround your friends (partners, spouses, children, counselees, work mates) with your love by using practical listening skills.

I hope too that you'll find deep respect for people vibrating off these pages and that it will stir your compassion for each other.

27

Beyond Skill...

My parents taught me as a child that when we picnicked in a park, fished along a stream, or walked a city street we should leave them in better shape than we found them. Before my first date my mother took me aside and applied the same philosophy: *"James, I want you to be the kind of person who treats women well. When you take her home to her parents, be sure she's in as good or better shape as when you picked her up."*

This basic family value stuck for me. I determined to walk though campsites and streets, through relationships with family, friends, strangers, and organizations in a way that would leave them in better shape than when I found them. And the book's listening skills are my toolkit for doing that.

We just got home from a family gathering of seventeen, all sizes, shapes, ages, etc. Sally and I ranged in our interactions from serious and lengthy listening (counseling) sessions to quickie listening feedbacks to quirky surface conversations — from playful banter to heavy loss issues. Our understanding of listening means that we are always ready to shift into deeper listening when it appears that someone needs it, when the political discussion calls for understanding rather than winning, or when relationships get strained.

But, you don't have to use listening techniques all the time. Every conversation or interaction does not call for trained listening. But knowing when and how to shift into your learned-listening-gear makes a major difference from the counseling office to random relationships.

But what does it take to encourage growth in people?

As a young pastor and counselor, I was nervous about my ability to help anyone. I studied many approaches to therapy. The more I learned, the more insecure and ineffective I felt.

At that time, academic battles simmered over which counseling and therapeutic styles were best. A group of researchers took on a study to determine the effective results of each school of psychology. What they discovered was this: That the personal qualities of the person doing the therapy were far more important than whatever technique they used. This doesn't mean that good technique and training don't matter, but it does mean that neither is a substitute for being mature and healthy.

Folks often seek counseling because their friends and relatives are lousy listeners or not very healthy. I've seen it over and over as I've worked to build therapeutic communities. Human beings become healthier in the presence of other healthy humans.

The study identified three key characteristics of the listener (counselor) that most influenced growth in people — *empathy, genuineness, and warmth.*

This came both as a surprise and a great relief to me. The findings in that research encouraged me to continue working with people.

While professionals do bring knowledge, skill, and a referral system to the diagnosis and treatment of the more difficult psychological problems, much of what they do consists of non-judgmental listening. You can use the same listening techniques to turn strangers into friends, friendships into healthier relationships, business associates into cooperators, and love-interests into partners.

If then you go beyond skill to increase your *empathy, genuineness, and warmth*, you'll tap into a reservoir of healthy humanness that will put wheels on your technique. And that's what I hope for you.

Empathy

The first of these characteristics, **empathy,** some call the "grace of God" quality in people. Stressed, flat-brained people do and say crazy things, but an empathetic person can see through "the crazies" into the pain and the person. If you can listen into other people's experience, you'll understand them and won't judge them. You'll develop concern about them and give them a better chance to become and stay healthier. Your insides will change toward them and *so will your behavior.*

Genuineness

People often say about **genuineness,** *"What you see is what you get,"* but most don't mean it. When our best friends won't tell us about the spinach in our teeth, they are not genuine and we don't get healthier around them.

Some people are more real than others. Their insides match their outsides, what they say is what they mean. Psychologists call this being congruent. If you can be this way with people in your listening relationships, it's like creating a substantial fund in your bank that others can draw on to invest in their own lives. (Being genuine however does not mean being "perfectly frank," that is, forgetting about empathy and warmth.)

Warmth

Finally, **warmth** is essential to growth, especially in a world where many people are more interested in themselves than in caring for others. (Narcissistic behavior has escalated off the charts in the last thirty years.) While warmth may not matter when the doctor removes an appendix, the doctor's bedside manner can nourish and relax us so our bodies heal quicker. Studies show that plants grow better in a warm, friendly, talking atmosphere. How much more true is that for human beings?

Let yourself be the kind of person with enough warmth to spare, so your spirit nurtures the environment around you. Then those in proximity will grow more fully as human beings.

When it works

Many of the folks who have read the book carefully to help with editing, reported that it caused them to re-examine the listening in their relationships.

One found herself in a spot with her husband that was a familiar pattern. It normally would have ended in a battle, a standoff, and distance for the next few days. She haltingly tried the listening techniques and they soon broke into companionable laughter (and understanding).

Another person, at a lengthy awards banquet, was seated next to a couple noted in their industry for being close-to-the-vest and open-with-very-few. *"Oh well,"* she thought, *"I'm stuck here. Might as well try what I've been reading."* She did and the pair opened up, let down their barriers, and shared their lives for the full two hours. Then they kept talking in evident enjoyment all the way to their taxis. They let someone into their lives and both listener and talkers gained a privileged gift.

Before finishing the first edition of this book, I was coming home from a conference in New York. As I approached the ticket handler, his communication was all non-verbal, that is, he looked worn and bedraggled. He slouched with weary eyes. *I acknowledged* what I saw, *"You look like you've had a really tough day...?"* He made no response I could see.

Then I told him that I had just met an old friend here at LaGuardia, found that we were on the same plane to Portland, and wondered if there was any chance we could sit together and visit on the long flight home.

Still no response. He didn't look up. He took our tickets, scribbled, stamped, stapled, poked at his computer, labeled our bags, and handed us our tickets as he reached for the next person's. In boarding we showed the flight-attendant our stubs and started turning right toward the cheap seats. She said, *"Oh no, you're in first class."* And we said, *"No, we're not, we're in economy."* And she repeated, *"No, you're not. You're in first class. See the seat numbers, 2A and 2B."*

I'm a bit of a skeptic. I looked back into economy to see if there weren't any seats together or if the plane might need balancing. Nothing. No reason I could see for the agent to have done that for us.

What happened? To this day I believe he switched us to first class because his unspoken pain had been heard with a simple listening response. I suspect that he had felt a human connection and responded to us in the way he could.

Acts of love, often beget acts of love.

Therapeutic or thera-noxious?

Everyone gets healthier, happier, and more confident around therapeutic people. In the presence of thera-noxious folk (I love that term), we feel less healthy and secure. We lose our energy, feel drained, and wonder whether our skirts are buttoned or our pants zipped.

When I see thera-noxious people heading my way, I want to hide. I know that after I spend time with them, I will feel a little less worthy and a little less capable. I do my best to listen to them, but they are a real challenge for me.

Therapeutics are so different. Even when I visit one of them in a hospital with cancer, I leave feeling more secure, capable, energized, and clear headed.

To enhance your maturity, make a list of the people you know who are therapeutic, that is, empathetic, genuine, and warm, with good listening skills. Hang out more with them. Learn from them and soak in their health so you more fully develop your therapeutic side.

I invite you to join me in continually learning to listen better, to communicate more clearly, and to grow *empathy, genuineness, and warmth.* Let this book increasingly help you be, in the words of my favorite psychiatrist, *"the kind of person in whose presence good things happen."*

Thank you for spending a chunk of your life reading and considering my thoughts about and experience with communication and personal growth. I hope the experience has been fun, enlightening, and a little challenging.

I trust now that in tight situations the flat-brain syndrome will pop into your mind and tickle your perspective. I can just see Talker-Listener Cards leaping from your wallet or purse to your mind or the table between you and those with whom you want to get along better.

It would please me if your relationships were deepened because of the time you've spent between the covers of my book. And may you toss Talker-Listener Cards like confetti on your friends, cohorts, and anyone you meet, so that their lives too can be enriched as well.

Acknowledgements

The first edition of my book owed its life to the many people whose impact forced me to think, reflect, learn, teach, and make it happen. It owed something as well to the Presbyterian Church that stresses learning and nurtured me. I'm grateful for my first family, Lorraine, Mike, and Lisa, where I began to realize that how we talked influenced how we got along.

Even after three years of seminary, I soon found in my first church that I didn't know much about helping people in trouble. Jack Walden, a neighboring pastor, bailed me out by listening to my frustrations, sharing his skills, and inviting me to join him in providing therapy for women who were on Oregon State's Aid to Dependent Children care. They needed more than a monthly check. With Jack my ear began its practical training in the kind of listening that encourages growth, insight, and new behaviors.

My second pastoral job allowed me time to specialize in growth-producing groups. I learned to tell the difference between feelings and thoughts from a pastor and psychologist, Dr. Thomas Carson Jackson. I discovered how to accurately reflect acceptance and empathy from my favorite psychiatrist, Dr. John L. Butler, who eventually became thesis advisor for my doctoral degree. An education specialist, Dr. Mike Giamatteo, gave me the first glimpse of the differences between the roles of talking, listening, and observing.

My first fear-filled teaching task came with a fishing friend and pastor, as Art Schwabe and I put bits and pieces of our learnings together and co-taught our first personal growth class. This led to teaching and leading more workshops where I developed the outlines of what you read here.

Where those folks challenged me and my ideas I had to dig deep to discover insights well beyond my own initial thoughts. To them I am eternally grateful.

In my second family, Sally and I struggled to learn about partnering in a marriage with a combined total of five children plus those they gathered and produced. That took me to new levels of thinking about life. Sally forever challenges me to practice what I teach and reflects and questions my thinking until it holds together.

Ah, and the writing. So many people helped as I developed my doctoral thesis-project. They took tests, reacted to my teaching and writing, typed and revised. Counseling clients put the methods to work, tested them, and reported back to me.

I'll mention a few of the names I remember and the rest of you know me well enough to forgive my faulty memory. Graphic artist George Ivan Smith designed the TLC and encouraged me to make it business-card size so people could easily keep it with their other cards. Early editing suggestions came from Wally Carey, Victoria Rystrom, and Ben Vose.

The next serious wave of full-service editing got kicked off by Martha Ragland, a writer friend, and then completed by Carmel Bentley, Joseph and Marie Kurtright, Bob McClellarn, and Connie Terwilliger. Sandy Larson came along with a fulsome edit, challenging my thinking and sharing her own. Sharon Mershon searched for typos. The reviewers' fields of work included psychology, ministry, law, counseling, social work, graphic design, real estate, business management, and geophysics.

My professional in-family writers, editors, and encouragers, Sally Rystrom Petersen and Lisa Marie Petersen, performed several outstanding editing runs through the book followed by Deb Pollard.

I am particularly appreciative of Jennifer McCord of Jennifer McCord Associates in Lake Forest Park, WA, who worked with and challenged me to make significant changes to ready the book for sale.

And thanks to Kim McLaughlin whose ideas started the cover and to Anita Jones of Another Jones of Missoula, MT, who finished it and then again updated it for the second edition. She also turned my scribbled drawings into friendly art and designed both editions.

The second edition owes its life to all those who've read, used, and shared their reactions with me. Eight years of feedback from readers convinced me of the need to update and expand *"Listen."*

Thanks to great editing on the revision form Candace Newman Holley, John Holley, Sally Petersen, and Marie Kurtright and also to Angie Wright for proof-reading.

A special thanks to Dwight Rice, D.Min., Ph.D. of the Center for Pastoral Counseling in Lynchburg, VA. Twelve years ago on assignment from Dwight, a student found my Talker-Listener material on our website. Dwight's support and encouragement have kept me writing and editing steadily since. With his mention of a third edition, I have opened a file for new ideas. Perhaps one day we will fish together instead of exchanging fish stories by email.

And finally, thanks to God who for me is the source of life, of love, and of all the creativity we enjoy.

About Jim Petersen

An experienced seminar and workshop leader, Jim Petersen developed his own practical techniques for improving communication and relationships. Among them are the Flat-Brain Theory of Emotions and the Talker-Listener Card, key tools featured in this book.

Dr. Petersen's material has benefited corporate clients, city governments, colleges and universities, the hearing-impaired community, students, teachers, parents, couples, and churches. His informal manner endears him to novices and experts alike.

He has taught personal growth, informal peer counseling, problem solving, motivation and decision-making, conflict resolution, life-planning, couples counseling, Biblical reflection, and discovering meaning through assessing life experiences. He provided pastoral leadership to three Presbyterian churches in Oregon over forty years. He was named Pastor Emeritus at Southminster Presbyterian Church in Beaverton Oregon, honoring his thirty-two year pastorate there.

In retirement he maintains a counseling practice as a Licensed Professional Counselor in the state of Oregon. He specializes in couples counseling and continues to teach classes on effective communication.

His degrees include Doctor of Ministry and Master of Divinity from San Francisco Theological Seminary in San Anselmo, California, and a Bachelor of Arts in mathematics from Lewis and Clark College in Portland, Oregon.

On a more personal level he has been an avid fisherman and plans his next book to be essays on his life-learnings from those experiences. He plays tennis and a mean game of ping-pong and lives and travels with his writer wife, Sally.

When Jim retired he thought he'd relax, fish, travel, and putter, not planning to continue counseling. But people just kept showing up so he did too. That provided the impetus for him to turn his dissertation material into this book – he wanted the people he counseled to have the advantage of some decent training in communication skills. So he fished less, sold a boat, let puttering tasks pile up around the house, and got wrapped up in this project. He says he's not regretted it for a minute. Although he *always* says that he plans to fish more next year.

You Can Help

Many of my readers have come to believe, with me, that listening in spite of stoppered ears, flat brains and other human frailties is an act of love. Such caring and gentle love, spreading person to person, is a powerful gift in trying times. Some have gone out of their way to help spread the gift of creative listening to others. They understand that when people ask, *"Why don't we listen better?"* it can be a plea for help.

So, if you would like to help:

- First and easiest, give Talker-Listener Cards to your friends with comments about what taking turns, listening first and talking second, does for you. Printing the TLC on the back of your business card turns your card into a *keeper* gift.
- Let folks know that I'm happy to send a sample book and Talker-Listener Card to professors, teachers, group leaders, grief counselors, and others who might use it in the training they do.
- Share with Stephen's Ministers, deacons, and other congregational care groups who operate in churches and focus on compassionate listening. Suggest they contact me for a free book, group discounts, and information on training.
- Talk with professional counselors about what the book has meant to you.
- Suggest *Why* as a good read for book groups.
- If you have a blog or website, write about how the book has been useful in your life and include a link to our website.
- Go to Amazon.com and/or your favorite eBook provider and write a brief review. This can really encourage others who would benefit from reading it.
- Write a letter to the editor or a review for your local newspaper and suggest they contact me.

Thanks for helping spread the word,

Jim Petersen

Email: Jim@PetersenPublications.com
Website: www.PetersenPublications.com

HOW TO ORDER

FREE:

If you don't have a card, give yours away, wear it out, or lose it...

I'll happily send you three business and one large size TLC on card stock, plus our eNewsletter with listening tips. (Email me your snail-mail address.)

If you want to print the TLC on the back of your business card or print the large card for classes...

I'll forward PDFs to you with permission to copy them. (Email me.)

PURCHASE FROM WEBSITE:

If you want larger quantities of TLCs that would break my bank, order from our website with a credit card or PayPal. Or, email me & we'll talk it over.

MORE BOOKS:

Order from Amazon, your favorite eBookstore, or our website.

For quantity pricing go to our website or email me.

Outside the USA:

Email me for shipping preferences and S & H costs.

CONTACT INFORMATION: Jim@PetersenPublications.com www.PetersenPublications.com

---

TALKER
I'm most bothered
I own the problem
GOALS • To share my feelings • To share my thoughts
Without • Accusing • Attacking • Labeling • Judging
© Dr. James C. Petersen
www.petersenpublications.com

LISTENER
I'm calm enough to hear
I don't own the problem
GOALS • To provide safety • To understand • To clarify
Without • Agreeing • Disagreeing • Advising • Defending
From: *Why Don't We Listen Better?*

TALKER
I'm most bothered
I own the problem
GOALS • To share my feelings • To share my thoughts
Without • Accusing • Attacking • Labeling • Judging
© Dr. James C. Petersen
www.petersenpublications.com

LISTENER
I'm calm enough to hear
I don't own the problem
GOALS • To provide safety • To understand • To clarify
Without • Agreeing • Disagreeing • Advising • Defending
From: *Why Don't We Listen Better?*

TALKER
I'm most bothered
I own the problem
GOALS • To share my feelings • To share my thoughts
Without • Accusing • Attacking • Labeling • Judging
© Dr. James C. Petersen
www.petersenpublications.com

LISTENER
I'm calm enough to hear
I don't own the problem
GOALS • To provide safety • To understand • To clarify
Without • Agreeing • Disagreeing • Advising • Defending
From: *Why Don't We Listen Better?*

TALKER
I'm most bothered
I own the problem
GOALS • To share my feelings • To share my thoughts
Without • Accusing • Attacking • Labeling • Judging
© Dr. James C. Petersen
www.petersenpublications.com

LISTENER
I'm calm enough to hear
I don't own the problem
GOALS • To provide safety • To understand • To clarify
Without • Agreeing • Disagreeing • Advising • Defending
From: *Why Don't We Listen Better?*